CAMBRIDGE LIBR

Books of enduring scholarly value

British and Irish History, Nineteenth Century

This series comprises contemporary or near-contemporary accounts of the political, economic and social history of the British Isles during the nineteenth century. It includes material on international diplomacy and trade, labour relations and the women's movement, developments in education and social welfare, religious emancipation, the justice system, and special events including the Great Exhibition of 1851.

Collections Relative to Systematic Relief of the Poor, at Different Periods, and in Different Countries

John Shute Duncan (1769–1844), keeper of the Ashmolean Museum in Oxford from 1823 to 1829, instituted a major reorganisation, and also donated his own library to the museum as the nucleus of a reference department. In addition to his writings on natural history, in 1815, he published (anonymously) this pamphlet, benevolence to the poor being one manifestation of his strong religious belief. In it, Duncan argues that in all nations from the ancient Hebrews to the Chinese, the Greeks and Romans to the peoples of modern Europe, either religious or ethical impulses have directed that charity should be offered to the poor. He describes (from written sources) the state of provision for beggars and the sick in Italy, Germany, France, Russia and Iceland, before turning to Britain, and concluding that, rather than seek government action, all people in comfortable circumstances should aid the 'worthy' poor via existing charitable establishments.

Cambridge University Press has long been a pioneer in the reissuing of out-of-print titles from its own backlist, producing digital reprints of books that are still sought after by scholars and students but could not be reprinted economically using traditional technology. The Cambridge Library Collection extends this activity to a wider range of books which are still of importance to researchers and professionals, either for the source material they contain, or as landmarks in the history of their academic discipline.

Drawing from the world-renowned collections in the Cambridge University Library and other partner libraries, and guided by the advice of experts in each subject area, Cambridge University Press is using state-of-the-art scanning machines in its own Printing House to capture the content of each book selected for inclusion. The files are processed to give a consistently clear, crisp image, and the books finished to the high quality standard for which the Press is recognised around the world. The latest print-on-demand technology ensures that the books will remain available indefinitely, and that orders for single or multiple copies can quickly be supplied.

The Cambridge Library Collection brings back to life books of enduring scholarly value (including out-of-copyright works originally issued by other publishers) across a wide range of disciplines in the humanities and social sciences and in science and technology.

Collections Relative to Systematic Relief of the Poor, at Different Periods, and in Different Countries With Observations on Charity

JOHN SHUTE DUNCAN

CAMBRIDGE
UNIVERSITY PRESS

CAMBRIDGE
UNIVERSITY PRESS

University Printing House, Cambridge, CB2 8BS, United Kingdom

Cambridge University Press is part of the University of Cambridge.

It furthers the University's mission by disseminating knowledge in the pursuit of education, learning and research at the highest international levels of excellence.

www.cambridge.org
Information on this title: www.cambridge.org/9781108083935

© in this compilation Cambridge University Press 2018

This edition first published 1815
This digitally printed version 2018

ISBN 978-1-108-08393-5 Paperback

COLLECTIONS

RELATIVE TO

SYSTEMATIC RELIEF

OF THE

POOR,

AT DIFFERENT PERIODS, AND IN
DIFFERENT COUNTRIES:

WITH

OBSERVATIONS ON CHARITY,

ITS PROPER OBJECTS AND CONDUCT,

AND

ITS INFLUENCE ON THE WELFARE OF NATIONS.

PRINTED BY
RICHARD CRUTTWELL, ST. JAMES'S-STREET, BATH;
AND SOLD BY
MURRAY, ALBEMARLE-STREET, LONDON.

1815.

COLLECTIONS ON CHARITY, &c.

—◦◦◦◦◦—

OUR duty towards our neighbour, the knowledge of which is called the Science of Ethics, is founded on our duty towards GOD. From his conftitution of our being we derive our fympathy, our benevolence, our fenfe of fitnefs, or of juftice, or of truth; our prudence, our felf-love, our reafon, and whatever elfe the partial views of theorifts can poffibly affign as the fundamental principle of moral action. From his conftitution of our being proceed all moral as well as all phyfical relations. We clearly perceive, no doubt, the relation between our lungs and the air, between our mufcles and our bones, between thofe of the jaw and the teeth, between thefe and the organs of deglutition, of digeftion, of fecretion, of abforption; between veins and arteries, arteries and lungs, between all and the heart. The relations between perceptions and fenfations, between the latter and appetites, between thefe and the affections of pleafure and difpleafure, between thofe and memory, between memory and emotions, paffions, habits, tempers, faculties, and energies, are not lefs manifeft. Our neceffary dependence on each other for our general well-being; the relations between appetites, emotions, and fexual attractions, between

beauty and love, between the love of parents and the
love of children and of kindred, between the love of
thefe and that of birth place and of country, are
equally apparent. Innumerable are the relations
between wants and qualities adapted to fatisfy them.
Varieties of fituation, of condition, of habit, are
attended with various and even oppofite wants ; yet
thefe fupply to each clafs both impulfe and facility to
relieve thofe of another. The weak require the aid
of the ftrong; but the continued gentle operation of
the weak has often a value above force. The flow
have need of the active; but deliberative perfeverance may prevail over vehemence. The refolute
needs the devices of the ingenious; the quick com-
biner, the calm fcrutiny of the patient inveftigator.
The rich and the poor have very different wants,
and poffefs mutual means of contributing to the welfare and happinefs of each other.

Society is the pre-ordained and inevitable refult of
the reagencies of mutual wants. The inequality of
conditions in fociety may be inferred, argumenta-
tively, as the neceffary confequence, or deduced,
hiftorically, as the known refult of the inequality of
bodily and mental powers.

The great Being who ordained thofe mutual
wants by which reafoning creatures are impelled to
focial union, has alfo ordained the modes of action
requifite to the production of that beneficial refult
which is fought to be attained by fuch union. It
is generally expedient, that each fhould fo contribute
to promote the well-being of another, that the welfare
of all may refult from fuch combined exertion. In
what manner each may beft exert his faculties to
the promotion of the general welfare, in conformity
to the laws of his Creator, natural or revealed, is a
queftion extending to all moral relations; one branch

[3]

of which is selected as the subject of the present inquiry, which will be principally directed to the duties of the rich toward the poor.

Duty is a course of conduct due or owing from one intellectual being to another. The principle of sympathy, a supposed instinctive sense of right, or the judgment requisite to an apprehension of propriety or utility, will equally accord with the injunction of Jesus Christ,—" Whatsoever ye would " that men should do to you, do ye even so to them." An obscure idea of mutual interest may enforce a general assent to the claim of mutual duty; but the assent to the claim is not an adequate motive to the performance. Philosophers have endeavoured to prove, by partial arguments, a most unquestionable truth,—that virtue is the pursuit of man's true interest. But the arguments which are derived only from the mutual interests of men are inadequate, because they cannot be applied, with promptness and certainty, to the determination of action. Mutual interests are undefined, perhaps undefinable. The consequent good which each might hope to derive in this world from doing to another as he might wish another to do to him, is by no means, in many cases, so clear as to furnish a sufficient impulse to right action. If each could see correctly the exact limits of his own true interest, and that of every other, this knowledge might probably supply an adequate motive to all moral conduct. But such sagacity does not belong to man, therefore it cannot supply the motive. The desire of immediate self-indulgence is a powerful and universal motive to action. The course of conduct which it suggests is commonly adverse to the welfare of others, and of the community. The prospect of contingent earthly advantage is notoriously inadequate to control it. All

B 2

syftems, therefore, which fuggeft motives to moral action, derived folely from a view of the mutual relations of mankind, are defective. But they are not merely defective, from the inadequacy of the motive; they are ftill more fo from the imperfect view which they take of thofe intellectual relations, from whence it was clear that fuch motive could only be deduced.

If it be demonftrable, that the great Author of nature has ordained man for the focial ftate ; it follows, that no view of focial relations can be complete, which does not comprehend the fundamental relation of each individual, and of fociety at large, to the Omnifcient and Omniprefent GOD. A due regard to this relation, though it may not fuggeft the precife courfe of conduct in each cafe which prudent deliberation may ultimately approve, will fupply the only adequate motive to control, in the firft inftance, the defire of felf-indulgence; fecondly, to direct the attention to the inveftigation of the duties belonging to the ftate to which we muft perceive ourfelves impelled by the irrefiftible law of our Creator; and thirdly, to urge us to the performance of thofe duties, on which we cannot fail to conclude that our own welfare, and that of other created beings, muft depend.

The law delivered by JESUS CHRIST bears this fupreme mark of divinity, it bids us refer every act to one unchanging teft. It directs us to inquire, how does this act appear at this moment in the view of the Supreme Ordainer, of the " Father that feeth in " fecret?"

The permanent diftinction of claffes in fociety, of the rich and the poor, is recognized throughout all parts of the facred writings ; and the rich are repeatedly exhorted to give abundant alms to the poor.

" Thou fhalt not harden thine heart, nor fhut thine
" hand from thy poor brother; but thou fhalt open
" thine hand wide unto him, and fhalt furely lend
" him fufficient for his need in that which he
" wanteth. For this thing the LORD GOD fhall
" blefs thee in all thy works. For the poor fhall
" never ceafe out of the land : therefore, I command
" thee, thou fhalt open thy hand wide unto thy
" brother, to the needy in thy land."

" When thou makeft a feaft, call the poor, the
" maimed, the lame, the blind; and thou fhalt be
" bleffed, for they cannot recompenfe thee ; but
" thou fhalt be recompenfed at the refurrection of
" the juft."

" Let thy alms be in fecret ; and thy Father
" which feeth in fecret, Himfelf fhall reward thee
" openly."

But the natural law which impels us to focial
union, not only points out the mutual duties neceffary to the general welfare, but alfo urges to the
performance, by connecting good and evil, prefent
and profpective, in experience and in hope, with the
obfervance and neglect of focial duties.

Detection in the act of evading, or of violating, a
plain unqueftionable duty, is univerfally attended
with pain. The burning pang of fhame, to efcape
from which life is often facrificed, follows the confcioufnefs of fuch difcovery, as furely as one vital
function conftantly fucceeds to another. Pride,
vanity, fenfuality, or thoughtlefs hilarity, may dif-
tract the attention, and beguile the pain ; but they
are fubject to control from *ennui*, from ficknefs,
and from approaching death. The confcioufnefs of
a right performance of duties, of poffeffing, in confequence of continual exertion, an improved power of
felf-control, of contributing to the welfare of many,

of increafing the general good, of meriting and of obtaining fervent gratitude, the admiration of the accomplifhed, the refpect of the wife, the love of the good, is univerfally attended with pleafure. This adaptation of pleafure and pain to certain acts dependent on our judgment and our will is a demonftration, above all modes of fyllogifm, of the eternal immutable foundation of all moral duties. It warns us to obey the ordinance of the all-feeing Ordainer; who furely beholds the fyftem which exifts but by his law; whofe detection no fecrefy can evade, no artifice deceive; whofe approbation muft furpafs all human applaufe, as the wonders of his works exceed the limits of his creatures' faculties. A more extended view of our phyfical and moral relations fuggefts a confident belief, which the revelation of CHRIST confirms, that our relation to the Author of natural and moral order will not ceafe with the diffolution of our forms in death; but that our conduct in this ftate of exiftence bears relation to our deftiny in another. That conduct which the order of nature fuggefts, the gofpel folemnly fanctions and commands; and denounces to thofe who violate the law, judgment after death; but to the obedient, happinefs in a life to come.

I have thus pointed out the true foundation of moral duty, with a view to imprefs on the minds of various perfons a conviction that, whatever be the theory of religion or of morals which their education or inquiry may induce them to adopt, the obligation is the fame in all, unchangeable, and indifpenfable.

It is, then, our duty towards GOD, as well as towards man, to promote the welfare of other men, according to our judgment and ability; duly applying our attention, our ingenuity, our knowledge, our strength, and our wealth, to this purpose. It is, however, reasonable, that this exertion should be limited by such a regard to our own comforts, as may secure us against any diminution of such ability.

A perception that a thing ought to be done, or a law which commands it, does not necessarily suggest the mode in which it should be performed. It is enacted, that an enemy should be opposed ; a marsh drained ; a public building erected. The modes must be devised by generals, by engineers, and architects: and in order that their designs may be well executed, men must be trained and exercised in the several occupations. If the precise mode of conduct, which is preferable on all occasions, were fully and clearly pointed out ; occasion for the exercise of reason would be wanting. This exercise of reason, to devise the best mode of performing an unquestionable duty, is necessarily the first step toward the performance.

But all have not equal power to devise, for the faculties of minds are various. All have not equal leisure to devise, for the conditions of society are various. It is, then, the plain duty of those who possess superior faculties, and superior leisure, to devote such faculties and leisure to the ascertainment of the modes most simply practical, and most widely beneficial.

A Moor purchases a number of slaves. Not knowing their language, he conducts them to a court surrounded with workshops, and opening to a garden. He exhibits implements of several trades, and garden tools; points to cloth and leather; to scissars, knives, thread, and other instruments ; to wood marked with lines for the saw; to boards and planes : places a scythe on a grass plot which requires to be mowed, a spade in unbroken soil. On one hand he shews comfortable apartments, with preparation for a repast:

on the other, narrow dungeons, with whips and chains.
He then departs, and leaves them to act according
to their comprehension of his figns. He returns
after an abfence of feveral hours, and finds that the
cloth and leather is untouched ; every implement
remains where he had left it ; neither fawing, nor
planing, nor digging, nor mowing, are performed.
He fends them to the dungeons, and provides coarfe
and fcanty fare. They cannot allege that their
hard fare and bad lodging might not have been
avoided, had they chofen to act according to the
figns which they could not fail to underftand. The
Moorifh mafter brings another party of flaves to the
fame place, makes the fame figns, and departs as
before. One prefently takes one implement, and one
another ; each according to his ftrength or fkill. The
taylor's, fhoemaker's, carpenter's, gardener's work
is done. The Moor returns, furveys the work, and
leads thefe flaves to the comfortable lodgings, and
to the refectory. The former party fee what paffes,
through the grates of their dungeons. They have
now increafed experience. Upon a fecond trial, they
will furely act like their induftrious fucceffors. But
of men, before whom Providence has placed wealth,
and leifure, and intellectual endowments ; who know,
from abundant experience, that the difufe of them
is attended with *ennui*, the mifufe with various
mifery, and with felf condemnation ; who know that
vice and luxury involve nations in ruin ; who are
fully affured that the labours of beneficence produce
double bleffings, both to the giver and the receiver;
that induftry and virtue render all focieties flourifhing
and happy ; how few profit by experience ! how few
devote their time to the performance of manifeft
duties ! Of men, with the gofpel of mercy in their
hands, with its myfteries frequent in their mouths,

how few imbibe the influence of its holy fpirit, the fpirit of fanctifying charity!

It is not intended to advance a vague general complaint againft the times, or to affert that benevolence is generally wanting. Perhaps no period, of equal refinement, luxury, diffipation, and corruption, ever comprehended an union of fo much benevolence with fo much felfifhnefs. The wand of charity divides the rock of avarice with a touch, and wealth flows forth like a torrent. Would that it could with equal facility diffufe life over the defert of indolence, and bring forth a healthful harveft of activity, without the ranknefs of prefumption, and of zeal, without the grofs weeds of fanaticifm.

The firft duty of thofe who poffefs wealth and leifure, towards God the author of moral order, and toward fociety, is the ftudy of the beft means of promoting the good of individuals, confiftently with that of the public.

Rules, founded on reafon and experience, for the direction of prudence toward the afcertainment and maintenance of the rights of individuals, of the public, and of the ftate, in relation to other ftates, compofe the fcience of legislation. Rules for the direction of the courage and activity of numbers, to purpofes of attack and defence, constitute the fcience of war. It is the duty of all who are, or who expect to become, ftatefmen, to study the fcience of legiflation; and of thofe who lead, or afpire to lead in battle, to study the science of war. But rules for the direction of charity toward the production of the greateft poffible happinefs in all ranks of fociety, have not been fo carefully collected and arranged, as to obtain the name of fcience.

As juftice, reduced to rules, becomes the fubject of legal fcience; fo charity, reduced to rules, may be

confidered as the fubject of the fcience of beneficence.
This fcience might have been fuperfluous in
patriarchal days, while yet the acknowledged ties of
kindred bound man to man. When the Deity gave
exprefs inftructions to law-givers, and law-ex-
pounders, in every moral and political difficulty, the
fcience of ethics was unneceffary.

The early adoption of the fyftem of flavery gave
a modification to the relations of rich and poor,
which made the number of independent poor much
lefs confiderable amongft the nations of antiquity,
with whom it feems to have prevailed univerfally,
than amongft thofe of modern Europe, where it is
now generally abolifhed. Hence, beneficence to the
poor, though generally recommended by the antient
moralifts, is not fyftematifed, or reduced to practical
rules for collecting and difpofing means, and for
combining operations, to the attainment of a definite
end. The fphere of fympathy was fo circumfcribed
by flavery, and fo darkened by religious error, that
thefe caufes fully fuffice to account for the tardy
advances of moral fcience, pointed out by Puffen-
dorff, and his commentator Barbeyrac. Religious
error has, in great meafure, yielded to the day-fpring
of chriftianity ; and flavery has fhrunk from its
advances. Its operations, however, like the great
changes of nature, though regular and conftant,
have been imperceptibly gradual and flow.

Plato, in the fifth book of his ideal Republic, introduces Socrates recommending the abolition of
the practice of enflaving captives taken in war, upon
the obvious principle of reciprocal advantage. But
his truths, intermixed with abftrufe reveries, were
not calculated to influence the practice of mankind.

The modification of flavery by facred law among
the Jews might be fuppofed to have elevated their

feelings, and to have enlarged their views in this refpect above thofe of other nations. It is probable, that fome of the firft and moft zealous Jewifh converts to chriftianity were of the Effene fect : whom Jofephus defcribes as men of auftere fanctity, avoiding towns and crowds; feeking retirement even in the defert; profeffing perfect equality before God, with property in common; devoted to pious meditation. Thefe were ready prepared to receive the commandments which filenced the Pharifees and Sadducees.* Matt. xxii. "Thou fhalt love the " Lord thy God with all thy heart, with all thy " foul, and with all thy mind. Thou fhalt love thy " neighbour as thyfelf. Whofoever fhall exalt him- " felf, fhall be abafed, and he that fhall humble " himfelf, fhall be exalted ?" Accordingly, an early effect of the progrefs of chriftianity was the difcontinuance of the practice of enflaving captives.

" As it was the cuftom of enflaving captives taken " in war, that was probably the foundation, and " certainty the fupport, for many ages, of this not " more iniquitous than impolitic fyftem ; fo it feems " that the difufe of the ancient practice of converting " captivity into flavery led the way to its ultimate " abolition."†

" Under the Saxon government, there were a fort " of people in a condition of downright fervitude ; " belonging, both they and their children, and effects, " to the lord of the foil, like *the reft* of the cattle or " ftock upon it."‡ It seems that in the feuds of

---

* Chriftianis in univerfum placuit bello inter ipfos orto captos fervos, non fieri. &c. Sed et Effenis a quibus ortum primi Chriftiani duxere. Grotius de Jure B. and, P. l. iii. c. 7. et Annot.

† Sir T. Eden, State of the Poor. p. 6.

‡ Blackftone, b. ii. c. 6.

thofe times, the poor, together with their children, were often feized by force, and fold for flaves.* The villeins of the feudal fyftem refembled the Spartan helotes, employed in ruftic works of the moft fordid kind, their rugged mafters efteeming war the only honourable employment. Thefe villeins were transferable by deed; and the lord might beat them with impunity, but not kill them.†
So in the Jewifh law, " if a man fmite his fervant " with a rod, and he die under his hand, he fhall be " furely punifhed; notwithftanding, if he continue a " a day or two, he fhall not be punifhed, for he is " his money."‡

Villenage gave way to the progrefs of refinement, and to the reformation of religion; fo that " when " virtually abolifhed by the ftatute of Charles II.§ " there was hardly one villein left in the nation. " Sir T. Smith, fecretary to Edward VI., teftifies " that he never knew any villein in grofs throughout " the realm; and the few villeins regardant that " were then remaining, were fuch only as had be-" longed to bifhops, monafteries, or other ecclefiaftical " corporations, in the preceding times of popery. " For the holy fathers, monks, and friars, had, in " their confeffions, and efpecially in their extreme " and deadly ficknefs, convinced the laity how dan-" gerous a practice it was for one chriftian man to " hold another in bondage; fo that temporal men

---

* Henry's Hiftory of Great-Britain, v. iv. p. 340.

† " He was liable to fome penalty, though generally but to a " fmall one. Such flaves could acquire nothing but their daily "maintenance. This fpecies of flavery ftill fubfifts in Ruffia, Po-"land, Hungary, Bohemia, Moravia, and other parts of Germany." —A. Smith, b. iii. c. 2, p. 88.

‡ Exodus xxi. 20.   § Blackftone, b. ii. c. 6, p. 96.

" by little and little, by reafon of that terror in their
" confciences, were glad to manumit all their villeins.
" But the faid holy fathers, with the abbots and
" priors, did not in like fort by theirs ; for they alfo
" had a fcruple in confcience to impoverifh and
" defpoil the church fo much as to manumit fuch as
" were bound to their churches, or to the manors
" which the church had gotten, and fo kept their
" villeins ftill."

But flaves and villeins were fecure from abfolute
want. Seneca, fpeaking of mutual kindnefs between mafters and flaves, fays,* " there are fome
" things with which a mafter muft provide his flave,
" as food and clothing; but no one will call this
" charity or kindnefs. Chryfippus fays, a flave is
" only a perpetual fervant. Diogenes had a flave
" who ran away.‡ The mafter was told where the
" flave was to be found, but he would not be at the
" pains to bring him back. ' If Manes can live
" independent of Diogenes,' faid the philofopher, ' I
" fhould be afhamed not to be able to live indepen-
" dent of Manes.' A family eftablifhment requires
" great expenfe ; food† is to be provided for many
" ravenous ftomachs, and clothing to be purchafed."

" In Arabia, where every man who is not a mafter
" is a flave, prompted by a regard for himfelf, as
" well as by better motives, the flave is folicitous to
" conciliate the regards of his mafter; who, influenced
" by the fame motives, is at equal pains to fecure the
" attachment and fidelity of his flave. The former

* De Beneficiis, c. 22. ‡ Seneca de Tranquillitate Animi, c. 8.

† " The experience of all ages and nations, I believe, demonftrates
" that the work done by flaves, though it appear to coft only their
" maintenance, is, in the end, the deareft of any."—A. Smith,
Wealth of Nations, b. iii. c. 2.

" counts with confidence on the faithful fervice of the
" latter, as he in his turn does on the care and kind-
" nefs of his mafter, and that at any rate he fhall
" never feel the want of food and raiment."

While the fyftem of villenage gradually funk into
decay, the poor had recourfe to private charity for
fupport. " Though it appears, by the mirrour,
" that, by the common law, the poor were to be fuf-
" tained by parfons, rectors of the church, and the
" parifhioners, fo that none die for default of fuf-
" tenance; and though by the ftatutes of 12 R. II.
" and 19 H. VII. the poor are directed to abide
" in the cities or towns where they are born, or fuch
" wherein they had dwelt for three years (which
" feem to be the firft rudiments of parifh fettlements);
" yet till ftatute 27 H. VIII. I find no compulfory
" method marked out for the purpofe. The mo-
" nafteries were at this time their principal refource;
" and among other bad effects which attended thefe
" inftitutions, it was not, perhaps, one of the leaft,
" that they fupported and fed a very numerous *and*
" *very idle poor*, whofe fuftenance depended upon
" what was daily diftributed in alms at the gates of
" the religious houfes. But upon the total diffo-
" lution of thefe, the inconvenience of thus encou-
" raging the poor in habits of indolence and beggary
" was quickly felt throughout the kingdom, and
" abundance of ftatutes were made in the reigns of
" Henry VIII. and his children, for providing for
" the poor and impotent; which, the preambles to
" fome of them recite, had of late years greatly in-
" creafed. To provide in fome meafure for thefe
" in and about the metropolis, Edward VI. founded
" three royal hofpitals; Chrift's and St. Thomas's,
" for the relief of the impotent through infancy and
" ficknefs; and Bridewell, for the punifhment and

" employment of the vigorous and idle. But thefe
" were far from fufficient for the care of the poor
" throughout the kingdom at large; therefore, after
" many fruitlefs experiments, by ftatute 43 Eliza-
" beth, overfeers of the poor were appointed in
" every parifh."*

But if the exiftence of the fyftem of flavery or
villenage made the neceffity of a fyftematic eftablifhment for the relief of the poor and impotent lefs
urgent than it feems to have become upon the abolition of fuch practices; yet it is moft certain, that the
poverty of freemen was, during the prevalence of
both, very abundant, and various modes were
adopted, in different countries and at different periods, for its relief.

The neceffity for mutual aid exifts to a great
extent in the moft uncivilized period. The fuccefsful hunter imparts to the lefs fortunate favage a
portion of the produce of the chafe. The earlieft
hiftories of all nations exhibit various pictures of
wretchednefs dependent upon charity : the maxims
of the earlieft moralifts, the dogmas of the minifters
of every diverfity of religion, the ordinances of legiflators, from the earlieft to the lateft periods, have
been directed to induce, to enjoin, to impel, thofe
who are bleffed with a fuperior fhare of the enjoyments of life, to extend fuccour to the poor and
the afflicted.

Perhaps the beft recommendation of any fcheme
for the advancement of any art or fcience, or of
any focial advantage, may be derived from a general
view of former efforts directed to the fame end, and
from exhibiting, (if poffible,) in the fcheme propofed, the good preferved, which has prevailed in,
and been common to, prior plans and undertakings ;

* Blakftone's Commentaries, b. i. c. 9, p. 359.

the defects removed, and benefits fupplied, which
have relation to the original principles, but were un-
attainable by means originally adopted.

A fhort furvey of dfferent maxims and means,
adopted in various times and countries, for the relief
of the poor, although we fhould difcover merely inadequate views and abortive expériments, may point
to general principles, and poffibly guide to fome
ufeful and practical conclufion.

Poor Laws, and Exhortations to Beneficence, of Moses.

It is a beautiful characteriftic of the law of Mofes,
that its foundation is natural affection, which it continually ftimulates to good, and fupplies with bonds
interwoven with every arrangement of focial life.
The love of kindred, and the love of their common
country, are fanctified and enforced with all the
energy of holinefs. The decalogue confifts of two
ftrongly-marked divifions. The firft is directed to the
fubjugation of felfifhnefs, by elevating the mind of
man to the contemplation of the great Spirit, the one
pure GOD. The fecond commences by directing
the benevolent affections to the neareft relative.

Servitude, as well as every other contract, is
limited to the term of fix years. " If thou buy
" a Hebrew fervant, fix years fhall he ferve thee,
" and in the feventh, he fhall go out free for nothing.
" If he came in by himfelf, he fhall go out by him-
" felf ; if he were married, then his wife fhall go
" out with him. If his mafter have given him a
" wife, and fhe have borne him fons and daughters,
" the wife and her children fhall be her mafter's ;
" and he fhall go out by himfelf." A maid fervant
who remains unmarried, is alfo to be fet free without money. Deut. xxi.

" At the end of every feven years, thou fhalt
" make a releafe. Every creditor that lendeth
" aught unto his neighbour, fhall releafe it : he fhall
" not exact it of his neighbour, or of his brother,
" becaufe it is the Lord's releafe. Of a foreigner,
" thou mayeft exact it again; but that which is
" thine with thy brother, thine hand fhall releafe ;
" *to the end that* there be no poor among you."
Deut. xv. 1, &c. Our tranflation is, " fave when
there is no poor " among you," which is not intelli-
gible. The tranflation above, is accordingly given
in the margin. The Greek is " Οτι εκ εςαι εν σοι
ενδεης :" and the Latin, " Quia non erit in te egenus."
" For there fhall not be a poor man among you."

In this fabbatic year all agriculture was to be
fufpended ; and all the fpontaneous products of the
earth to be left to the poor, the orphan, and the
ftranger. Exodus xxiii. 10. Alfo, Lev. xxv. 6.
This fallowing may poffibly have been fervi-
ceable to the foil. The regulation certainly tended
to form provident habits; for the maintenance of the
population during this year wholly depended on
ftores previoufly provided ; and the habit of profpective care might have been fecurity againft times
of dearth.

The fiftieth year, called Jubilee or Yobel, becaufe
it reftored every thing to its priftine ftate, provided
alfo for the poor. " Ye fhall hallow the fiftieth
" year, and proclaim liberty throughout all the
" land unto all the inhabitants thereof: it fhall be
" a jubilee unto you ; and ye fhall return every man
" unto his poffeffion ; and ye fhall return every man
" unto his family." Thus conveyances in fee to a
man and his heirs for ever were forbidden ; and
freeholds were only transferable for a period of
forty-nine years. Jews are likewife forbidden to

fell themfelves as perpetual flaves; but they may engage to ferve a ftranger till the year of the next jubilee. This year always following a fabbatarian year, was a year of no produce; and extraordinary exertion was requifite to provide againft it. "Ye "fhall not fow, neither reap that which groweth of "itfelf in it. If thy brother be waxen poor, and "hath fold away his poffeffion, and have none to "redeem it; in the jubilee he fhall return to his "poffeffion."

"If thy brother be waxen poor, and be fold unto "thee, thou fhalt not compel him to ferve thee as a "bond fervant, but as an hired fervant; and he "fhall ferve thee unto the year of jubilee, and then "fhall he depart from thee, both he and his children, "&c. Moreover, of the children of the ftrangers "that do fojourn amongft you, of them fhall ye "buy, and of their families: and ye fhall take them "as an inheritance for your children after you to "inherit them for a poffeffion. They fhall be your "bondfmen for ever: but over your brethren the "children of Ifrael ye *fhall not rule with rigour.*" Leviticus xxi.*

"And if thy brother be waxen poor, and fallen "in decay with thee; then thou fhalt relieve him: "yea, though he be a ftranger, or a fojourner; that "he may live with thee. Take thou no ufury of him, "or increafe; but fear thy GOD; that thy brother "may live with thee. Thou fhalt not give him thy "money upon ufury, nor lend him thy victuals for "increafe. I am the LORD your GOD, which brought

---

* On this point, Wilhelm Zepper, in his *Legum Mofaicarum Forenfium Explanatione*, obferves, "Though thefe civil laws now "ceafe, yet the moral principle remains, that mafters and miftreffes "fhould be mild and gentle with their fervants; for fhall the condi-"tion of thofe, for whofe fake CHRIST died, be worfe than that of "thofe who lived before his blood was fhed for all?"

" you forth out of the land of Egypt, to give you
" the land of Canaan, and to be your GOD."
Leviticus xxi. 35, 36.

This charge to charity, without ufurious referve,
is delivered with peculiar folemnity, by the duplication
of the admonition, and of the warning " I am
" your GOD."

" If there be a poor man, of one of thy brethren
" —thou fhalt not harden thine heart, nor fhut
" thine hand from thy poor brother : but thou
" fhalt open thy hand wide unto him, and fhalt
" furely lend him fufficient for his need. Beware
" that there be not a thought in thy wicked heart,
" faying, The feventh year, the year of releafe is at
" hand ; and thine eye be evil againft thy poor
" brother, and thou giveft him nought ; and he
" cry unto the LORD againft thee : and it be fin
" unto thee. Thou fhalt furely give him ; and thine
" heart fhall not be grieved, when thou giveft unto
" him ; becaufe, that for this thing the LORD thy
" GOD fhall blefs thee in all thy works, and in all
" that thou putteft thine hand unto.*   For the poor
" fhall never ceafe out of the land : therefore I
" command thee, faying, thou fhalt open thine hand
" wide unto thy brother, to thy poor, and to thy
" needy, in thy land." Deut. xv.

" After a layman had paid his firft tithes to the
" Levites, he was obliged to fet afide a fecond tenth,
" or exchange it for an equivalent in money, with
" an addition of a fifth part above the value ; and to
" bring this to Jerufalem, and there make a feaft,
" and invite, befides his friends and relations, the
" priefts and the Levites.—*Another tithe* was to be

---

* This may be reconciled with the former fentence : " There
" fhall not be a poor man among you," by confidering thofe words
as imperative,—Let not the poor continue in his diftrefs.

" fet by, every third year, and be confumed in
" feafts at home, to which they were obliged to
" invite the Levites, the poor, fatherlefs, widows,
" and ftrangers. *Perhaps* this tenth differed in
" nothing from the former, but only in this, that
" one was fpent at home every third year, and the
" other at Jerufalem on the other two years, being
" a kind of Euchariftical Agapæ, which the Jews
" therefore called Mofher Oni, and the Greek
" Πτω οδεκατη, the tenth of the poor." Univ.
Hift. vol. i. b. i. c. 7.

Gleanings were to be left for the poor. " When
" ye reap the harveft of your land, thou fhalt not
" make clean riddance of the corners of thy field
" when thou reapeft, neither fhalt thou gather any
" gleaning of thy harveft : thou fhalt leave them
" unto the poor, and to the ftranger. I am the
" LORD your Gor " Lev. xxiii. 22. " And
" thou fhalt not glean thy vineyard, neither fhalt
" thou gather every grape of thy vineyard ; thou
" fhalt leave them for the poor and ftranger. I am
" the LORD your GOD."

The Effenes, a philofophical fect among the Jews,
are faid, by F. Jofephus, to have governed all their
acts in this life, with a conftant reference to another.
" Thefe men are defpifers of riches : it is a law
" among them, that thofe who come to them muft
" let what they have be common to the whole order;
" infomuch that among them all there is no ap-
" pearance of poverty." In general, " they do
" nothing, but according to the injunctions of their
" curators. Only thefe two things are done among
" them, at every one's own free will ; which are, to
" affift thofe that want, and to fhew mercy. For
" they are permitted of their own accord to afford
" succour to fuch as deferve it, when they ftand in

" need ; and to beftow food on thofe that are in dif-
" trefs. But they cannot give any thing to their
" kindred without the curators." Wars of the
Jews, book ii. c. 8.

Systematic Beneficence in Ancient China.
Confucius. Modern China.

The Jefuits, who have tranflated into Latin the
" Maxims of Confucius," dedicated to Louis XIV.,
in the prefixed life, ftate the philofopher to have been
born 551 years before CHRIST ; and particularly
extol his modefty, in profeffing that the doctrine
which he delivers is not his own, but that of two
admirable monarchs and legiflators, Yao and Xun,
who lived fifteen hundred years before him. Thefe
monarchs are faid to have devoted their lives to GOD
and the poor ; " ut cælo fervirent, et egentioribus
" fubvenirent." The hunger of my people is my
hunger, faid Yao, and the fin of my people is my fin.*
The foundation of good government, fays Confucius, is to be laid in the good conduct of domeftic
affairs. For how fhall he exact rectitude from
fubjects, who has never obferved, nor maintained it
at home ? " If the king has honoured his parents,
" and the elders of his relatives, at home; the exam-
" ple of his obedience will influence his people,
" and infure their reverence and fubjection. If the

* The birth of Mofes is commonly faid to have been 1371 years
before CHRIST. The reign of Yao is 2337 A. C.; fomewhat prior
to the fuppofed period of the erection of the Egyptian pyramids.
It is not impoffible, that the wifdom, both of Mofes and of Yao,
might be derived from the patriarchal fount. It is alfo poffible,
that the precepts of the Jewifh lawgiver may have found their way
to China, before the days of Confucius, and have been blended
with thofe of Yao and Xun.

" king be humane and charitable toward the
" orphans and the helplefs of his houfhold, his
" people will imitate his conduct, and every one
" will be a cherifher of the infirm and friendlefs."
P. 25. b. i.   A note adds, " Chriftian Europe may
" well admire the ancient piety of thefe heathens."
Their books of offices make frequent mention of the
practice of Yao and Xun, and indeed of other
monarchs, to change their drefs of folemnity, after
the offering of facrifices, and to go about amongft
thofe who were infirm from age, affording them, with
their own hands, various kinds of aid: Nor was this
affiftance confined merely to the aged, for it is
exprefsly faid to have been extended to all the
wretched, to widows, to orphans, the dumb, the
blind, the maimed, and the difeafed. " Let this rule
" be the meafure for your conduct to others. Re-
" member what you wifh others to do towards you,
" or what you wifh them not to do, they each and
" all wifh you to do, or not to do, towards them.
" What you condemn in your fuperiors, do not to
" your inferiors ; what you have noted hateful in
" your predeceffors, let not your fucceffors find
" caufe to blame in you ; what you blame in thofe
" on your right, do not to thofe on your left. In
" a word, do not to another, what you would not
" that he fhould do to you. A prince, obferving
" this rule, will have one heart and one foul with
" his people : he will be more juftly ftiled their
" father, than their Lord." P. 26. l. i. " Let
" a monarch limit his expenditure, taking away
" fuperfluous and ufelefs occafions of wafte. But
" let him be bountiful to his fubjects, who need his
" aid, extending a paternal care, raifing the afflicted
" in want, in hunger, in ficknefs, or other cala-
" mity : fo fhall his fubjects venerate and love him

" as a father." P. 4. l. ii. Czu Cum, a difciple of Confucius, confults him, whether the piety or virtue of a rich man is to be eftimated according to his alms. "It is not virtue," fays Confucius, " unlefs " the principle or motive of action be holinefs." " That fanctity, charity, or piety, which I require, " O my difciple, is a fixed habit or affection of the " mind, confonant with reafon, whereby a man " wholly fubjugates all felfifh feelings, and becomes " ever anxious for the good of others; identifying " the good of his neighbour with his own, rejoicing " in his profperity, and grieving for his adverfity, as " if it happened to himfelf. This was the aim of " Yao and Xun; yet they owned that their efforts " were unequal to the accomplifhment of this great " purification."

From thefe remarkable fentences it fufficiently appears, that a confiderable revenue was applied to the relief of the infirm and needy in China in the earlieft times; and the principles of charity were well underftood.

Barrow eftimates the population of modern China at three hundred millions, allowing two hundred and fifty-fix perfons to a fquare mile. They are fubject to dreadful famines, by which " a whole province is " fometimes half depopulated; wretched parents are " reduced, by imperious want, to fell or deftroy their " offspring, and children to put an end, by violence, " to the fufferings of their aged and infirm parents." Thefe calamities he attributes, among other caufes, to the divifion of land to all, that all may barely provide for themfelves the articles of firft neceffity for fubfift-ence. " There are no great farmers who ftore their " grain, to throw into the market in feafons of fcarcity. " In fuch feafons the only refource is that of the " government opening its magazines: this is feldom

" adequate to the wants of the people." " Although
" in China the public law be not eftablifhed, of the
" *jus trium liberorum*, by which every Roman ci-
" tizen, having three children, was entitled to certain
" privileges and immunities; yet every male child
" may be provided for, and receive a ftipend, from
" the moment of his birth, by his name being en-
" rolled on the military lift." This may, perhaps,
be not only a convenient mode of eafing the burthen
of large families to the poor, but may likewife
prove to be the moft effectual and leaft oppreffive
method of raifing recruits for fleets and armies.

M. De Paw, fpeaking of the Jefuits' account of
the Chinefe population, obferves, " Il faut que le
" P. Parenin fe foit convaincu, pendant le fejour
" qu' il a fait à la Chine, que la fureur de mutiler
" les enfants eft encore plus commune qu'on ne
" pourroit le croire; puifqu' il tache d'expliquer
" par la comment Polygamie peutetre si fort en
" vogue dans un pays où il ne nait certainement
" pas plus de filles que de garçons. (Lettres Edi-
" fiantes, 26 Receuil.) Mais comme prefque tous
" les enfants qu'on y etouffe, qu'on y jette dans les
" rivieres, où qu'on porte à la voirie, font des filles,
" cela laiffe fubfifter la difficulté dans fa force; car
" enfin on y maffacre plus d'individus du fexe
" feminin qu'on n'y chatre de males.—Il y a à la
" Chine une multitude d'hommes qui vivent dans le
" celibat ; on y compte plus d'un million de moines
" dont la plupart font Mendians, & dont il n'y a
" aucun qui foit marié : les voleurs qui inondent les
" provinces n'ont pas de famille : enfin les maitres ne
" permettent pas le mariage aux efclaves, et le nombre
" des efclaves eft tres grand. '

Barrow calculates that near nine thoufand infants
are annually deftroyed in Pekin alone. " It is

" probable that extreme poverty and hopeless in-
" digence, the frequent experience of direful famines,
" and the scenes of misery and calamity occasioned
" by them, acting on minds whose affections are not
" very powerful, induce this unnatural crime, which
" common custom has encouraged, and which is not
" prohibited by positive law. Almost all the in-
" fants that are exposed are females, who are the
" least able to provide for themselves, and the least
" profitable to their parents; and the practice is
" most frequent in crowded cities, where not only
" poverty more commonly prevails, but so many
" examples daily occur of inhumanity, of summary
" punishments, acts of violence and cruelty, that the
" mind becomes callous, and habituated to scenes
" that once would have shocked, &c."

" How weak in reality must be the boasted filial
" affection of the Chinese for their parents, who
" scruple not to be the murderers of their own
" children. Filial piety among them may be rather
" considered in the light of an ancient precept, car-
" rying with it the weight of positive law, than the
" effect of sentiment."

" I am informed, that foundling hospitals do exist
" in China, but that they are on a small scale, being
" raised and supported by donations of individuals;
" and their continuance is, therefore, as precarious as
" the wealth of their charitable founders."—Travels
in China, c. iv.

The allotment of small portions of land, by way
of or in lieu of poor-rates, appears to promote a
kind of starving industry, which co operates, with the
custom of infanticide, to force the growth of a most
wretched population. Charity can never thrive
amidst customs, against which reason, not less than
humanity, revolts.

Charity amongst other ancient and modern Asiatics.

The beſt maxims and regulations of civil polity of the ancient Egyptians may, probably, be incorporated with the laws of Moſes. " Their laws are " highly commended by Strabo and Diodorus; and " it is none of the leaſt commendations of them, that " Solon and Lycurgus borrowed ſo many of their " conſtitutions from them, and for the prudent ma- " nagement of their government; as the continuance " of their ſtate ſo long in peace and quietneſs is an " invincible demonſtration of it; ſo the report given " of them in ſcripture adds a further teſtimony to it, " for therein the King of Egypt is called ' the ſon " of the Wiſe.' Isaiah xix. 11. Móses, probably, " excelled the moſt renowned of the Grecian phi- " loſophers in that very learning wherewith they " made ſo great a noise in the world, which was " originally Egyptian; as is evident in the whole " ſeries of the Grecian philoſophers, who went, age " after age, to Egypt to get ſome ſcraps of that " learning there, which Moſes could not but have " full meals of, becauſe of his high place, great " intereſt, and power in Egypt." Stillingfleet's Orig. Sacræ, b. ii. ſ. 7.

The laws and maxims of religion delivered to the Perſians by Zerduſht or Zoroaſter, in the days of Guſhtaſp or Hyſtaſpes, or of Darius his ſon, about five hundred years before CHRIST, were clearly borrowed from the Jewiſh code. Zerduſht appears to have been a pupil, aſſociate, or ſervant, of ſome Jewiſh prophet or prieſt, probably of Ezra. The maſs of ſingular extravagance, entitled Zendaveſta, tranſlated into French from the ancient language by

Monſieur Anquetil du Perron, although very curious, ſeems leſs calculated to procure reſpect for
the name of Zoroaſter, than the abridgement of his
doctrines in modern Perſian, called the Sad-der,
tranſlated into Latin by Mr. T. Hyde.* The ex-
hortations to charity are frequent, but often accompanied with fantaſtic qualifications. The work is
divided into one hundred chapters or gates, as the
name Sad-der imports. Gate 21. " It is the duty
" of the religious at all meal times to feed the faith-
" ful, that is to ſay, the virtuous and pious, but not
" the vicious ; for it is a principle of the true religion,
" that to feed the hungry, with a pious motive, is an
" act of high merit, if goodneſs in others, and not
" ſin, be thereby promoted."

Gate 35. " When you eat bread, ſet apart three
" mouthfuls for the dogs ; and when your bread is
" eaten, give theſe morſels to a dog, and beat him
" not; for of all the poor creatures through land
" or ſea, none is poorer than a dog."

Gate 25. " Abſtain from immoderate faſting;
" for to be without food from morning to night is
" not good, nor preſcribed by religion ! Our faſting
" conſiſts in this, to abſtain from ſin."

The latter has a plainneſs of good ſenſe, which
ſeems to belong to a ſtructure of different character
from that of the former gate.

Among the precepts of Zerduſht, relative to the
duties of prieſts, enumerated in the Ancient Univerſal
Hiſtory, vol. ii. b. 1, p. 79, is the following :
" He (the prieſt) is to take the layman's tithe, i. e.
" the tenth of all that he has, but not to his own

---

* Veterum Perſarum eorumque Magorum liber Sad-der, In-
terprete Thomâ Hyde, S. T. D. Ling. Hebr. in Univ. Oxon. Prof.
Reg. &c. A collection of Canons and Precepts of Zerduſht, made
by a Deſtur, or High Prieſt, in verſe.

"ufe; for he is to confider himfelf as the almoner of
" God, who makes ufe of him only to difpenfe to the
" poor the tribute paid by the rich."

In the Alcoran, recommendations of charity occur
frequently. The following is an entire chapter,
the 117th.

" What thinkeft thou of him who denieth the
" future judgment as a falfehood? It is he who
" pufheth away the orphan, and ftirreth not up others
" to feed the poor. Wo be unto thofe who pray,
" and who are negligent at their prayer; who play
" the hypocrite, and deny neceffaries to the needy."

In chap. 4. " Serve God; fhew kindnefs unto
" parents, and relations, and orphans, and the poor,
" and your neighbour who is of kin to you, and alfo
" your neighbour who is a ftranger. We have
" prepared a fhameful punifhment for unbelievers,
" who beftow their wealth in charity to be obferved
" of men."

Chap 76. " The juft fhall drink of a cup of
" wine, mixed with the water of Cafur (or cam-
" phor), a fountain whereof the fervants of God
" fhall drink. Thefe give food unto the poor, and
" the orphan, and the bondman, for his fake;
" faying, we feed you for God's fake only, we
" defire no recompenfe from you, nor any thanks.
" Wherefore God fhall reward them with a garden,
" and filk garments; and youths, which fhall con-
" tinue for ever in bloom, fhall go round to attend
" them; and they fhall be adorned with bracelets of
" filver; and their Lord fhall give them to drink of a
" pure liquor, &c." Koran, by Sale.

Preliminary Difcourfe, fec. 4. " Kalif Omar
" Ebn Abd'al Aziz ufed to fay, that prayer carries
" us half way to God, fafting brings us to the door
" of his palace, and alms procure us admiffion.

" Hafan, the fon of Ali, and grandfon of Moham-
" med, is related to have thrice in his life divided
" his fubftance equally between himfelf and the poor,
" and twice ·to have given away all he had.
" Alms, according to the prefcriptions of the Ma-
" hommedan law, are to be given of five things:
" 1 of cattle, 2. of money, 3. of corn, 4. of fruit,
" 5. of wares fold. Of each of thefe a certain
" portion is to be given in alms, being ufually
" one part in forty, or two and a half per cent.
" But no alms are due for them, unlefs they amount
" to a certain quantity or number, nor until a man
" has been in poffeffion of them.eleven months."

In modern Perfia religious beggars appear to
abound, encouraged by general indolence, ignorance,
and fuperftition.

Mr. Moriér, in his Journey through Perfia, &c.
fays, " A circumftance connected with the more per-
" manent fuperftitions of Perfia occurred during the
" firft part of our ftay at Bufhire. A derveifh
" fettled himfelf for many days at the door of the
" affiftant refident's houfe, and did not quit it till
" he had extorted from the envoy a donation of ten
" rupees. Thefe men wander from place to place,
" and, as their demands are fanctioned by long
" ufage, they levy, wherever they go, their efta-
" blifhed dues. Mr. Bruce told me, that on his
" firft arrival a derveifh came to him, and afked him
" the fum of ten piaftres; he was refufed, but he
" perfifted that he would not depart till he fhould
" receive it. He accordingly ftationed himfelf at

---

* Les Afiatiques devancerent les autres peuples. Ils eurent les
premiers des efpeces d'hopitaux, qu'on nomma Maraftins. Rhazes
etoit à la tete de celui de Bagdad; Sabur Ebn Schaled en dirigeoit en
chef un autre; excepte les voyageurs et indigens, les malades
n'etoient admis qu' en payant.—Magazin Encycl. Juillet 1813.

"the door, and commenced his conjuring, crying
" Hag, Hag, Hag, unceafingly for days and nights,
" till he had worked himfelf up into a frenzy, in
" which his cries became quite horrible. To get
" rid of the nuifance, Mr. B. was glad at laft to pay
" the price which his tormentor originally charged.
" Mr. Manefty, the Eaft-India Company's refident
" at Buflorah, was attacked more formidably, and
" defended himfelf with more perfeverance, but
" without better fuccefs. A derveifh afked for one
" hundred piaftres, and being of courfe refufed,
" fettled himfelf at the door, and remained there two
" years; when Mr: M. was forced to yield, and he
" paid the fum required. Lord Teignmouth, in an
" interefting paper in the Afiatic Refearches, vol. iv.
" p. 334, mentions a fimilar cuftom, (Sitting Dherna)
" in a different religious order. Brahmins, even in
" Calcutta, have been known to obtain charity or
" fubfiftence from the Hindoos, by pofting them-
" felves before the door of their houses, with a
" declared refolution to remain there until their fo-
" licitations fhould be granted. The religious men-
" dicants of India have fometimes affembled in a
" body of five thoufand men."—A Journey through
Perfia, &c. by James Morier, efq.

Poverty was an objeft of early legiflative notice in
India. The maxims and regulations refpefting it
(as in the Zendavefta) are mixed with a ftrange far-
rago of fuperftitious mummery. See the laws of
Menu, fon of Brahma, in the works of Sir W. Jones,
vol. viii. on the mixed claffes, and times of diftrefs.
43. "The following races of Cfhatriyas, by their
" omiffion of holy rites, and by feeing no Brahmans,
" have gradually funk among men to the loweft of
" the four claffes: Paund'racas, Paradas, Pahlavas,
" &c. All thofe men who fprung from the mouth,

" the arm, the thigh, and the foot of Brahma, but
" who became outcasts by having neglected their
" duties, are called Dafyus, or plunderers. Their
" abode muft be out of the town. Their clothes
" muft be the mantles of the dead." [This feems to
be an *ex poft facto* denunciation, defcribing the
exifting ftate of the poor at the time.] " Their
" difhes broken pots. They muft roam from place
" to place. Let food be given to them in potfherds,
" not by the hands of the giver. Let them not
" walk by night in cities." 75. " Giving to the
" poor is among the fix prefcribed acts of the first-
" born clafs." The Levite, the Deftour, and the
Brahman, have, doubtlefs, a common origin. 96.
" A man of the loweft clafs, who through covetouf-
" nefs lives by the acts of the higheft, let the king
" inftantly banifh." 101. " Should a Brahman,
" afflicted, and pining through want of food, choofe
" rather to remain fixed in the path of his own duty,
" than to adopt the practice of Vaisyas, he may
" receive gifts from any perfon whatever; for by no
" facred rule can it be fhewn that abfolute purity can
" be fullied." 104. " He who receives food, when
" his life could not otherwife be fuftained, from any
" man whatever, is no more tainted by fin than the
" fubtil æther by mud." But, 109. " Among the
" acts generally difapproved, namely, accepting
" prefents from low men, &c.; the receipt of pre-
" fents is the meaneft in this world, and the moft
" blamed in a Brahman after his prefent life." Yet
in the next chapter on penance it is faid, " Thefe
" nine (defcriptions of) Brahmans (in fickness, on
" a journey, defiring to maintain parents or a pre-
" ceptor, &c.) let mankind confider as virtuous men-
" dicants, called Snatacas; and to relieve their wants,
" let gifts of cattle or gold be prefented to them in

" proportion to their learning." On Œconomicks.
190. " A twice-born man (a Brahman), void of true
" devotion, and not having read the Veda, yet eager
" to take a gift, finks down together with it, as
" with a boat of ftone in deep water." 226. " Let
" each wealthy man continually perform the facred
" rites : if he meet with fit objects of benevolence,
" let him conftantly beftow gifts on them, both at
" facrifices and confecrations, to the beft of his
" power, and with a cheerful heart." 228. " Such
" a gift, how fmall foever, beftowed on requelt,
" without grudging, paffes to a worthy object, who
" will fecure the giver from all evil." 236. " Let
" not a man be proud of his rigorous devotion ;
" having made a donation, let him never proclaim it;
" by proclaiming a largefs, its fruit is deftroyed."

*Maxims and Regulations, relative to Poverty and
Charity, in Ancient Greece.*

Individuals differ greatly in capacity, in quick-
nefs of fenfibility, in power of attention, and confequently in acquirement. Nations differ no lefs in
thefe, and other phyfical and moral qualities. But
thefe are differences of degree, not of kind. The
fame circumftances, at different periods, and in different countries, will generally be found to operate as
caufes nearly in the fame manner. Similar events
excite fimilar emotions ; fimilar wants lead to the
adoption of fimilar expedients. The moral maxims
which fympathy has approved in China or Peru will
hardly be alien to the bofom of an Englifhman.
Want and infirmity belong to man in all ftages of
fociety. Inftinctive fympathy, and probably fome
faint traces of primitive revelation, or fupernatural
inftruction, prompt all men to devife means for their
relief. Some barbarians are faid to deftroy the

fick and decrepit, to fave them from the fangs of
wild beafts. Men oppreffed by famine have agreed
to facrifice a part of their number to preferve the
remainder. But fuch inftances of defperate extremity afford no generally applicable exception to the
obferved influence of focial fympathy. A fimilarity
of inftitutions, having relation to circumftances common to all nations, might be expected to occur in
each, even if facred writings, and common tradition,
did not point to a common origin.

A moft ancient law of the Athenians commands*
charity to ftrangers. It is referred to Buzyges, who
firft taught the ufe of the plough. The temple of
the Eumenides, and that of Minerva, and another
confecrated to Thefeus, afforded afylum to diftreffed
ftrangers. In the market-place, was an altar to
Mercy.† It is noticed by Diodorus Siculus, in a fine
fpeech of Nicolaus, an aged Syracufan, pleading
againft a propofal of Diocles to flaughter the Athenian generals their prifoners in cold blood, and con-
trary to the faith of their capitulation. The oration contains many pathetic paffages, recommending
mercy towards the affl éted. " Let not this praife be
" denied to your country, O Syracufans! wherever
" its glory fhall be recorded amongft mortals, that
" you have vanquifhed the Athenians not only by
" your arms, but by your clemency. It will thus
" appear, that they who boaft their fuperiority in
" civilization to all others, are efpecially beholden
" to your benevolence ; and that the nation which
" firft confecrated an altar to mercy, found mercy
" itfelf in this city of Syracufans." Diod. Sic. Bib.
Hift. l. xiii. p. 559. This altar is faid to have

---

* Κοινωνειν κατα τον βιον υδατος η πυρος.
    S. Petiti, Leges Atticæ, p. 55. 557.

† Αθηναιοις δε εν τη αγορα—και Ελεου βωμος.   *Pausanias.*

D

been founded by the defcendants of Hercules. It is nobly defcribed by Statius, in lines which may be wifhed to have proceeded from the pen of Virgil, that they might be more familiarly known.

> Urbe fuit mediâ, nulli conceffa potentum,
> Ara Deûm ; mitis pofuit clementia fedem,
> Et miferi fecêre facram. Sine fupplice nunquam,
> Illa novo ; nullâ damnavit vota repulsâ.
> Auditi quicunque rogant ; noctefque diefque.
> Ire datum, et folis numen placare querelis.
> Nulla autem effigies ; nulli conceffa metallo,
> Forma Deæ ; mentes habitare et pectora gaudet.
> Semper habet trepidos. Semper locus horret egenis
> Cætibus ; ignotæ tantum felicibus aræ. *Theb. lib.* 12.

> Moft facred mid the facred city ftands
> An ancient altar, rais'd by Mercy's hands.
> No God of high Olympus gives it name ;
> Hallow'd by woe, by woe advanc'd to fame.
> Wretches from wretches catch the cheering found,
> Proclaim its praife, and throng the fhrine around.
> Vainly by none is earneft prayer preferr'd ;
> Egyptian, Greek, the free, the flave, is heard.
> By night, by day, uncheck'd the crowd appears,
> Groans are their off'rings, their libations tears.
> Before no form of ftone or bronze they bow ;
> A God of fpirit hears the foul-fraught vow.
> A God, whofe aid no gilded gifts can lure ;
> His favour'd fhrine, the hallow'd heart and pure.
> Here mis'ry only bends ; the calm and gay
> Know not the fane, its vot'ries, or their way.

Here the diftreffed of various defcriptions, ftrangers and fugitive flaves, affembled, where facrifice was offered at the public expence, ιερα τα δημοτελη.* The Athenian law was particularly indulgent to flaves. They might at any time become free, by paying a known ranfom : they might fue their mafters for cruelty, and compel them by law to part with them to others. Freed flaves were bound to affift their proftates, προςʃαʃης or patron ; who, on their failure, might fue them in an action, called

* Commentaries in Petit. Leges Atticos, p. 9. Ditto, p. 178. 179.

δικη αποςʃασιου. He, on his part, was bound to aid them in diftrefs.

Hofpitality to diftreffed ftrangers was the boaft of Grecian cities at all periods ; and no doubt was much abufed by rambling mendicants. Even in the days of Homer, their tales were heard with diftruft, but their wants were relieved with readinefs.

> Small is the faith the Prince and Queen afcribe,
> Replied Eumæus, to the wandering tribe ;
> For needy ftrangers ftill to flatt'ry fly,
> And want too oft betrays the tongue to lie.* *Od. b. xiv.* 145.

Antinöus, the fuitor, obferves,

> Enough of thefe our Court already grace,
> Of giant ftomach and of famifh'd face.   *b. xvii.* 455.
>
> From all thou begg'ft, a bold audacious flave ;
> Nor all can give fo much as thou canft crave.   535.

But Ulyffes replies,

> The Gods affert the poor.

And fome of the Court obferve,

> What if, in this low difguife,
> Wander, perhaps, fome inmate of the fkies.
> They, curious oft of mortal actions, deign,
> In forms like thefe, to round the earth and main ;
> Juft and unjuft recording in their mind,
> And with fure eyes infpecting all mankind.†   580.

Maffinger, in the Virgin Martyr, probably without a thought of Homer, has,

> " Look on the poor
> " With gentle eyes, for in fuch habits often
> " Angels defire an alms."

* Ulyffes remarks, p. 18,

> Πτωχω βελτιον εςι κατα πλολιν περ κατ' αγρες,
> Δαιτα πλωχευειν.

† Ovid introduces Jupiter declaring,

> Summo delabor Olympo,
> Et Deus humanâ luftro fub imagine terras.
> *Metam. l. i.* 213.

Eumæus fays,

> It never was our guife
> To flight the poor, or aught humane defpife ;
> For Jove unfolds our hofpitable door ;
> 'Tis Jove that fends the ftranger and the poor. *B. xiv.* 65.

The ancient Greeks had temples to Zeus Xenius, Jupiter, the ftranger's friend, and Apollo Theoxenius ; and facred rights are mentioned, inftituted by Caftor and Pollux Theoxenia, to fuftain hofpitality to ftrangers. Plato admonifhes to protect ftrangers of all kinds, τιμωντες ξενιον Δια, in honour of Jove, the protector of all.* At Athens and Sparta, there were public officers, called *proxeni* and *proftatæ,* who provided *proxenia* for new comers. Xenophon, in his Anabafis, mentions feveral cities which fent *xenia,*‡ or provifions, for the retreating Greeks : l. 5 and 6. Public eftablifhments for the reception of ftrangers in Crete, called *andreia* or *fyffitia,* with fleeping apartments called κοιμητηρια, are mentioned by Athenæus; and *phyditia,* and *copides,* and *æela,* of a fimilar nature, among the Lacedæmonians.† Paufanias mentions

> And wandering for the fame purpofe with Mercury ;
>> Immenfa eft finemq; potentia cœli
>> Non habet.
>> Jupiter huc fpecie mortali, cumque parente
>> Venit Atlantiades.
>>
>> Mille domos adiere ; locum requiemq; petentes,
>> Mille domos claufêre feræ ; tamen una recepit.|
>> *Metam. l.* 8. 63.

* Προς γαρ Διος εισιν απαντες,
  Ξεινοι τε, πτωχοι τε.   Ξ. 38.

‡ See Gulielmi Stuckii Antiquitates Conviviales, l. i. p. 90.

Και ξενια Διος πολλαι τιμαι και μεγαλαι.
                                    Plutarch de exilio

† The public repafts were called by the Cretans *andreia,* but the Lacedemonians ftyled them *phyditia,* either from their ten-

the temple of Æfculapius at Epidaurus, as a kind
of medical eftablifhment, to which the fick reforted,
apparently, indeed, rather for divine than human
aid. But it feems that women who came pregnant,
were not allowed to lie in there; nor was there any
fhelter, in which the dying might be received; and
the grove of the God was not allowed to be
polluted by death: but in the days of Paufanias,†
one Antoninus, a man of fenatorial rank, raifed
buildings there for thefe purpofes. '' The poor,''
faysMenander, '' are always deemed to be under the
'' fpecial protection of the Gods.''

Stobæus has made a large collection of complaints
on poverty, and of confolations under it, from numerous Greek writers. '' A poor man,'' fays Di-
philus, '' is of all the happieft; no apprehenfion of
'' change for the worfe can torment him.'' '' O
'' wretched poverty,'' fays Theognis, '' why, fitting
'' on my fhoulders, doft thou debafe my body and
'' my foul.'' He quotes Phintios, a daughter of Calli-

dency to friendfhip and mutual benevolence, *phyditia* being ufed
inftead of *philitia*, or elfe from their teaching frugality and parfimony, which the word *pheido* fignifies. There were fifteen
perfons to a table, or a few more or lefs. Each of them was obliged
to contribute monthly about a bufhel of meal, eight gallons of
wine, five pounds of cheefe, two pounds and a half of figs, and a
little money, to buy flefh and fifh. If any of them happened to
offer a facrifice of firft-fruits, or to kill venifon, he fent a part of it
to the public table. *Plutarch, Life of Lycurgus.*

Cratinus, in Athenæus, fays,   εκη
Πασι τοις ελθυσιν εν τη κοπιδι θοινασθαι καλως.
All comers feafted nobly in the Copis.

† A. D. 170. Antoninus appears not to have been a chriftian,
for he built temples to Hygeia, and to Æfculapius, and Apollo.
Corinthiaca, lib. ii. p. 135.

Αu νομιζονϑ' οἱ πενηλες των θεων.
Menander, in Stobæo, ferm. 93.

crates, a writer on female temperance. " If a poor
" man reafon thus with himfelf, If I marry and fall
" fick, how fhall my wife be maintained? I would
" advife him not to marry."

Although it was confidered as a facred duty to
affift ftrangers in diftrefs, yet idlenefs and voluntary
mendicity were, throughout all antiquity, fufficiently
fcandalous. Under the almoft military difcipline of
Sparta, all were employed, and all were publickly
fed. In Egypt, by the laws of Athens, and of
other Grecian cities, a man was pronounced unfit
to live, who was not ufefully employed.* Yet the
infirm poor were in no danger of ftarving, nor were
they under an abfolute neceffity of feeking precarious
fupply from cafual charity. Every man of property
had a number of poor dependents called *pelatæ*,
Πελᾶαι, or Θῆζες, fimilar to the *clientes* of the
Romans; the patron was either *proftates* or *epi-
tropos*: the latter feems to be a patron of fuperior

* 4 Ælian 1. Cleanthes, the ftoic philofopher, is faid to have
been brought to trial before the Areopagus, for living in idlenefs;
and to have been acquitted, upon proof that he worked fometimes
for a gardener, and fometimes for a woman who was a baker.
Di. Laert. 7.

The Δργιας Δικη was very fevere: by the laws of Draco, idlenefs
was punifhed with death. A flave who would not work, might ftarve.
Μη εξειναι αργον τρεφειν οικετην. *Pelit. Com. in Leg Att.* 185.

Plato of Laws, b. 11. Let no one be a beggar in our city; but
if any one fhall undertake to do fo, collecting a livelihood by vain
fupplications, let the overfeers of the market drive him from
the market; the officers of police from the ftreets of the city. Let
the country magiftrates drive him from the country, even beyond
our borders, that the ftate may be purged of fuch an animal for ever.

Ifocrates declaiming againft democratic anarchy, and extolling
the ancient aominiftration of the republic, in the days of Solon,
obferves, that then no one was in danger of ftarving, no one brought
fhame on the city, by begging of paffers in the ftreets; but now,
he adds, the craving poor exceed in number thofe who poffefs the
means of fubfiftence. *Ifoc. Orat. Areopag.*

character.* If a man loſt his patron, he might ſeek
another ſervice, or ſell himſelf as a ſlave. By a law†
againſt the expoſure of children at Thebes, parents
who could not maintain their offspring were commanded to bring them to the magiſtrates, who
ſhould rear ſuch children as public ſlaves.‡ Slaves
of the public, engaged in public works, appear to
have been numerous in all ancient ſtates. Men
falling into poverty from infirmity, which rendered
it impoſſible to engage in ſervile occupation, might
obtain public relief. Suidas ſays, '' thoſe who were
'' approved by the ſenate, were allowed daily two
'' oboli ; ſome ſay only an obolus ; but Philochorus
'' ſays, nine drachmæ a month.'' Sacred feaſts
were numerous : in the beginning of every month,
feaſts of Hecate§ were placed in the ſtreets for the
poor. At the Panathenæa, every Athenian colony
contributed an ox. Feaſts of Theſeus gave occa-

* Petit. Com. in Leges Atticas, p. 181.

† Ælian. V. Hiſt. l. ii. c. 7.

‡ Æſchines, amidſt invectives againſt Demoſthemes, mentions
a ceremony in which the children of thoſe who had died in battle,
having been educated at the public expenſe, were preſented in
complete armour (at full age) to the people in the Theatre of
Bacchus. A herald proclaimed, that in return for their education
at the publie coſt, clothed in their panoply, they were ready to
follow the ſteps of their fathers, to glory or death, for their country.

Προσελθων ὁ κηρυξ, και παρασησαμετος les ορΘ-αυς ων οι παleρεs
ησαν εν τω πολεμω τετελευτηκοles νεανιsκus πανοπλια κεκοσμημενus,
sκηρυτle το καλλιsον κηρυγμα και π. οsτρεπlικωτατον προs αρετην, &c.
Κατα ΚΤΗΣΙΦΩΝΤΟΣ, των παλαιων Ρητορων λογοι. Fol. H.
Steph. p. 75.

§ Ariſtophanes' Plutus. Cumberland's Tranſlation, p. 204.

Chremes. '' You need only conſult Hecate, to know whether
'' wealth or poverty be preferable. She will tell you that the rich
'' ſend her every month a ſupper, but that the poor ſnatch it away,
'' before it is laid upon the able.''

fion to public diftribution.　Add to thefe **Chariftia**
and Encœnia.*　A portion, indeed, of moft facrifices
feems to have been allotted to the poor.　But from

Chremes defcribes an Athenian beggar.　He addreffes Poverty.
" With what good canft thou fupply mankind, except blifters on
" the legs from the public bagnio fires, and the cries of half-ftarved
" children and old women ! together with an army of lice, gnats,
" and fleas, too numerous to be muftered ; which humming round
" our heads torment us, awakening us, and faying, Arife or ftarve.
" Moreover, inftead of clothes, we fhall have rags; inftead of a bed of
" down, we fhall have one of rufhes, full of bugs, which will awaken
" us out of the foundeft fleep; inftead of a carpet, we fhall ' have
" a rotten mat; and inftead of a pillow, we fhall prop our heads
" with a ftone.　As to our food we fhall exchange bread for mallow
" branches, and frumenty for the leaves of radifhes.　Our feats
" will not be chairs, but the head of a broken jar; and laftly we
" fhall be even compelled to use one fide of a broken pitcher inftead
" of a kneading-trough."
　　Poverty.　" You have not been defcribing my life, but canting
" forth the life of beggars."

* A fpecimen of ancient mummers, going about on holidays to
collect trifling charities, is preferved by Athenæus.　It may prove
amufing to obferve their refemblance to the chaunters at this day
in honour of Bifhop Blaize, the faint of wool-combers, &c. and
collectors of fmall gifts on the eves of feveral holidays.—Athenæus
Deipnofoph. l. viii. c. 15, t. iii. p. 326, ed. Schweighaufer.
　" Have the goodnefs, friend Ulpian, or any of you gentlemen
" philologifts, to explain the allufion of Ephippius in the verfe
" addreffed to the Coroniftæ, or Crow Mummers,

　　' To-morrow we'll dine on the veal of the crow.'

　" It refers," faid Plutarch, " to a Rhodian cuftom, which is par-
" ticularly mentioned by Phœnix of Colophon, a writer of Iambics,
" who defcribes certain men going about to collect donations for
" the crow, and finging or faying,

　' My good worthy mafters, a pittance beftow,
　Some oatme l, or barley, or wheat, for the crow;
　A loaf, or a penny, or e'en what you will,
　As fortune your pockets may happen to fill.

　' From the poor man a grain of his falt may fuffice,
　For your crow fwallows all, and is not over nice;
　And the man who can now give his grain, and no more,
　May another day give from a plentiful ftore.

　'Come, my lad, to the door, Plutus nods to our wifh,
　And our fweet little miftrefs comes out with a difh.

various fluctuations of circumstances, bad feasons,
&c. great numbers were continually diftreffed.

> She gives us her figs, and fhe gives us a fmile,
> Heav'n blefs her! and guard her from forrow and guile,
> And fend her a hufband of noble degree,
> And a boy to be danced on his grand-daddy's knee;
> And a girl like herfelf, all the joy of her mother, *
> Who may one day prefent her with juft fuch another.
> God blefs your dear hearts all a thoufand times o'er!
> Thus we carry our crow-fong to door after door;
> Alternately chaunting we ramble along,
> And we treat all who give, or give not, with a fong.'

And the fong ever concludes,

> ' My good worthy mafters, your pittance beftow,
> Your bounty, my good worthy miftreffes, throw.
> Remember the crow! he is not over nice,
> Do but give as you can, and the gift will fuffice.'

Chelidonizing, or fwallow-finging, is another method of collecting eleemofynary gifts among the Rhodians; of which Theognis,
fpeaking of facred rites practifed at Rhodes, fays, " the collection
" of alms, which the Rhodians call Chelidonizing, takes place in the
" month Boedromion, or Auguft. It is fo named from the cufto-
" mary fong."

> ' The Swallow, the Swallow is here,
> With his back fo black, and his belly fo white;†
> He brings on the pride of the year,
> With the gay months of love, and the days of delight.
> Come, bring out your good humming ftuff;
> Of the nice tit-bits let the Swallow partake;
> Of good bread and cheefe give enough,
> And a flice of the right Boedromion cake;
> Our hunger, our hunger it twinges;
> So give, and give quickly, good mafters, I pray;
> Or we'll pull off the door from its hinges,
> And ecod! we'll fteal young madam away,
> She's a nice little pocket-piece darling;
> And faith! 'twill be eafy to carry her hence;‡
> Away with old prudence fo fnarling,

---

* και τω γερονίι παίρι κουρον εις χειρας
    και μηίρι κουρην εις τα γουνα κατθειν.

† Επι γαςερα λευκα καπι νωτα μελαινα.

‡ μικρα μεν εςι ραδιως μεν οισομεν.

Money and corn were collected by public taxes for monthly diftribution, Σιτηρεσιον εμμηνον.

Charitable diftributions, analogous to the Roman *sportulæ*,* were called δειπνα εν σπυριςι, fuppers in bafkets: on thefe occafions meat, διανομην κρεως, and money, διανομην αργυρε, were given.

Friendly focieties, for common benefit and fupport, appear to have been of ancient inftitution, called Εταιρειαι and Συσσιζια. At Naucratis, a city built in Egypt by the Milefians, were daily feafts cele-brated in the Prytanæum,‡ a place dedicated to ftate affairs, from whence any one might obtain portions

> ' And tofs us down freely a handful of pence.
>   Come, let us partake of your cheer,
> And loofen your purfe-ftrings fo hearty ;
>   No crafty old grey-beards are near,
> But fee, we're a merry boy's party,
>   And the Swallow, the Swallow is here !'

This benevolence, or voluntary contribution, was inftituted by Cleobulus of Lindos, at a time when public neceffity drove the Lindians to the expedient of foliciting a general fubfcription.

* *Sportula* is faid to be derived from Σπαρζον a rufh.—Dr. Potter confiders δειπνα εν σπυριςι as rather correfponding with our Pic Nics than with the Roman *sportulæ*. Vol. ii. c. xvii. p. 355.

‡ Not only the famous Prytanæum at Athens, but all public places confecrated to feafting were called Πρυζανεια. On the Κυνοσαργες hill, near Athens, was an ancient temple dedicated to Hercules, in which foundlings were educated at the public expenfe. " Quia vero nothus putabatur Hercules, ideo nothi qui neque pater-" no neque materno genere cives erant exercebantur."—Suidas. Κυνοσαργ. Plutarch, in the life of Solon, fpeaks of a law of Pifi-tratus for the public fupport of foldiers maimed in battle. In Suidas, Art. Πρυζανειο , is a fhort notice of Γερωνια at Athens dedicated to the maintenance of thofe who had grown old and infirm in the fer-vice of the public. Vitruvius mentions *Gerufiæ* applicable to the fame purpofe. " Crœsi domus quam Sardiani civibus ad requief-" cendum ætatis otio ; feniorum collegio gerufiam dedicaverunt." —*Vitruv. Architectura, l.* ii. *c.* 8.

of food, and allowances of wine, to carry home.
Athens was at firſt divided into four tribes or wards;
theſe were trebly ſubdivided into Τριτ]υς, Εθνος,
and Φρατρια; "and each of theſe into thirty Γενη,
"or families. Theſe were called alſo Οργεονες,
"becauſe they participated of the ſame ſacrifices and
"worſhipped the ſame Gods together." The number of the tribes were afterwards encreaſed to twelve.
"The better to maintain a mutual correſpondence,
"and for the promotion of good fellowſhip and
"kindneſs amongſt them, they had public feaſts firſt
"inſtituted by Solon, where they all met together,
"and made merry. Theſe meetings were named from
"the perſons aſſembled at them; if the whole tribe
"came together, they called it δειπνον φυλετικον;
"if only one φρα]ρια, it was δειπνον φρα]ρικον.†
The frequency of theſe feſtive meetings was no doubt
favourable to the poor, and they probably multiplied
in proportion as the number of the poor increaſed,
yet without any tendency to produce a diminution of
the aggregate of poverty. The facility of obtaining
caſual aid moſt probably produced an oppoſite effect,
by relaxing induſtry.

The poor were chiefly Μετοικοι, ſojourners, who
were ſubject to taxation; or freeborn citizens, who
were under a neceſſity of ſerving for wages,
Θητες or Πελα]αι. The natural effect of luxury,
and of diſſolute morals, ſeems to be a general relaxation of uſeful exertion; and a conſequent rapid increaſe in the number of the poor. Alms, however,
profuſely ſcattered from the tables of luxury, excite
little gratitude, ever leſs in proportion as they are
indiſcriminate. The continued augmentation of the
maſs of craving poverty, in a correſponding ratio to

† Potter's Archæologia Græca, c. iii. p. 51.

the sloth and selfishness of the rich, is the disease which necessarily brings destruction on free states; and was, no doubt, a great moral cause of the decline and fall of the Grecian republics.

Maxims and Regulations, relative to Poverty and Charity, in Ancient Rome.

Hospitality to strangers was sanctified by religious honour in Rome, as well as in Greece. The Ζευς ξενιος of the one was the Jupiter Hospitalis of the other.

Jupiter, hospitibus nam te dare jura loquuntur.   *Virg. Æn.* i.

Ante fores horum stabat Jovis hospitis ara.   *Ovid. Met. l.* x. 224.

Testatus jusque fidemque
Hospitiique Deos.   *Metam. l.* v. 45.

Cicero writes to his brother Quintius, " Non faciam " ut illum offendam ne imploret fidem Jovis hospitalis."

As the Greeks had buildings for the reception of strangers, which Plato notices in his book of laws, called ξινωνες καταγωγαι, &c. by the Phrygians, ανδρανες, and by the Cretans, κοιμητηρια, so the Romans had their edifices called *hospitalia;* of which we find this mention in Vitruvius, l. vi. " Let *domunculæ*, wings or pavilions, be built on " the right and left of the great mansion, for the re- " ception of strangers; having separate entrances, " and beds, and other convenient accommodations, " that they may not occupy the colonnades." This building is noticed by Livy, who says, Sextus Tarquin, when he paid his fatal visit to Lucretia, was " post cœnam in hospitale cubiculum deductus."

" Nothing seems so truly accordant to the nature " of man," says Cicero, " as beneficence and libe-

" rality. Yet much caution is requifite for its di-
" rection. For it is needful to confider, firft,
" whether the benefit propofed may not be ultimately
" injurious to the object of our benevolence; and
" fecondly, whether it may not be injurious to others.
" Then prudence requires a due limitation of our
" bounties by the confideration of our means; and
" finally, it is our duty to make a juft eftimation of
" the moral character of thofe whom we are inclined
" to benefit.* Some exercise beneficence with ve-
" hement temerity, without judgment or limit,
" impelled by ardent imagination as by a ftrong and
" fudden gale. Bounties proceeding from fuch a
" fource are not, by any means, to be eftimated fo
" highly as thofe which, proceeding from due deli-
" beration, are beftowed with fteady perfeverance."
Cicero de Off. l. i. 49.† Cicero's maxims on
this fubject are excellent. He fhews the duty of
confulting the welfare of thofe moft nearly connected
with us, and the natural expanfion of benevolent
affection from the domeftic circle; firft to friends,
then to our country, and finally to all mankind.
" Although every virtue excites us to admiration, and
" allures us to regard with affection thofe who pof-
" fefs it, yet juftice and liberality above all muft be
" acknowledged to produce this effect. What can

* That which GOD himfelf does, (fays Seneca, c. xii of
Benefits,) we are fure is well done: and we are no lefs fure that for
whatfoever he gives, he neither wants, expects, nor receives any
thing in return; fo that the end of the benefit ought to be the advantage of the receiver; and that muft be our fcope without any
by-regard to ourfelves. The perfon, the matter, the manner, and
the time, are circumftances abfolutely neceffary to the reafon of the
action : there muft be a right judgment in all refpects, to make
it a benefit.

† Plutarch (in his Sympofiacks) fays, it was a rule amongft the
Pythagoreans not to take a burthen from their fellow, but to help
him to bear it. This was to exclude idlenefs.

" be a firmer bond of love and union than a confor-
" mity of good difpofitions. They in whom the
' fame affections are found to refide, delight in each
" other no lefs than each in himfelf; and muft be
" be in the way to attain to that point which Py-
" thagoras pronounces to be the perfection of focial
" love, in which many become one. No doubt the
" beft ftate of fociety muft be that which is held to-
" gether by benefits fpontaneoufly and mutually
" given and received, which at once diffufe mutual
" delight, and derive ftability from fuch commu-
" nion."—*De Off. l. i.* 56.‡ No expreffion of
philanthropic feeling can equal the pathetic lines of
Juvenal, fat. 14.

> Molliffima corda
> Humano generi dare fe natura fatetur
> Quæ lacrymas dedit. Hæc noftri pars optima fenfus.†
> —— —— Quis enim bonus aut face dignus
> Arcanâ, qualem Cereris vult effe facerdos,
> Ulla aliena fibi credat mala? Separat hæc nos
> A grege mutorum, &c.

> Nature who gave us tears, by that alone,
> Proclaims, fhe made the feeling heart our own.
> And 'tis our nobleft fenfe—
> For who, that to the purity afpires
> Which Ceres for her fecret rites requires,
> Feels not for others' woes? This marks our birth,
> Our great diftinction from the beafts of earth. *Giffard.*

The line of Terence is become proverbial,

> Homo fum, humani nihil a me alienum puto.

Cicero, as well as Seneca, admonifhes that flaves
fhould, on every account, from motives of humane
fellow-feeling, no lefs than of policy, be treated with
kindnefs. " Let us remember that juftice is due
" even to the loweft, even to flaves," *De Off. l. i.* 41.

---

† " Neque ullâ re longius abfumus a naturâ ferarum in quibus
" ineffe fortitudinem fæpe dicimus—bonitatem non dicimus."—
De Off. l. i. 50.

Of flaves, fome were public, fome private. The private were fecure from want, while their mafters had the means of fupporting them. The public, of courfe, were fupplied from the public purfe. They formed a large body of poor; they were *libertini*: and were named after captured provinces from whence they came, or from mafters who gave them manumiffion, or from conquering generals. "Quippe "late fufum id corpus; hinc plerumque tribus, "decurias, minifteria magiftratibus, et facerdotibus "cohortes etiam in urbe confcriptas." Tacitus, lib. xiii. They were fcribes in public offices, meffengers, lictors, criers, &c. Livy, lib. xxvi. "Scipio, after "the conqueft of Carthage, enrolled 2000 men as "public flaves or workmen, with hopes of being "fhortly fet at liberty, if they would engage ftre- "nuoufly in military occupations." Pliny writes to Trajan, "Shall I employ, as centinels or watchmen, "the public flaves of thefe cities, or give them a "military guard." Trajan replies, "Let us purfue "the practice of the province, and employ the public "flaves." A Roman public flave might antiently convey by will one half of his property. Thefe perfons acquired confiderable fortunes in public fecu- rities, and acted as notaries and as bankers; this was prohibited by a law of Arcadius and Honorius.

Titus Popma, de Operis Servorum, enumerates above one hundred different offices of private flaves. They appear to have received a payment, at the rate of four modii of corn by the month. The allowance was called *Demenfum et Diarium*. They differed in degrees, *difcrimina quædam.**

"Sunt famulis fplendorque fuus." Claudian, l. i. in Eutrop. Servitude was foothed and relaxed by numerous holidays. Auguftus treated his with a holiday on the birth-day of Servius Tullius, who was

born of a female flave. On the Saturnalia, it is
well known, the flave and his mafter changed places
for a day ;

Saturnalia dicam,
Feftaque fervorum cum famulantur heri.   *Aufonius.*

A cuftom of moft humane origin. This feftival was
at firft confined to one day in the year, (*Liv. ii.* 2 1.)
but was afterwards extended by Caligula to five
days. Anciently, any one might manumit, or give
compleat freedom to, his flaves ; but this was found,
in procefs of time, to be fraught with ferious inconvenience. It brought an immenfe number of poor
dependent on the public rates. " When many
" worthlefs and profligate perfons, being freed by
" their mafters, invaded the rights of citizens,
" various laws were made to check the licenfe of
" manumiffion. No mafter was allowed to free by
" his will above a certain number, in proportion to
" the number which belonged to him ; but he was
" not allowed to give freedom to more than 100 ;
" even though he poffeffed 20,000, which number
" is faid to have been the property of fome indivi-
" duals." *Athen. Diepnos.* vi. 20. Hence Seneca
fpeaks of " vafta fpatia terrarum per vinctos colenda,
" et familia bellicofis nationibus major." *De
Ben. viii.* 10.

The inftitution of the relation of Patron and Client
may be confidered as an ancient poor law ; of vaft
importance to the ftate, as it tended to reftrain the
neceffity of application for fupport, to the public
purfe ; and of peculiarly interefting character, as it

* Sive vicarius eft qui fervo paret, uti mos
Vefter ait, feu confervus.
Hor. Sat. l. ii. s. 7. b. 79.

† Adams's Roman Antiquities, p. 40.

exhibits the engagement of pride in the caufe of humanity, and the humiliation of dependence almoft removed by the force of mutual obligations. The concife view of it given in Adams's Roman Antiquities, p. 30, fuits my purpofe better than a longer detail. " That the patricians and plebeians m'ght be connected " together by the ftricteft bonds, Romulus ordained " that every plebeian fhould chufe from the patricians " any one he pleafed as his patron or protector, " whofe client he was called, *quod eum colebat*. It " was the part of the patron to advife and to defend " his client ; to affift him with his intereft and fub- " ftance; in fhort, to do every thing for him that a " parent is ufed to do for his children. The client " was obliged to pay all kind of refpect to his " patron, and to ferve him with his life and fortune " in any extremity." *Dionys.* ii. 10.

It was unlawful for patrons and clients to accufe, or bear witnefs againft, each other; and whoever was found to have acted otherwife, might be flain by any one with impunity, as a victim devoted to Pluto and the infernal gods. Hence, both patrons and clients vied with one another in fidelity and obfervance; and for more than 600 years we find no diffentions between them. *Ibid.* Virgil joins to the crime of beating one's parent, that of defrauding a client. *Æn.* vi. 605. It was efteemed highly ho-nourable for a patrician to have numerous clients, both hereditary, and acquired by his own merit.*
Hor. Ep. ii. 1. 103. *Juv.* x. 44.

Freed flaves became clients to thofe by whom they were manumitted. " Patrons retained various rights " over their freedmen. If the patron was reduced

---

* As feudal lords were proud of the number of followers of various connexions, whom they could bring into the field, or reckon of their clan, owing homage, and claiming aid.

E

" to poverty, the freedman was bound, in the fame
" manner as a fon, to fupport him, according to
" his abilities. And if a patron failed to fupport
" his freedman when poor, he was deprived of the
" rights of patronage." [No doubt as profligacy
increafed, the number of diftreffed patrons fo deprived, and of diftreffed freedmen driven to feek fupport
from the public purfe, became very great.]
" If a freedman died inteftate, without heirs, the
" patron fucceeded to his effects."
" Thofe freedmen who proved ungrateful to their
" patrons, were condemned to the mines (ad
" lautumas) ; and by a law of the Emperor Claudius,
" were reduced to their former flavery." Suet.
Claud. 25. Adams's R. A. 42.

Clients, and others of inferior condition, were frequently not invited to partake in fuppers or feafts,
but to receive a fportula.*

The fportula† was fo called from little rufh
bafkets, in which cakes and prepared meats were at
firft diftributed ; afterwards, money to procure the
food was given ; and finally, the term was often
ufed to fignify any public or private bounty, or
diftribution of food or money.

The bounty which was at firft extended to clients,
and to humble friends, when individuals were en-
riched by the plunder of provinces, and Roman
citizens furpaffed all monarchs in wealth and magnificence, became a coveted object to crowds of various
fuppliants. The pomp of oftentatious hofpitality
difdained the toil of difcrimination ; the temptation

---

* Sometimes they were furprifed by a cœna recta, when a fpor-
tula was expected.
    Promiffa eft nobis fportula recta data eft.   Martial.
† Plautus in Menæchm.
Sportulam cape, et argentum. Eccum tres nummos habes.

bore down the fmall remains of independent dignity, and great numbers, who ought to have blufhed at fuch meannefs, poffeffing themfelves abundance, con-defcended to mix with the multitude, and fhare in the lavifhed profufion. The rich joftled the poor, and robbed them of their due. Juvenal fays, Sat. i. 95,

> Nunc fportula primo
> Limine parva fedet turbæ rapienda togatæ.
> Ille tamen faciem prius infpicit, et trepidat, ne
> Suppofitus venias ac falfo nomine pofcas.
> Agnitus accipies. Jubet a præcone vocari
> Ipfos Trojugenas: nam vexant limen et ipfi
> Nobifcum. Da Prætori: da deinde Tribuno.
> Sed libertinus prior eft.‡

To how degraded a ftate was the moral feeling reduced at this period. It is not to be wondered at, that fuch a people were incapable of freedom. Dryden's tranflation preferves the force of the original :

> Clients of old were feafted; now a poor
> Divided dole is dealt at th' outward door;
> Which by the hungry rout is foon difpatch'd;
> The paltry largefs too feverely watch'd
> Ere given; and every face obferv'd with care,
> That no intruding gueft ufurp a fhare.
> Known you receive; the crier calls aloud
> Our old nobility of Trojan blood,
> Who gape among the crowd for their precarious food.
> The prætor's, and the tribune's, voice is heard;
> The freedman joftles, and will be preferr'd;
> Firft come, firft ferved, he cries, &c.
>
> But‡ fince our knights and fenators account
> To what their fordid begging vails amount;
> Judge what a wretched fhare the poor attends,
> Whofe whole fubfiftence on thofe alms depends.
> Their houfhold fire, their raiment, and their food,
> Prevented by thofe harpies; when a wood

‡ Cum tu laurigeris annum qui fafcibus intras
 Mane falutator limina mille teras ?
 Quid faciam, &c. &c.   *Martial. Ep. lib. x.*

Of litters thick befiege the donor's gate,
And begging lords, and teeming ladies, wait
The promis'd dole. Nay fome have learnt the trick,
To beg for abfent perfons; feign them fick,
Clofe mew'd in their fedans, for fear of air :
And for their wives produce an empty chair,—
This is my fpoufe, difpatch her with her fhare,
'Tis Galla,—let her ladyfhip but peep ;—
No, sir, 'tis pity to difturb her fleep.

Strangers received *xenia* and *apophoreta*, gifts
of various kinds, according to their quality or their
neceffities : the poor, a bare fupply of aid; perfons of fome confequence, an exhibition of the
donor's fplendour under the guife of hofpitality.*
Teffera or tickets, of wood and ivory, were given to
thofe who had received bounty. Thefe were marked
and broken ; half being retained by the giver ; the
other half, when brought again, entitled the bearer
to a certain allowance ; the *teffera frumentaria*, for
meal ; the *teffera nummaria*, for money ; and *teffera*
hofpitales, in memory of extended hofpitality.*

> Summula ne pereat quâ vilis teffera venit,
> Frumenti.   *Juv.*
> Scabiofum tefferula far, poffidet, &c.   *Perfius.*

Baths were articles of firft neceffity in Greece and
Rome ; they were among the firft offerings of hofpitality.   Homer notices them in many places.
" CHRIST reproaches the Pharifee,' *Luke vii.* 44,
" Thou gaveft me no water for my feet."   Bethefda,
or Beth-Chefda, the houfe of mercy, appears to have
been a public bath. Pool, in his Annotations, obferves,
that the erection of fuch baths for the common
people was an act of peculiar humanity ; their
complaints in hot countries requiring frequent bath-
ing.   Public baths were called *balnea* and *therma*;

* Gul. Stuckii Ant. Con. l. i. 94.

† Stuckii, Ant. Con. de Balneis, p. 216.

private, *balnea.** It is faid, that there were above
eight hundred public baths, of different kinds, at
Rome: among the chief, were thofe of Agrippa.‡
Dio. liii. "Moriens Agrippa populo hortos et
"balneum a fe denominatum legavit, ut gratis
"lavarentur." Nero conftructed fome of great extent.—*Martial, l. vii. p. 33.*

> Quid Nerone pejus
> Quid thermis melius Neronianis?

Spartian defcribes the public baths of Caracalla.
"Vixit diu in odio populi Antoninus quamvis et
"veftimenta populo dedit, unde Caracallus eft dictus,
"et thermas magnificentiffimas fecerit."

It is well known that public games were very frequently, at all periods of the Roman ftate, gratuitoufly
exhibited to the people. The Circus Maximus, firft
built by Tarquinius Priscus, and furrounded with
magnificent porticos by Julius Cæfar, is faid to have
been a mile in circumference, and capable of holding,
fome fay 150,000, fome 380,000 perfons. Juvenal
fays contemptuoufly of the Roman people,

> Duas tantum res anxius optat,
> Panem et Circenfes.

The calendar of ancient Rome abounded in holidays no lefs than that of modern Rome. Sacrifices
were commonly concluded with feaftings. A part
of the facred offerings were due as among the Jews,

---

* Cafalius de Urbe Roma, p. 314, c. xviii. &c.—"Talia et
"tam exacte prifci Romani et aliæ Ethnicæ gentes servare confue-
"verant circa corporum ablutiones in balneis. Per fanguinem
"autem Chrifti expiatione deinde factâ in terris diminutæ plurimum
"fuere hujusmodi ablutiones apud Chriftianos, quoniam innatus
"fœtor in corporibus hominum per baptifmum pulfus receffit: ut
"apud Card. Baron, &c."—De Judæorum autem fætore refert Am-
mianus Marcell. l. i. Cum Marcus Imp. Paleftinam pertranfiret,
Egyptum petens, fœtentium Judæorum tædio percitus fuit, &c.—
Caf. 321.

‡ Pliny, lib. xviii. c. 15.

to the prieft, a part was confumed at home, and a part given to the poor.

Sacra tulere fuam, parseft data cætera menfis.

Ovid. Met. 12.

Septemviri Epulones were appointed to prepare the public facrifices and feaftings. On folemn occafions, efpecially at funerals, a diftribution of raw meat was made for the people, called *vifceratio.* But the grand fupply for the wants of the Roman populace was the *frumentatio,* the public diftribution of corn. This feems to be the bread which, Juvenal fays, divided their affeftion with the fports of the Circus.

To this purpofe, *pra annoná,* no doubt was applied a great portion of their numerous and heavy taxes; *vectigalia; portorium,* port duties ; *decumæ,* tithes; *fcriptura vigefima hæreditatum,* a twentieth on inheritances, [a tax, which has this great merit, that it does not diminifh any man's aftually poffeffed property: our legacy tax is on the fame principle, and might, perhaps, be ufefully extended to freehold property.] *Vigefima quinta mancipiorum,* a twenty-fifth on flaves: *centefima,* a hundredth on things fold.

The colleftion and diftribution gave employment to various public officers. The cenfors reviewed the populace, to afcertain the number of thofe to whom *teffera frumentariæ,* corn tickets or bread tickets, were delivered.

The public diftributions, *erogationes,* (fometimes of food, fometimes of money inftead,) have been defcribed very much at large by feveral writers, of laborious refearch. See the Effay of Vincentius Contarenus de frumentariâ largitione, in Grævius's Thefaurus Antiq. Romanarum, v. viii.; in which he difcuffes the prior differtation of Juftus Lipfius. The frumentation, corresponding to the Greek σιτηρεσιον,

was gratuitous diftribution of *annona*, annually collected food. This bounty* was of very ancient date,
even from the firft expulfion of the kings, and commonly managed to keep the people in good humour.
Pliny, lib. xviii. refers the inftitution to Manius Martius, the ædile. The diftribution was one of the
official employments of the ædiles. It feems that
the contribution was originally voluntary, and the
diftribution arbitrary, at the will of the fenate. This
mode might fuffice for Rome, while a fmall town ;
but for Rome advancing to the proud title of queen
of the world was impracticable. The tribunes of
the people, feeking wealth and popularity by the
meafure, no doubt, but with fufficient reafon, demanded that the fyftem fhould be defined and regulated by law, that the contribution fhould no longer
be precarious, and that the diftribution fhould be
regular and conftant. By a law, propofed by Caius
Gracchus, it was enacted, that the poor fhould receive
the diftributed corn at a very fmall price.‡ He alfo
divided the public lands among the poor citizens, on
condition that they fhould pay a fmall rent into the
treafury. The fenate inveighed againft him as a
flatterer of the populace; but afterwards extolled
Drufus, his chief opponent, who difcharged the lands
even of that acknowledgement. They alfo, to pleafe
the people, decreed that the corn diftribution fhould
be gratuitous; limiting the monthly maximum to five
modii. This allowance was called *menftruum.* A
daily diftribution to the prifons was called *diurium.*

* It was at different times called *largitio, donativum, congiarium,*
&c. and the diftribution was fometimes made by iffuing *teſſeræ
frumentariæ;* fometimes a delivery of loaves, *panes gradiles,* the
applicants afcending fteps to receive their *dole,* as feen on the
medals of Liberalitates Auguftorum.—*See Spanheim, v. ii. p.* 531—
533, *and authorities there cited.*

‖ Plutarch's Life of C. Gracchus.

It may be fuppofed that the price fixed by Gracchus
was fo fmall as to have been little more than nomi-
nal; as Cicero fays, in his oration for P. Sextius:
" Frumentariam legem C. Gracchus ferebat. Re-
" pugnabant boni quod et ab induftriâ plebem ad
" defidiam avocari putabant, et ærarium exhauriri
" videbatur." And in 2 De Officiis: " C. Gracchi
" frumentaria magna largitio fuit, exhauriebat igi-
" tur ærarium." Another law for a corn diftribution appears to have been propofed by Marius;
and another by L. Apulius Saturninus. This laft,
we learn from Cicero, was rejected, as tending to
exhauft the treafury. The former law feems to
have been fufpended at that time, U. C. 653.
Confufion prevailed during the contefts of Sylla and
Marius. Sylla died, U. C. 675. Till 680, the
fenate held out againft the paffing a new corn law;
but a great effort was then made to obtain it, and
the confuls, C. Cassius and Terentius Lucullus,
paffed one. The allowance, indeed, feems to have
been at all times a fcanty one, and the whole affair
to have been miferably conducted. In the fpeech
of Marcius, reported by Salluft, we find objections to
the principle of the law. " Thefe clamourers for
" the corn law feem to eftimate the value of our com-
" mon liberty at the paltry price of their five *modii;*
" a bare prifon allowance; enough juft to keep a
" man from ftarving, but not to maintain vigour;
" not to provide independence of other fupply.
" The idle, who might look for this as a maintenance,
" would be wretchedly difappointed." To antici-
pate the defigns, and to counterbalance the popularity, of Cæfar, Cato, in 691, advifed the fenate to
pafs an extended law for the public diftribution.
The ordinary annual expense appears, in Plutarch's
life of Cato, to have been feven hundred and fifty

thoufand aurei.* Julius Cæsar made a furvey of the
lower claffes, with a view of regulating the diftribution. It was a fubject worthy of his genius, but
fcarcely compatible with his ambition. Auguftus,
to conciliate the people with his affumption of imperial dignity, greatly increased the allowance, iffued
teſſeræ nummariæ, or money-tickets, and appointed a
præfectus frumenti, or general overfeer. He befides
fold out corn at reduced prices, and gave out that he
had exhaufted two vaft paternal eftates‡ by his private liberality to the Roman people, (perhaps equivalent to above one hundred millions fterling;) but
Dio fhews that his expenditure was, in fact, from the
public purfe, and included the army payments.
Nero made his burning the city a pretext for plun-
dering the treafury; and for a time demanded a
fmall payment to be made by or for each who fhould
receive the corn allowance, which in fact was a fmall
diminution of the aid to each. Under Trajan the
diftributions were profufely great, and children were
admitted as claimants, called *pueri alimentarii.* Books;
containing lifts of thofe entitled to receive the allow-

* "Pecuniæ vis effufa quotannis in has largitiones quæ funt
"DCCL aureorum millia. επεισε τον Συγκλητον απονειμαι σιῖηρεσιον
"αυλοις εμμηνον εξ ου δαπανης μεν επιακοσιαι πενῖηκονῖα μυριαδες
"προσεγινονῖο τοις αλλοις αναλωμασιν."—*Plutarch. Cato.*

"Singulæ Græcorum mvriades mille aureis noftris fcutatis re-
"fpondent."—*Contarenus. Græv. v. viii. p.* 948.

‡ "Quanquam enim cum fæpe alias Auguftus tum fupremo
"teftamento profeffus eft abfumpta a fe in rempublicam duo pa-
"terna patrimonia, et fupra quaterdecies millies quod ex tefta-
"mentis amicorum perceperat, (quæ minimum funt trecenties
"quinquagies centena aureorum millia, vel ut nunc vulgó loquitur
"quinque et triginta milliones;) arguitur tamen femel et iterum
"mendacii a Dione, l. 46; ut qui militibus pecunias divifent λογω
"μεν οικοθεν εργω δε ε των κοινων, verbis de fuo reapfe de publico."
—*Vincent. Contareni, c. iii. Græv. v.* 8.

N. B. An *aureus* contained 146 grains; 42 were coined from a
pound of gold in the days of Auguftus.

ance, were depofited with the *præfectus annonæ.*
Hadrian and Antoninus followed the example of
Trajan. Fauftina, the emprefs of Antoninus Pius,
extended peculiar benevolence to the *puellæ alimen-
tariæ,* charity girls, and inftituted fchools for their
education; one of which, at Prænefte, occupied a pa-
vilion attached to the Temple of Fortune, one of the
moft magnificent of ancient edifices. (See *Monfauçon,
v. ii. pl.* 19.) Some beautiful medals of Fauftina
bear on one fide her portrait, and on the other,
groupes of *puellæ fauftinianæ.*—*(*See *Spanheim de
præftantia & ufu Nummifm. Antiq. vol. ii. pl.* 19.)
Lampridius, in his life of Alex. Severus, mentions
fimilar eftablifhments founded by that emperor, and
entitled by him, in honour of his mother, *Puellæ
Mammæanæ.** In imperial Rome, the fpring head of
public benefit was to be traced to the emperor as to
a mountain, which collected on its height the heavenly moifture, to pour it down in fertilizing ftreams
over the fubjacent nations. We have accordingly
fine medals, recording the bounty of the Cæfars,
Liberalitates Auguftorum.—*(Spanheim, Ant. Num.
v. ii. p.* 533.)

The bounty which policy devifed, which ambition
extended, and pride oftentatioufly vaunted, the advancing influence of Chriftianity fyftematized.

The Roman *Valetudinarium* was an infirmary
attached to the houses of the rich for the ufe of fick
dependents, and poffibly occafional ftrangers. The
term is alfo applied to a military hofpital. It has been
faid, that no eftablifhment exifted in ancient Rome
on a more extended plan. But the expreffion of

---

* This life is afcribed, by a MS. in the Palatine Library, to Spartian.
It is obferved of Alex. Severus, p. 132, "Clamabat fæpius, quod
" a quibufdam five Judæis five Chriftianis audierat et tenebat ; idque
" per præconem quum aliquem emendaret dici jubebat; quod tibi
" fieri non vis, alteri ne feceris."

Seneca feems to mark a difference between a *valetu-dinarium* of a general nature, and one attached to a great man's houfe. " Si intraffem Valetudinarium " exercitatus et fciens, aut domum divitis, non idem " imperaffem omnibus per diverfa ægrotantibus." It, indeed, ftrictly oppofes the *valetudinarium* to the houfe of the rich, therefore may fignify that the diforders of the poor in the *valetudinarium* require a different treatment from thofe of the rich in the *domus.* Yet in epift. 27, he fays, " tanquam in " eodem valetudinario jaceam de communi malo tecum " colloquor, remedia communico." This feems to refer to a kind of place in which he and his friend might have come together, without a total change of condition from freedom to flavery. I find, in Pitif-cus's Lexicon, art. Valetudinarium, " Macer juris-" confultus inter munia tribuni recenfet infpicere va-" letudinarios : Vegetius principum tribunorumque et " comitis, &c." It was the duty of a military tribune or military chief, whatever might be his title, to in-fpect the ftate of the fick foldiers in their infirmary.*

---

* Velleius Paterculus extols Tiberius, Pliny, Trajan, Tacitus, Germanicus, for their care in this refpect. Hyginus, who lived under Adrian, and Vegetius, who lived under Valentinian II give defcriptions of military, hofpitals attached to camps. Hyginus alfo mentions *veterinarium* for the wounded and difeafed cattle.

The firft founder of a general poor-houfe, it feems, was the Emperor Alexis Commenus; combining an afylum for orphans, for maimed foldiers, and aged poor of every defcription.

In the eleventh and twelfth centuries, hofpitals innumerable, for leprous patients, were eftablifhed. " In Galliâ non erat minimus " pagus, in quo non effent elephantiacorum hofpitia."—*Fallop de Morb. Gall. p.* 664. Muratori fpeaks of their dedication to St. Lazarus, from whence Lazaretto and Lazaroni; but Volney thinks the name of the houfe and patient to be derived from El-hezar, a hofpital for the blind at Cairo.

The Emperor Conftantine dedicated great fums to the endow-ment of hofpitals in his new feat of empire. Sampron and Eubulus, two rich Byzantines, employed their fortune in the like manner at the fame time. The Emperor Julian followed his uncle's example,

Whatever might be the care of the poor in ancient Rome, it is not to be doubted, that it was fublimely extended, and for a long time, ufefully directed, by the early chriftians. If any thing like a public hofpital exifted, of pagan conftruction, either its peculiar title was merged in that of the temple to which it was attached, as the building of the fenator Antoninus connected with the temple of Æfculapius, or it was of too humble a conftruction to have attracted the notice of defcribers of Rome and of Conftantinople.* " But," fays Dr. Ryan, (in his Hiftory of the Effects of Religion on Mankind,†) " Mark the happy change wrought by chriftianity " on the condition of all the diftreffed, in the courfe " of a few centuries! Conftantinople alone, which " had not one charitable houfe (at leaft no one is " mentioned, in the defcription of public edifices, in " the firft volume of Byzantine Hiftory,) in the end " of the fourth century, contained afterwards above " thirty ; for the accommodation of orphans, of found- " lings, of the fick, of ftrangers, of beggars, of per- " fons in a leprofy, of the aged, and other perfons in " diftrefs. Thefe houfes were called *orphonotrophia,* " *brephotrophia, nofocomia, xenodochia, lobotrophia,* " *pandochia, ptochia, ptochotrophia, penetotrophia, and* " *gerontocomia ;* Greek words expreffive of the purpofes

and employed his phyfician Oribafus for that purpofe. The famed Belifarius, after he had freed Rome from the Goths, con- ftructed two magnificent hofpitals. St. Jerome or Hieronymus mentions Fabiola, a Roman lady of the fourth century, as the firft, who, having founded an hofpital, devoted her whole time to attendance on the fick.—*Mag. Encyclop.* 1813.

* Scrip. Byzantini, v. 1 and 22.; and Publius Victor de urbis Rom. regionibus.

† E. Ryan, D. D. Hift. &c. v. ii. 28. ‡ Scrip. Byzan. v. 21.

" for which thefe houfes were inftituted.† As thefe
" inftitutions did not exift in Greece before the efta-
" blifhment of chriftianity, thefe words do not occur in
" lexicons for interpreting the ancient Greek authors,
" but frequently in the writings of the Greek chriftians,
" and in the gloffaries which explain them.*" " Upon
" the whole, it does not appear, that there was any
" public place in ancient Rome for the reception of
" the poor or fick, the widow or the orphan;
" whereas, in the feventeenth century, there were
" twenty-five magnificent houfes in Rome for thefe
" humane purpofes. In ancient Rome, they had no
" inftitutions for the fupport of orphans. [It ought,
however, to be remembered that the Prætors were
bound by the Attilian, Prætorian, and Titian laws,
to provide proper guardians for all orphans.] " In
" chriftian Rome, they had two for their fupport in
" the laft century." " In Saxony, and in the chief
" cities of Spain and Italy, there were three religious
" orders for the relief of diftrefs, one of which was
" called the Servants of the Deceafed."‡ In France

† Regulations refpecting them, are found in the Novellæ Conftitutiones of Juftinian. *Nov.* 131. *c. x. and c.* xv.

* Dr. Ryan's Hift. of Eff. of Rel. on Mankind, §. iii. 30.—
This muft be taken with fome limitation, for Ξενων and *xeno-
dochium* are of the fame import; and *pandochium*, an inn, occurs in
the gofpel, and muft have exifted before, or the term could not
have been underftood.

‡ Rofini, lib. viii. c. 17. de Tutelis.—Medical men, however,
received falaries from a public fund. Their duty was to
attend on all the fick of a city. They were called *fufceptores*,
their patients *fufcepti*. Guido Pancirollus Tractatus de magiftratibus municipalibus in Grævii Thes. Ant. Rom. " Medicos
" quoque qui ægrotantes curarent, certo ipfis falario præftituto
" conducebant; neque in hoc præfes provinciæ interveniebat,
" fed curiales ipfi quos morum probitate et artis peritia fpectatos
" cognoviffent eligebant." See collections on this fubject in a joint
effay of M. Percy, Baron de l'Empire, &c. and M. Willaume,
membre de la Legion d'Honneur, on this queftion "Les anciens

there was an order of females, devoted to nurfe-
tending the fick; concerning whom Voltaire ex-
claims, with wonder and fatisfaction, " How noble
" to fee perfons of the tender fex, and diftinguifhed
" by birth, as well as by youth and beauty, ftoop to
" the meaneft offices in the hofpitals, for wretches
" whofe appearance is mortifying to human pride,
" and fhocking to humanity."

It cannot be a fubject of wonder, that the divine
fpirit of mercy, which characterizes the gofpel,
fhould have caufed the early chriftians to abound in
love, and in good works, toward the infirm and needy.
The baneful influence of fuperftition could, however,
fo far pervert even this holy fpirit, as to make it
the means of cherifhing much idlenefs in after times,
greatly counterbalancing its benefits, from the abandonment of right reafon.

Several parts of the New Teftament, in addition
to the parable of Lazarus, fhew that mendicants were
frequent at the gates of the temples, and the doors
of the rich, and in the ftreets. They chofe their
convenient ftations :* which, we learn from Juvenal,

avoient ils des établiffemens publiques en faveur des indigens, des
enfans orphelins ou abandonnés, des malades, et des militaires
bleffées; and s'ils n'en avoient point qu'eft ce qui en tenoit lieu.
Millin Magafin Encyclopedique. Juillet 1813.

* The Sublician bridge, feems to have been a convenient place.
Mendici in ponte Sublicio ftipem petere folebant. *Seneca de vitâ
beatâ. c. xv.*

De mendico male meretur qui dat ei quod edat aut bibat, nam
et illud quod dat perdit, et producit illi vitam ad miferiam.
Plautus in Trinummo.

Codex Juftiniani, lib. 11. tit.25. De mendicantibus validis. Impp.
Gratianus, Valentinianus, et Theod. A. A. A. ad Severum P. U.

Cunctis quos in publicum quæftum incerta mendicitas vocaverit
infpectis, exploretur in fingulis et integritas corporum et robur
annorum: atque inertibus et abfque ullâ debilitate miferandis

were called contemptuoufly *profeuchæ*, προσευχαι, mumping corners. They were characterifed by the mat on which they lay, the ftaff, the dog, and the bag for offals. Juvenal, praying for exemption from the beggar's lot, fays,

> Sit tuta feneçtus—a tegete et baculo.   *S. ix.* 140.

And Martial, laughing at cynick philofophers affecting the mendicant appearance—

> Ne mendica ferat barbati prandia nudi.   *l.* 14.
>
> Dormiat et tetrico cum cane, Pera rogat.   *Ep.* 81.

> The very bag's, afhamed to bear
> The filthy fcraps of beggar's fare;
> And would difcard, if it could ftir,
> The ragged rogue and fhaggy cur.

Euftathius, in a note on Odyfs. P. fays, that fome were called, in Greek, Aγυρ]αι or Mη]ραγυρ]αι, becaufe they went about collecting charity in the name of the holy mother Rhea. Erafmus, on the proverbial term, *mithragyrtes*, obferves, that beggars were fo called, who went about pretending to Egyptian myfteries, and impofing on the vulgar. Apuleius, indeed, fays Stuckius, in his "Convivial "Antiquities," to which work I am obliged for many curious references, fhews that thefe vagabonds refembled thofe of later times, who carried about relics of faints, for petty gain, and impudent pretence to piety. C. v. 146. The ancients were not without even their mendicant friars.

" In the old defcriptions of lazy mendicant priefts, " among the heathens, who ufed to travel from houfe

---

neceffitas inferatur, ut eorum quidem quos tenet conditio fervilis proditor ftudiofus et diligens dominium confequatur : eorum vero quos natalium fola libertas perfequitur colonatu perpetuo fulciatur quifquis hujusmodi lenitudinem prodiderit ac probaverit falvâ dominis in eos actione, qui vel latebram forte fugitivis vel mendicitàtis fubeundæ confilium præftiterunt.

" to houfe with facks on their backs, and from an
" opinion of their fanctity, raife large contributions
" of money, bread, wine, and all kinds of victuals,
" for the fupport of their fraternity, we fee the very
" picture of the begging friars, who are always about
" the ftreet on the fame errand. Stipes æreas
" immo vero, et argenteas multis certatim offeren-
" tibus finu recepere patulo, necnon et vini cadum
" et lactis, et cafeos avidis animis corradentes,
" et in facculos huic quæftui de induftriâ præparatos
" farcientes." *Apul. Metam. l.* 8. " Cicero, in his
" book of Laws, reftrains this practice of begging
" or gathering alms to one particular order of priefts,
" and that only on certain days; becaufe, as he fays,
" it propagates fuperftition, and impoverifhes families.
" Stipem fuftulimus, nifi eam quam ad paucos dies
" propriam, Ideæ matris excepimus. Implet, enim,
" fuperftitione animos exhaurit domos." *Cic. de leg.*
l. ii. 9—16. From Middleton's Letter from Rome.

In Juftinian's Novellæ Conftitutiones, *Auth. Coll.*
vi. Tit. 9, *Novell. lxxx. c. v.* 162,* " it is enacted,
" that perfons able in body, belonging to other

‡ Pope Sixtus V. had once determined to expel every one from
Rome, who had not a fortune, or could not get a livelihood by
their labour. But thinking this would be a cruel meafure, he un-
dertook the building of great edifices, to employ all idle hands.
The more effectually to prevent the city from being filled with
beggars, he would not fuffer foreigners to come and live there,
except they brought a certificate that they were able, by fome trade
or profeffion, to maintain a family: ftrictly forbidding the clergy
to marry any one that had not a proper licence and teftimonial to
that effect from the magiftrate; and the laity, on pain of being fent
to the gallies, to promife marriage before they had prefented themfelves to fuch magiftrates as were appointed to examine their circumftances; who, if they found them in danger of falling into
poverty, or not able to maintain children, were not only to prohi-
bit their marrying, but in cafe they perfiftedin their defign, to banifh
them out of the city. And when it was told Sixtus, that many
thoufands had been already banifhed upon that account, he faid,
" It was better to depopulate a city, than have it inhabited by
" beggars."

" places, but lingering in Rome without vifible
" means of fupport, fhall be fent back, if of fervile
" condition, to their mafters, if free, to their provin
" ces." Chapter 5, *on mendicants*, decrees,
" But if they are natives or citizens, and found in
" body, but without adequate means of fupport,
" they muft not be permitted to become a burthen
" to the land, but muft be delivered without delay
" to the furveyors of the public works, that they
" may be provided with employment; to the over-
" feers of the ovens, to gardeners, or to men of
" different occupations; in fome of which they may
" be able to engage and earn a maintenance; chang-
" ing a life of idlenefs for one of ufefulnefs. But
" if any fhall refufe to work at the feveral trades
" or occupations to which they fhall be fo appointed,
" let them be banifhed from our royal city. This
" we decree in our mercy, left, driven by idlenefs to
" crime, they become liable to heavier penalties,
" and the feverities of our courts of juftice. But
" thofe who are debilitated by cafual injury, by fick-
" nefs, or by age, if they be citizens, we permit
" to remain without moleftation in our city, and to
" be placed on the lift of the penfioners of the pious;"
[probably of the chriftians; or failing in this refpect, we may fuppofe, to avail themfelves of the
fportulæ, frumentationes, &c.] " But we command
" that enquiry be made refpecting others fo maimed
" and infirm, as to the occafion of their coming to
" this place, that they may not fit idle in our ftreets;
" and that if it fhall appear right and fit, they may
" be conveyed back to their proper provinces."

The dead poor, whofe friends could not afford
the expenfe of a funeral, were carried to their
graves, by men called *vefpæ* or *vefpillones*. " Qui
" Sexto Pompeio auctore fic dicebantur, quod vef-

" pertino tempore eos efferrent qui funebri pompa
" duci propter inopiam nequibant." *Rofini Ant.
Rom. l. v. c.* 39.

The ancients, Romans as well as Greeks, had
numerous clubs and affociations many, no doubt,
for mere purpofes of feafting, but even from thefe
diftributions were made to their poorer neighbours ;
but feveral appear to have been founded on the
principle of promoting charity. They were called
collegia and *fodalitates.* " Sodales, Auguftinus vult,
" dictos quafi fimul edales." *Stuckius.* A fraternity
of a religious kind is faid to have been inftituted by
Romulus, in honour of his union with Tatius the
Sabine king. Numa inftituted colleges or companies
of the different trades, mafons, goldfmiths, &c.
appointing peculiar folemnities of ceremony for their
meetings and facred rites, to cherifh peace and love
amongft the citizens. *Plutarch, Life of Numa.* It
was afterwards found, that the different focieties
promoted faction, rather than peace ; and laws were
paffed, at different times, to regulate them and to fupprefs them. Tarquinius Superbus fuppreffed them.
After his expulfion, they were revived. A great
number were fuppreffed by decree of the fenate,
in the confulfhip of Q. Cæcilius and Q. Martius.
There were then above five hundred different
clubs in Rome. Nine years after, P. Clodius reftored them, and added many new ones, collegia
(fays Cicero) " ex omni fæce urbis et fervitio conci-
" tata." Cæfar, when dictator, fuppreffed, Auguftus
reftored, many.

Pliny writes to the Emperor Trajan, " The free
" and confederate city of Amifus" [a colony of Athenians, in the province of Pontica,] " enjoys, by your
" indulgence, the privilege of being governed by its
" own laws. A memorial having been there pre-

" fented to me, concerning a charitable inftitution,
" I have fubjoined it to this letter, that you may
" confider, fir, whether, and how far, this fociety
" ought to be licenfed or prohibited." *Letter* 93.

Letter 94. Trajan to Pliny. " If the prayer of
" the petition of the Amifeni, which you have
" tranfmitted to me, concerning the eftablifhment of
" a charitable fociety, be agreeable to their own
" laws, which, by the articles of alliance, it is fti-
" pulated, they fhall enjoy; I fhall not oppofe it;
" efpecially if thefe contributions are employed, not
" for the purpofes of riot and faction, but for the
" fupport of the indigent. In other cities, however,
" which are fubject to our laws, I would have all
" affemblies of this nature prohibited."*

From this flight view of ancient charity and policy,
it is fufficiently apparent, that the principle of benevolence was not wanting among the Greeks and
Romans; that the regulation of the poor has been
attended with confiderable difficulty at all times;
that confiderable funds were conftantly applied to the
relief of the infirm and indigent; and that in proportion as great wealth has been accumulated in few
hands, and luxurious habits have widened the diftinction between the higher and lower claffes; want,
beggary, and idlenefs, have extenfively encreafed;
and the demands for a permanent fupply been pro-
portionately urgent.

---

* The learned Cafaubon, in his obfervations upon Theophraftus,
informs us, that there were at Athens, and other cities of Greece,
certain fraternities which paid into a common cheft a monthly
contribution toward the fupport of fuch of their members who had
fallen into misfortunes; upon condition, that if ever they arrived
at more profperous circumftances, they fhould pay into the
general fund the money fo advanced. *Melmoth's tranflation.*

*Charities of Naples, and other towns of Italy,
from Eustace's Travels, &c.*

" The hofpitals of Naples reflect much honour
" on the charity of the inhabitants.   Thefe eftablifh-
" ments are very numerous, and adapted to every
" fpecies of diftrefs to which man is fubject, in mind
" or body.   Many of them are richly endowed, and
" all clean, well attended, and well regulated.   One
" circumftance, almoft peculiar to Italian hofpitals
" and charitable foundations, contributes effentially
" to their fplendour and profperity; it is, that they
" are not only attended by perfons who devote
" themfelves entirely, and without any interefted
" views, to the relief of fuffering humanity; but
" that they are governed and infpected, not nomi-
" nally but really, by perfons of the firft rank and
" education, who manage the interefts of the efta-
" blifhments with a prudence and affiduity, which
" they feldom, perhaps, difplay in their own domeftic
" economy.   Befides, to almoft every hofpital is
" attached one, and fometimes more, confraternities,
" or pious affociations, formed for the purpofe of
" relieving fome particular fpecies of diftrefs, or
" averting or remedying fome evil.   Thefe confra-
" ternities, though founded upon the bafis of equa-
" lity, and of courfe open to all ranks, generally
" contain a very confiderable proportion of noble
" perfons, who make it a point to fulfil the duties
" of the affociation with an exactnefs as honourable
" to themfelves, as it is exemplary and beneficial to
" the public.   Thefe perfons vifit the refpective
" hofpitals almoft daily, inquire into the fituation and
" circumftances of every patient, and oftentimes
" attend on them perfonally, and render them the
" moft humble fervices.   They perform thefe duties

" in difguife, generally in the drefs or uniform worn
" by the confraternity, for the exprefs purpofe of
" diverting public attention from the individuals,
" and fixing it on the objeƈt only of the affociation.
" Of charitable foundations in Naples, the number
" is above fixty. Of thefe, feven are hofpitals, pro-
" perly fo called; thirty at leaſt are confervatories,
" or receptacles for helplefs orphans, foundlings, &c.;
" five are banks for the relief of fuch induſtrious
" poor as are diſtreſſed by the occafional want of
" fmall fums of money; the others are either fchools
" or confraternities. The incomes of moſt of thefe
" eſtabliſhments, particularly of the hofpitals, are in
" general very confiderable, but feldom equal to the
" expenditure. The annual deficiency, how great
" foever it may be, is abundantly fupplied by do-
" nations, moſt of which come from unknown be-
" nefaƈtors. The two principal hofpitals are, that
" called *Degli Incurabili*, which, notwithſtanding its
" title, is open to fick perfons of all defcriptions, and
" conſtantly relieves more than eighteen hundred;
" and that of *Della Santa Annunziata*, which is im-
" menfely rich, and deſtined to receive foundlings,
" penitent females, &c. &c. and faid fometimes to
" harbour two thoufand. To each belong, in the
" firſt place, a villa, and in the fecond, a cemetery.
" The villa of the firſt is fituated at Torre del Greco,
" and is deſtined for the benefit of convalefcents,
" and fuch as labour under diſtempers to which the
" poorer clafs are liable, and arife from conſtant con-
" finement, and the want of pure air. The cemetery
" is, in a different way, of at leaſt equal advantage to
" public health. It was apprehended, and not
" without reafon, that fo many bodies as mſt be
" carried out from an hofpital, efpecially in unhealthy
" feafons, might, if depofited in any church or church-

" yard within the city, infect the air, and produce or
" propagate contagious diseases. To prevent fuch
" evils, the fum of 48,500 ducats, raifed by volun-
" tary contribution, was laid out in purchafing
" and fitting up for the purpofe a field, about half-
" a-mile from the walls of the city, on a rifing
" ground. A little neat church is annexed to it,
" with apartments for the officiating clergy, and
" the perfons attached to the fervice of the cemetery;
" and the road that winds up the hill to it is lined
" with cypreffes. The burial-ground is divided
" into three hundred and fixty-fix large and deep
" vaults, one of which is opened every day in the
" year, and the bodies to be interred depofited in
" order. Thefe vaults are covered with flags of
" lava, that fit exactly, and completely clofe every
" aperture. The bodies are carried out at night
" time by perfons appointed for the purpofe, and
" every precaution taken to prevent even the
" flighteft chance of infection. All is done gratis,
" and the expenfes requifite fupplied by public
" charity. It is to be regretted, that this method
" of burying the dead has not been adopted in every
" hofpital and parifh in Naples, and indeed in every
" town and city, not in Italy only, but all over Europe.
" It is really lamentable, that a practice fo difgufting,
" not to fay fo pernicious, as that of heaping up
" putrid carcafes in churches, where the air is ne-
" ceffarily confined, and in church-yards in cities,
" where it cannot have a free circulation, fhould be
" fo long and fo obftinately retained. It would be
" difficult to difcover one fingle argument, drawn
" either from the principles of religion, or the
" dictates of reafon, in its favour, while its in-
" conveniences are vifible, and almoft tangible.

" When a patient in a hofpital has recovered
" his health and ftrength, and is about to return to
" his ufual occupations, he receives from the efta-
" blifhment a fum of money fufficient to compenfate
" for the lofs of time and labour, unavoidable during
" his illnefs; a moft benevolent cuftom, and highly
" worthy of imitation. A long illnefs or danger-
" ous accident deprives a poor labourer or artizan
" fo long of his ordinary wages, and throws him
" fo far back in his little economy, that he cannot,
" without great difficulty, recover himfelf, and re-
" gain a ftate of comfort. From this inconvenience
" the fmall fum granted by the charity of the hof-
" pital relieves him; and reftores him to his trade in
" health, ftrength, and fpirits.—The *Confervatorii*
" are fchools opened for poor children of both fexes,
" where they are educated, fed, and taught fome
" handicraft or other. Some are in the nature of
" working-houfes, and employ a prodigious number
" of indigent perfons of both fexes, in feparate
" buildings, while others are devoted entirely to
" children, educated principally for mufic. Thefe
" latter inftitutions have produced fome, or rather
" moft, of the great performers and mafters of the
" art, who have figured in the churches, or on the
" ftages, of the different capitals of Europe, for the
" laft hundred years. Paefielli, Caffarelli, and Per-
" golefe, were formed in thefe feminaries. And,
" indeed, Naples is to Italy, what Italy is to the
" world at large, the great fchool of music, where
" that fascinating art is cultivated with the greateft
" ardour; an ardour oftentimes carried to an ex-
" treme, and productive of confequences highly
" mischievous, and degrading to humanity.—Of
" the numberlefs confraternities, one eminently
" worthy of notice is that, whofe motto is *Succurre*

" *Miferis*; the members of which make it their duty
" to vifit condemned criminals, prepare them for death,
" accompany them to execution, and give them a
" decent burial. They carry their charitable at-
" tentions ftill farther, and provide for the widows
" and children of thefe unhappy wretches. This
" fociety was originally compofed of fome of the firft
" nobility of the city; but the tyrant Philip, influenced,
" it feems, by motives of political fufpicion, forbad the
" nobles to enter into fuch affociations, and in parti-
" cular, confined the one we are fpeaking of to the
" clergy.—The congregation *De S. Ivone* confifts of
" lawyers, who undertake to plead the caufes of the
" poor gratis, and furnifh all the expenfes neceffary
" to carry their fuits through the courts with effect.
" To be entitled to the affiftance and fupport of this
" affociation, no recommendation or introduction is
" required. The perfon applying has only to prove
" his poverty, and give in a full and fair ftatement of
" his cafe.—*Congregazione della Croce*, compofed
" principally of nobility to relieve the poor, and im-
" prifoned, and particularly to bury the bodies of fuch
" diftreffed and forfaken perfons when dead.—The con-
" gregation *Della Sta. Trinita dei Pellegrini* is des-
" tined, as its name imports, more particularly for the
" relief of ftrangers, and is compofed of perfons of all
" claffes, who meet in its affemblies, and fulfil its du-
" ties, without diftinction. It is governed by five per-
" fons, one of whom prefides, and is generally a pre-
" late or high officer of ftate ; the others are a
" nobleman, a citizen, a lawyer, and an artizan. All
" the members attend the hofpital in rotation, each for
" a week, during which they receive ftrangers, wafh
" their feet, attend them at table, and ferve them with
" the humility, and with more than the affiduity, of
" menials.—The *congregation of Nobles*, for the relief

' of the bafhful poor. The objeft of this affociation
" is to difcover and relieve fuch induftrious perfons, as
" are reduced to poverty by misfortune; and have too
" much fpirit, or too much modefty, to folicit p blic
" affiftance. The members of this affociation, it is
" faid, difcharge its benevolent duties with a zeal, a
" fagacity, and what is ftill more neceffary for the ac-
" complifhment of their objeft. with a delicacy and
" kindnefs truly admirable. All thefe confraternities
" have halls, churches, and hofpitals, more or lefs
" grand and extenfive, as their objeft may require,
" or their means allow."*

What a bleffed abode of piety and charity is Naples, if Mr. Euftace prefents us with a faithful picture!
Can this be the town fo fcandalized by other travellers, the feat of the moft corrupt and profligate
court in Europe, difgraced by the worft government,
worft exercifed, by nobility and gentry the moft depraved, and commonly the moft wretchedly degraded?
The above quotations are merely introduced to fhew
that, whatever may be the ftate of religion, government, morals, and police, the fums annually devoted
to the relief of the infirm and poor are not fo fmall
as to warrant the vain fuggeftion which many delight
to propagate, that the facrifice of property to the
fupport of the poor in England, by the operation of
the poor's law, is greatly difproportionate to that

* " Even in the very refpeft in which Naples is fuppofed to be
" moft deficient, I mean in regard to chaftity, there are inftances of
" attention to morality, not to be equalled in any tranfalpine capital.
" For inftance, there are more retreats open to repentant females,
" and more means employed to fecure the innocence of girls expofed
" to the dangers of feduction by their age, their poverty, or by the
" lofs, the neglect, or the wickednefs, of their parents, than are to be
" found in London, Paris, Vienna, and Peterfburgh united. Of this
" latter defcription, there are four hundred educated in one confer-
" vatorio ; and not only educated, but when fit for marriage, por-
" tioned out according to their talents." *Euftace's Travels.*

which common humanity devotes to that object in other countries.

That the legal allotment of a portion of the public revenue to the support of thofe whofe labour has been or may be beneficial to the public, and whofe powers of exertion are fufpended or deftroyed by age or ficknefs,—to infants deprived of parental protection,—to ideots and lunatics,—is, in any view of national policy, more difadvantageous to the community, than the leaving all who are in want to feek at large for the charity of individuals, is a conclufion, to which, I conceive, an obferver could never be led by an examination of the ftate of the poor, and the effects of charity in Catholic countries. The notices of the ftate of the poor, to be found in the journals of travellers, are indeed rare and fcanty ; but the remarks of a furious panegyrift of Italian charities will probably lead thofe who are capable of confidering the fubject without Romifh prejudices, to inferences very different from thofe of the author. Baretti (Account of Manners and Cuftoms of Italy, v. ii. p. 100, &c.) fays, " the benevolence of the modern Romans muft have " been very great, and have continued through " many generations; fince it is afferted, that the united " revenues of all the Cardinals refiding in Italy, " which, upon a medium, may be reckoned at 4000l. " each, do not amount to the third part of the " revenues poffeffed by the hofpitals in that fingle " city. Nor is the admittance into our hofpitals " rendered difficult, by cavilling or narrow regu- " lations, as is often the cafe in other countries, " where charity is fo diligently anatomifed, that " many good things are not done, for fear improper " objects fhould partake of them. *The Italians fcorn* " *fuch paltry difcriminations*, and every perfon who is, " or will be, an object of their charity, is by them

" confidered as poor enough to deferve a fhare of it.
" Therefore, in the greateft part of our hofpitals,
" every object of mifery is freely received; nor is
" there any enquiry ever made, whether it is in his
" power to procure affiftance at home.

" With regard to the foundlings, thofe that carry
" them to the proper hofpitals, put them in an engine
" at the door, ring a bell to give notice that a child
" has been brought, and go about their bufinefs;
" and the poor infant is immediately taken care of:
" nor is there any enquiry ever made after their
" parents. So that thofe who cannot maintain their
" children, as well as thofe who will not, may fend
" them there without the leaft hindrance, certain
" that the public charity will fupply their want of
" ability and *tendernefs.*"

" But Italian charity is ftill of a more extenfive
" nature, and embraces other objects befides thofe
" that are only fit for hofpitals. Many are the funds,
" and fome them very confiderable, whofe produce
" is yearly fhared into competent fums, and diftri-
" buted under the name of portions to poor maidens,
" when they are willing to marry, or defirous to take
" the veil."

" Befides the funds thus applied, we have others,
" inftituted to prevent the extortions of ufurers; by
" which the diftreffes of the poor are extremely
" aggravated in other countr es. From thefe funds
" the poor generally receive two-thirds of the value
" of their pledges, without paying intereft for fmall
" fums, and only one or two per cent. for fums con-
" fiderable. Should they forfeit their goods, they
" are fold by auction, and the furplus paid them.
" Why do not all nations adopt this Italian fcheme
" of relieving their poor, ever fubject to the rapacious
" extortions of hard-hearted Jews, or mercilefs

" pawnbrokers ?" [*Anfwer*. Becaufe the fcheme offers a bounty on improvidence; and as it muft be conducted at a great expenfe, and without profit, the funds neceffary to its fupport may be more beneficially bestowed.]

" I need not mention that other kind of charity, " fo common among the Italians, of giving alms to " ftreet-beggars. This great fault of ours is gene- " rally known, thanks to thofe ultramontane poli- " ticians, who have fo often blamed us for it in their " wife accounts of our country, pretending that this " practice of ours encourages idl·nefs, and of courfe " deftroys induftry. To this heavy charge I have " *nothing* to anfwer, but that I hope my countrymen " will never adopt fuch outlandifh politics!" An anfwer worfe than nothing. He eftimates the popu- lation of Italy at fourteen millions: the number of friars at 84,000, and the proportion of mend·cants to non-mendicants as 3 to 1. It were vain, indeed, to reafon on the evils of a life of beggary, w th one who can vindicate the devotion to it of fo large a portion of his country's population.

Of the Roman charities, the two moft celebrated are, the Hofpital for Pilgrims, and *Monte della Pietá*, or Bank for Pledges. Cafalius, in his work *De Urbe Româ*, defcribes the former with enthufiaftic eulogy. Salmon, in the hiftorical defcription of ancient and modern Rome, has this notice of them. " St. " Philippo Neri, when fecular, feeing how much the " poor pilgrims fuffered, who came to Rome, from " various parts, *to vifit the fepulchres of the apoftles*, " *and obtain indulgences*, no one giving them lodging; " the pious youth, with fixteen of his companions, " began the great work of hofpitality in the church " of S. Salvatore in Campo, forming a contraternity, " under the title of the Holy Trinity, for the

" purpofe of exercifing charity toward their neigh-
" bours, and adminiftering relief to poor pilgrims.
" They received all pilgrims with the greateft be-
" nevolence; and wafhing their feet, gave them
" food and lodging for three nights. D. Elena
" Orfini, a Roman lady, gave a houfe for the ac-
" commodation of female pilgrims, and this charitable
" work has continued ever fince. Here are bufts of
" Clement VIII. and XI. and that of Bened. XIV.
" &c. as brothers and benefactors of this pious work,
" who, by their affiftance and good example of at-
" tending upon and wafhing the pilgrims' feet, have
" infpired others to the fame. Befides thefe, the
" poor convalefcents are received here, who have left
" the hofpitals; relief being afforded them for three
" days, and longer, if neceffary." [As the days of
pilgrimages, it may be hoped, are nearly at an end,
this charity may probably in future be wholly applied
to relieve the diftreffes of the refident poor, inftead
of giving bounties to indolent wanderers.] " In
" order to avoid the great extortion exacted by the
" Jews for pledges of the chriftians, and to relieve
" thofe in neceffity, in 1539, by perfuafion of Gio-
" vanni Calvo, prior of the conventual friars, a
" company of wealthy perfons was formed, who
" depofited a certain fum of money to eftablifh a
" bank, in order to lend money to the poor, who
" brought pledges for fecurity of their debts, with-
" out taking any intereft. This company being
" approved by Paul III. he elected St. Charles Bor-
" romeo* protector, who formed the ftatutes. Sixtus

* The Cardinal Charles Borromeo, called St. Charles, having
been canonized in 1610, and having merited all earthly honour by
a life dedicated to the glory of GOD in the benefit of mankind, en-
joined the inftitution of charitable affociations throughout all the
parifhes of his diocefe, the archb.fhopric of Milan, *in folievo de
poveri infermi*, for aid and fupport of the fick and difabled. In

" V. gáve a place in the ſtreet Coronari for this
" purpoſe.   Clement VIII. removed them, and
" granted the palace inhabited by Urban VIII. when
" cardinal, in which are the Bank for Depoſits, and
" apartments for the ſuperintendants.   The money
" lent, amounting to thirty crowns, is gratis; but
" above that ſum, two crowns are paid annually for
" every hundred.   The pledges are kept here for
" eighteen months, then ſold by public ſale, and the
" money lent ſtopped; but the overplus of the gain
" is returned to the owners of the pledges."—*Salmon's
Ancient and Modern Rome, vol. ii. p.* 152.

It may be worth while here to preſent a few plain
obſervations on Italian charities, by a very enlightened
French traveller, *Lalande, Voyage en Italie, vol. v.
c. ix. p.* 166.

" Il y a des fondations dans pluſieurs egliſes pour
" diſtribuer à chaque fête ſolennelle des dots aux
" pauvres filles, ſoit pour prendre le voile, ſoit pour
" ſe marier ſelon leur gout.   La ſomme eſt fixée, de
" même que le nombre des filles qui viennent en
" proceſſion pour la reçevoir.   Ces charités, ſi fre-
" quentes et faites ſi mal-apropos, ſont un des grands
" vices du gouvernement ou elles entretiennent la
" faineantiſe.——Quand une fille du commun à la

the collection of rules of one of theſe ſocieties, " Regole per li
" aſcritti alla carità criſtiana in ſollievo, &c. nella parochia di S.
" Bartolomeo ſotto il pa rocinio di S. Luigi Gonzaga," it is ſtated,
that a large aſſociation of perſons of either ſex are devoted to the
objects of the inſtitution, to daily and nightly attendance on the ſick
poor with zeal and diligence, no leſs beneficial to the bodies of the
ſufferers, who receive their bounteous aid, than to their own ſouls.
    Mr A. Young (*Travels in France, &c.* 4to. *p.* 645) ſays, arti-
cle Milan, " charitable foundations in the city only amount to
" 3,000,000 livres, (87,500l. ſterling.)   In the great hoſpital, there
" are commnoly from 12 to 1500 ſick.   The effect is found to be
" exceedingly miſchievous, for there are many that will not work,
" depending on theſe eſtabliſhments."   " The population of Milan
" is ſaid to be 116,000."—*Watkins's Travels, Letter* 24.

" proteƈion du batard de l'apoticaire d'un cardinal,
" elle ſe fait aſſurer cinq ou ſix dots dans cinq ou
" ſix egliſes, et ne veut plus apprendre ni a coudre
" ni a filer, &c.

" Il n'y a preſque point de jour, ou dans quelques
" un des principaux couvens de religieux on ne
" diſtribue de la ſoupe à la porte à tous ceux qui la
" viennent demander: le grand nombre d'hopitaux
" qu'il y a dans Rome, et la facilité d'avoir le pain
" la ſoupe et l'aumône dans les couvens, y entreti-
" ennent la faineantiſe et la mendicité ; et c'eſt une
" choſe qui revolte que le grand nombre de mendians
" dont on eſt aſſailli dans les rues de Rome, ainſi que
" dans celles de Naples: on y regrette bien la bonne
" police de Londres, qui a ſu debarraſſer totalement
" les rues et les egliſes de cette vermine inſupportable
" pour les citoyens, et honteuſe pour un etat. Au
" reſte c'eſt bien pis à Naples," &c.

Charities in Germany.

The degraded charaƈer of the poor throughout
the greater part of Germany renders it difficult to
colleƈ faƈts reſpeƈing them from the narratives of
travellers. In Travels through Germany, written
by Baron Rieſbeck, and tranſlated by the Rev. Mr.
Maty, publiſhed 1787, it is ſaid, " All the charities
" (of Vienna) depend upon the Court alone for their
" ſupport. We meet here with no curé of St.
" Sulpice, to raiſe 300,000 livres a year for the relief
" of the neceſſitous. The Archbiſhop Migazzi is as
" bigoted, and as dependant on the papal hierarchy,
" as Beaumont ; but he gives no millions of livres
" yearly out of his income to ſecret diſtreſs, as the
" good Archbiſhop of Paris does. The Empreſs's
" benevolence, of which religion is the principle,

" approaches to profufion; fhe refufes relief to none
" who ftand in need of her affiftance. Her fteward
" has hardly any thing to lay before her but ac-
" counts of charities. Her liberality particularly
" fhews itfelf towards widows, efpecially fuch as are
" of high birth. Her partiality to high birth makes
" her defirous that every perfon fhould live up to his
" or her rank. With refpeft to the public foun-
" dations, the library, fchools, hofpitals, and poor-
" houfes, coft her immenfe fums. I am affured, that
" the debts fhe has contraƈed by this liberality, (if
" they are juft debts, the liberality is at the expenfe
" of her creditors,) amount to upwards of twenty
" millions of guilders ; and one of my friends in-
" formed me, that fhe gives away three millions per
" annum in private charity. Who would imagine
" now, that under fo worthy a charaƈer merit often
" ftarves, whilft large fums are lavifhed upon the
" worthlefs ? The prejudices of religion have fo far
" gotten the better of her natural difpofition, as to
" make her refufe affiftance to an officer who had
" been crippled in her fervice, unlefs he would em-
" brace the Catholic religion !"

In Madame de Stael's eloquent and difcriminating
work on Germany, the poor could not be wholly
unnoticed. If they occupy but a fmall fpace, the
defeƈt is in the fubjeƈt, not in the writer.* Her
remarks are confined principally to Hamburgh.
Having noticed the fchools of Peftalozzi, for the
improvement of the poor throughout Germanic
Switzerland, fhe defcribes fimilar inftitutions of
Mr. Fellenberg, in Hamburgh. " He caufes village

* Defcribing the Prater, (the Hyde-Park of Vienna,) fhe favs,
" you never meet a beggar at thefe promenades ; none are to be
" feen in Vienna. The charitable eftablifhments there are regulated
" with great order and liberality ; private and public benevolence
" is direƈted with a great fpirit of juftice."

" fchoolmafters, to be taught according to Peftalozzi's
" method. The labourers who cultivate his grounds
" learn pfalm tunes; and the praifes of GOD are heard
" throughout the country, fung by fimple but har-
" monious voices, celebrating nature and its Author.
" In fhort, M. de Fellenberg endeavours, by every
" poffible means, to form between the fuperior and
" inferior claffes a liberal tie; a bond which fhall
" not be merely dependent on the pecuniary interefts
" of the rich and the poor. It is not enough to be
" occupied in promoting the welfare of the lower
" claffes, with a view to ufefulnefs only: they fhould
" alfo participate in the enjoyments of the imagina-
" tion and the heart. It is in this fpirit, that en-
" lightened philanthropifts have taken up the fubject
" of mendicity at Hamburgh. Neither defpotifm,
" nor fpeculative œconomy, have any place in their
" charitable inftitutions." [N. B. Speculative œconomy muft here be taken in a very limited fenfe, to
avoid abfurdity.] "It was their wifh, that the
" unfortunate objects of their care fhould them-
" felves defire the labour which was expected from
" them, as much as the benefactions which were
" granted them. As the welfare of the poor was
" not with them a mean, but an end, they have not
" ordered them employment, but have made them
" defire it. We conftantly fee in the accounts of
" thofe charitable inftitutions, that the object of their
" founders was no lefs to make men better, than
" to render them more ufeful. Such is the high
" philofophical fpirit of liberty and wifdom, which
" reigns in, and gives peculiarity of character to, this
" ancient Hanfeatic city. There is much real bene-
" ficence in the world, and he who is not capable
" of ferving his fellow-creatures by the facrifice of
" his time, and of his inclinations, voluntarily con-

" tributes to their welfare with money : this is ftill
" fomething, and no virtue is to be difdained. But
" in moft countries, the great mafs of private alms
" is not wifely directed ; and one of the moft emi-
" nent fervices which the Baron de Voght, and his
" excellent countrymen, have rendered to the caufe
" of humanity, is that of fhewing how, without new
" facrifices, without the intervention of the ftate,
" private beneficence may be rendered fufficient
" for the relief of the unfortunate. That which
" is effected by individuals is particularly fuited to
" Germany ; where every thing taken feparately is
" better than the whole together. Charitable infti-
" tutions ought, indeed, to profper in the city of
" Hamburgh. There is fo much morality amongft
" its inhabitants, that for a time they paid their
" taxes into a fort of trunk, without any perfon
" feeing what they brought ; thefe taxes were to
" be proportioned to the fortune of each individual,
" and when the calculation was made, they were
" always found to be fcrupuloufly paid. Might we
" not believe, that we were relating a circumftance
" belonging to the golden age, if in that golden age
" there had been private riches and public taxes ?"
[A circumftance, it muftbe owned, rather improbable.]

A very interefting extract from the Report of the
Eftablifhment at Hamburgh, in 1799, is publifhed
in the 12th Report of the Society for bettering the
condition of the poor. No. 10. It contains feveral
facts, bearing ftrong internal evidence of authenticity,
and refults of extenfively ufeful application.

In 1789, the ftreets of Hamburgh were crowded with beggars, many of them ftrangers;
all in great diftrefs ; the modeft
and deferving perifhing un-
heard and unknown, for want

In 1799, fcarcely a beggar
was to be feen ; every neceffitous inhabitant receiving, under
kind and regular care and infpection, fure and beneficial
relief. In ten years, 3081

of a fhare in that relief which the ftreet beggar anticipated by fraud and importunity. 446 perfons were in the houfe of correction, befides prifoners.

5. The diftreffes, and the conduct of the poor were almoft unknown, except to a few clerical and medical men. When the directors and infpectors made their firft inquiries, they vifited fome narrow courts inhabited entirely by beggars, loft to fociety, and fcarcely preferving the human form; courts, which benevolence approached with a degree of alarm and horror.

10. There were 7391 paupers, 4087 women, 1079 men, and 2225 children, befides perfons in hofpitals. Mendicity, fpreading like infection, and paralyfing the induftry and energy of the poor, was become an epidemic difeafe among the lower claffes of life.

poor ftrangers were relieved and returned to their places of habitation. Not more in the whole than 147 perfons in the Houfe.

5. There are now 180 Infpectors; five phyficians, and five furgeons, who regularly vifit every part of Hamburgh. Each houfe is numbered, and there are 2200 poor perfons employed (perhaps this means fome one in every houfe, or nearly fo, to which the benefit of the charity has extended) to bring the infpectors immediate information of any diftrefs or diforder in the city. Thus are vice and mifery diminifhed among the poor; and virtue and patriotifm increafed among the rich.

10. There are (1799) at prefent 3090 paupers, fed and clothed, and obliged to do fuch work as they are capable of. Of thefe, 1692 are aged perfons, from 60 to 100 years of age; 1097 maimed or difeafed perfons of middle age, and 401 children, the greater part of whom are very young.

The members of this inftitution in Hamburgh voluntarily engaged themfelves to pay each a fine, in cafe of fuch deviation from the true principles upon which the poor ought to be affifted, as the giving indifcriminate alms, without inveftigating and afcertaining the wants of the object. *Account of Management of Poor in Hamburgh, by Mr. Voght,* p. 15.

Mandeville remarks of Holland, (Fable of Bees, Remark 2.) " The country is fo fmall and po-
" pulous, that there is not land enough (though

" hardly an inch of it is unimproved) to feed the tenth
" part of its inhabitants. The Dutch endeavour
" to promote as much frugality among their fubjects
" as poffible, not becaufe it is a virtue, but becaufe
" it is, generally fpeaking, their intereft." However, our lateft traveller in Holland (Sir John Carr,
1807) obferves, " I found that the received opinion
" of there being no beggars in Holland is erroneous.
" I was frequently befet by thefe fons and daughters
" of forrow or idlenefs, who preferred their petition
" with indefatigable purfuit, but in fo gentle a tone,
" that it was evident they were fearful of the
" police. There are fo many afylums for paupers,
" that a Dutchman, acquainted with the legiflative
" provision made for them, always confiders a
" beggar as a lawlefs vagabond. Holland is juftly
" celebrated for its public charities. In Rotter-
" dam, before the laft war, there were many bene-
" volent inftitutions, fome of which have inevitably
" languifhed, and others expired, in confequence of
" the ufually impoverifhing effects of long hoftility."
The devaftation of the continent, the general confequence of debility from bad government, and of the
overwhelming violence of mad ambition, renders all
enquiry into exifting inftitutions ufelefs.* Whenever
good government fhall be eftabl:fhed in any portion of
Europe, which an internal combination of force, or
the confent of the furrounding countries, fhall render
worthy to be called a ftate; then ufeful inftitutions for
the indigent and infirm will, no doubt, be eftablifhed,
differing probably in many particulars from thofe
which have hitherto been known on the Continent,
except perhaps in Hamburgh.

* This and fome fimilar paffages were written, while the Continent of Europe was almoft wholly fubject to Bonaparte, his brothers,
and generals. Thanks to GOD for the heart-cheering change !

In a moſt valuable book, entitled " Inquiries con-
" cerning the Poor, by John M'Farlan, D. D. one
" of the miniſters of Canongate, Edinburgh, 1782,"
p. 202, c. viii. the obſervations on the police of
Holland, relating to the poor, are highly intereſting.
For a full extraƈt of the laws of the United Provinces
reſpeƈting the poor, he refers to Poſtlethwayte's Diƈt.
of Commerce. He ſhews the good effeƈt of general
ſimple manners; of frugal and ſober habits, prevalent
throughout all claſſes ; of the attentive encouragement of induſtry by example and reward; and the
benefit of a rigorous police repreſſing mendicity.
" There are (he admits) a few vagrant beggars, but
" theſe are ſeldom natives. In every great town,
" there is a public correƈtion houſe, in which
" the proviſion allowed is of the pooreſt kind;
" even for this they are compelled to work. They
" earn their hard fare by raſping lignum vitæ, &c.
" No corporal puniſhment can be ſo great a terror
" to perſons of a ſlothful or of a vicious diſpoſition.
" But, ſeƈt. ii. where there are ſo many thouſands
" employed in the meaneſt occupations, there muſt
" be a great number daily reduced to indigence,
" from cauſes which no induſtry and no foreſight
" could have prevented. The poor of this deſcrip-
" tion ought to be provided for, and perhaps there is
" no country in the world, where greater attention
" is paid to them than in this.
    " The immediate charge of the poor is committed
" to the Conſiſtory, compoſed of the elders and dea-
" cons of the church, who are generally of the
" moſt reſpeƈtable and intelligent claſs of citizens.
" They are at particular pains to enquire into the
" characters, the circumſtances, and the real ſtate
" of all the poor within their diſtriƈts. They have
" hoſpitals, like our charity work-houſes, for the

" poor. They have alfo *Proveniers*, cheap lodging
" and boarding houfes."

Public taxes, and the rate of wages, are faid to
be higher in Holland, than even in Great-Britain.
Money for the poor is chiefly raifed by collections in
the churches, where every fermon contains an appeal
to the charity of the congregation. " The elo-
" quence of the preacher, it is faid, contributes much
" to the amount of the collection ; but the fobriety
" and regularity of the people may be confidered
" as a more certain caufe of its abundance. There
" are fome fmall taxes impofed, for the benefit of
" the poor,—on public diverfions, on markets, on
" marriages, and on private baptifms. In garrifon
" towns, the Sovereign allows a tax for the poor
" to be collected from every perfon going out or
" coming in at the gate during divine fervice, and
" at certain other fixed hours. In fome places,
" orphans are hired from hofpitals to attend fune-
" rals; thus the pomp becomes a charitable fund.
" The expenfe of the hofpitals is in general defrayed
" by the intereft of a capital ftock, which the
" overfeers have accumulated from legacies, inherit-
" ances of thofe who die in the houfe, donations,
" favings, and, chiefly, profits of the work done in
" the houfe."

" Befides the ftated and weekly collections, there
" are more general contributions made by the
" Confiftory ; who go about, particularly four times
" in the year, when the holy facrament is admi-
" niftered, and folicit every family from whom alms
" may be expected "

From a review of the Dutch poor laws and regulations, (Dr. M. juftly obferves,) "it does not appear
" that they are materially different from our own.
" The admired method of their providing for their

" poor feems to arife rather from the ftrict execution
" of the law, and the fidelity of the adminiftrators,
" than from any peculiar excellency of the laws them-
" felves. Were we equally attentive in maintaining
" a ftrict police, and in a frugal and judicious diftri-
" bution of the poor's money, there is reafon to
" think that the poor might be better provided for,
" and more eafily maintained, in England than in
" Holland."

The ftate of mendicity in one remarkable town
is detailed with an interefting minutenefs, which
demands the peculiar attention of thefe who feel
anxiety for the improvement of the general condition
of the poor. I refer to *Count Rumford's Hiftory
of the Public Eftablifhment for the Poor at Munich
in Bavaria.* "Laws (fays he, c. i.) were not
" wanting to oblige each community in the country
" to provide for its own poor ; but thefe laws had
" been fo long neglected, and beggary had become
" fo general, that extraordinary meafures, and the
" moft indefatigable exertions, were neceffary to put
" a ftop to this evil. The number of itinerant beg-
" gars of both fexes, and all ages, as well foreigners
" as natives, who ftrolled about the country in all
" directions, levying contributions from the indus-
" trious inhabitants, ftealing and robbing, and
" leading a life of indolence and the moft fhamelefs
" debauchery, was quite incredible ; and fo nume-
" rous were the fwarms of beggars in all the great
" towns, and particularly in the capital, fo great
" their impudence, and fo perfevering their impor-
" tunity, that it was almoft impoffible to crofs the
" ftreets without being attacked, and abfolutely
" forced to fatisfy their clamorous demands. And
" thefe beggars were in general by no means fuch
" as, from age or bodily infirmities, were unable by

" their labour to earn their livelihood; but they
" were, for the moſt part, ſtout, ſtrong, healthy,
" ſturdy beggars; who, loſt to every ſenſe of ſhame,
" had embraced the profeſſion from choice, not ne-
" ceſſity ; and who not unfrequently added inſolence
" and threats to their importunity, and extorted that
" from fear, which they could not procure by their
" arts of diſſimulation." They filled the public
walks and the churches, diſturbing all acts of devotion; and ruſhed into private houſes, of which the
ſtreet-doors were for a moment left unguarded.
They continually expoſed their children in the ſtreets,
that their unaffected cries might attract pity. P.
19. " A beggar who goes about from houſe to houſe
" to aſk for alms, has many opportunities to ſteal.
" No wonder that thieving and robbing ſhould be
" prevalent, where beggars are numerous. That
" this was the caſe in Bavaria will not be doubted
" by thoſe who are informed, that in the four years
" immediately ſucceeding the introduction of the
" meaſures adopted for putting an end to mendicity,
" and clearing the country of beggars, thieves, rob-
" bers, &c. above ten thouſand of theſe vagabonds,
" foreigners and natives, were actually arreſted, (with
" the aid of four regiments of cavalry,) and delivered
" over to the civil magiſtrates; and that in taking
" up the beggars in Munich, and providing for thoſe
" who ſtood in need of public aſſiſtance, no leſs than
" 2600 were entered upon the liſts in one week;
" though the whole number of the inhabitants of
" the city of Munich, probably, does not amount to
" more than 60,000, even including the ſuburbs."
The funds for a very extenſive eſtabl ſhment to
provide work for the able-bodied and unemployed,
and various aid for the infirm poor, were " derived
" from the following ſources: Firſt, from ſtated

" monthly allowances from the Sovereign out of his
" private purfe, from the States, and from the Trea-
" fury or chamber of finances. Secondly, and
" principally, from the voluntary fubfcription of the
" inhabitants." [This muft be equivalent to a poor's
rate.] " Thirdly, from legacies left to the inftitu-
" tion; and fourthly, from feveral fmall revenues
" arifing from certain tolls, fines, &c. appropriated
" to that ufe." " During a late journey in Italy,
" (p. 110,) I vifited Verona; and becoming ac-
" quainted with the principal directors of two large
" and noble hofpitals, *La Pietá* and *La Misericorde*,
" in that city; the former, containing about three
" hundred and fifty, and the latter near five hundred,
" poor; I gave them an account of the arrange-
" ments that had been made at Munich, and took
" the liberty of propofing fome improvements, par-
" ticularly in regard to the arrangements for feeding
" the poor." While employed in building a new
kitchen in the hofpital of *La Pietá*, the Count propofed to furnifh them with clothing from his houfe
of induftry at Munich, and adds, " a few days be-
" fore I left Munich to come to England, I had the
" pleafure to affift in packing up, and fending off
" over the Alps, by the Tyrol, fix hundred articles of
" clothing, of different kinds, for the poor of Verona;
" and hope foon to fee the poor of Bavaria growing
" rich, by manufacturing clothing for the poor of
" Italy." Why not to fee the poor of Italy growing wife enough to manufacture for themfelves?
Count Rumford's detail refpecting the eftablifhment
at Munich is followed by an effay on fundamental
principles of eftablifhments for the poor, containing fome juft and important remarks, to which I
fhall refer hereafter.*

* See Appendix.

Spain an1 *Portugal*, under the worſt of governments, and worſt of adminiſtrations, and worſt of ſuperſtitions, have ſunk into an atrophy of ſocial principle. The higher claſs, proud, indolent, and bigoted, ſcarce regard the lower as beings of the ſame ſpecies ; the lower, a nation of beggars, deſtitute of moral ſympathy, have abundantly exhibited their unconcern at the ruin of the higher, by their readineſs to ſubmit to the yoke of a foreign tyrant.

Southey ſays of Liſbon, " the ſtreets are infeſted " by a nuiſance more intolerable than their nightly " darkneſs, or their eternal dirt,—the beggars. I " never ſaw ſo horrible a number of wretches, made " monſtrous by nature, or ſtill more monſtrous by " the dreadful diſeaſes that their own vices have " contraſted. You cannot paſs a ſtreet without " being ſickened by ſome huge tumour, ſome miſ- " ſhapen member, or uncovered wound, carefully " expoſed to the public eye. Theſe people ſhould " not be ſuffered to mangle the feelings, and inſult " the decency, of the paſſenger: if they will not " accept the relief of the hoſpital, they ſhould be " compelled to endure the reſtraint of the priſon. " I do not extend my cenſure to that multitude of " beggars who weary you at every corner with ſup- " plications for the love of GOD and the Virgin ; " theſe wretches, ſo many and ſo miſerable, do in- " deed occaſion harſh and ungentle feelings, not " againſt them, but againſt that depraved ſociety, " that diſinherits of happineſs half the civilized " world."

In *Townſhend's Journey through Spain* it is obſerved, that the country is depopulated from the various evil conſequences of bad government. The *regidors,* police magiſtrates, purchaſe their offices, and indemnify themfelves at the expenfe of the poor and induftrious. The number of convents is nearly nine thoufand. Perfons bound to celibacy by vows are eftimated at near two hundred thoufand Speaking of Seville, he fays, " In traverfing the ftreets I " was ftruck with the multitude of beggars clothed " in rags, and was at firft inclined to attribute this " to the decay of trade; but. upon examination, I " found a more abiding caufe in the diftribution of " alms at the Archbifhop's palace, and at the gates " of twenty convents, daily, and without diftinction, " to all who make application for relief. Such " mifplaced benevolence is a bar to induftry, and " multiplies the objects of diftrefs, whofe numbers " bear exact proportion to the provifion fo made " for their fupport."

Mr. T. notices, in his account of Cadiz, three hofpitals for the fick; in one of which they have fix thoufand patients, and lofe annually on an average one tenth. There is alfo a Retreat, or Afylum, for forty-feven Widows. But the moft interefting of their public eftablifhments is the *Hofpicio*, or general workhoufe. In it are received the poor of all defcriptions, young and old, the blind, the lame, idiots and infane. The average number of perfons maintained in the houfe appears to be eight hundred and fifty-five. " Forty-five looms and fixteen ftocking- " frames are provided for their fervice, with a fuffi- " cient number of fpinning-wheels, working benches, " tools for carpenters, turners, fhoemakers, aud " taylors, a twifting-mill, a fpinning-jenny, and a " machine for carding cotton." The expenfe of the houfe for the year 1786 was equal to 13,850*l.* The food for each individual appears to have amounted in the year to 6*l.* 7*s.* 4*d.*; clothes to 13*s.* 8*d.*; but the average expenfe of the eftablifh-

ment will give 14*l*. 8*s*. 7*d*. for the expenfe of each,
not including the produce of his labour. This
produce; befides its proceeding from but a part of
thofe who are on the eftablifhment, as the infirm of
all kinds contribute nothing by induftry, is much lefs
profitable than that of ordinary manufactories.
" People deprived of liberty univerfally eat too much,
" and work too little. This, beyond a queftion, is
" the cafe at Cadiz in the *Hofpicio*, in which they
" have ninety-two holidays allowed them, and in
" which the expenfe of food and raiment is double
" what it fhould be."

" The *Hofpicio* of Barcelona originated in 1582,
" when the poor began to occupy the ferious atten-
" tion of all the governments of Europe. With the
" houfe of induftry is united the Hofpital of Mercy.
" In this eftablifhment they provide for children of
" parents who are burthened with a numerous off-
" fpring, for beggars, and for other objects of
" diftrefs. Their average number is 1436: about
" one thoufand able to work, three hundred idiots,
" and the reft little children. The whole expenfe
" of them is about 48,200 livres Catalan, or about
" 5164*l*. fterling, per annum. The king allows for
" each pauper fourteen maravedis per day, to pur-
" chafe a ration of bread. Thefe are nearly equal
" to one penny fterling. The voluntary contribution
" amounts to about 15,000 livres Catalan, and the
" deficiency is made up by the bifhop. The produce
" of their labour fcarce exceeds the rate of one penny
" each per day; yet this is greater than the average of
" our workhoufes in England. Although no paupers
" can be better fed, better clad, or better lodged, or
" can meet with greater tendernefs when they are
" ill, they cannot readily forget their lofs of liberty.
" All thefe comforts, therefore, are defpifed, when

" compared with freedom ; and few, befide the moft
" decrepit, would remain within thofe walls. if they
" could be permitted to beg their bread from door
" to door. This principle, however, is productive
" of much good ; for moft of the young men in
" Barcelona, of any worth or fpirit, form themfelves
" into clubs for mutual relief, nearly upon the plan
" adopted by our friendly focieties in England,
" leaving none but the moft improvident and worth-
" lefs to be difgraced by confinement among fools
" and madmen."

Of an unprofitable falt-petre work at Madrid
Mr. T. obferves, " I have no doubt that motives of
" benevolence may have contributed to keep this
" voracious monfter at Madrid, and the apprehenfion,
" that were it not cherifhed and fupported, a multi-
" tude which is now fed by their attendance upon
" it would be reduced to famine. Of all employ-
" ments for the poor, that which is moft uncertain is
" leaft defirable ; and little is that to be encouraged,
" which in fummer decoys them from the harveft,
" and when winter comes turns them adrift to remain
" inactive till the return of fpring. The manufac-
" ture at Madrid feeds four hundred only in the
" winter, and when they fhould liften to the calls
" of agriculture, employs from thirteen hundred to
" four thoufand. If thefe are not wanted for the
" labours of the field, and can find no conftant work
" in profitable fabrics, it is plain that they have been
" needlefsly drawn into exiftence, and that the popu-
" lation fhould be fuffered to fink gradually, till it
" has again found its proper level. The principle
" hereby eftablifhed is of great importance to man-
" kind, and yet feems to have been little underftood."
This is the principle which Mr. Malthus has fince,
with great ability, invefligated and illuftrated.

Institutions for the Poor in France.

France, before the Revolution, loudly vaunted its
fuperiority to all other nations in all the arts of
civilized life; and its claims, however arrogantly
afferted, were, in fome refpects, generally allowed.
Its writers, moral and political, were numerous,
eloquent, and fagacious. Several of their works
powerfully recommend charity, and review correctly
the relations of the rich and poor. Its inftitutions
were numerous and coftly; and religious devotees,
of both fexes, often bound themfelves by vows to the
arduous duty of adminiftering to the wants of the
difeafed poor, in hofpitals, in garrets, and in cabins.*
Were the poor of France better fuftained, were its
hofpitals better regulated, were its charities better
directed, than thofe of other nations? A few extracts
from the few books which I am able to procure, may
beft anfwer thefe queftions.

Le Mercier, Tableau de Paris, chap. 266, *edit.
Amfterdam* 1782. " Et comment voulez vous, que
" cette ville, qu'on appelle fuperbe, ne pullule pas des
" mendians, autant de taches dans la legiflation d'un
" peuple. Il ne faut pas pour cela les etouffer,
" comme on a fait dans ce qu'on nomme depots.
" C'eft une cruauté abominable et grauuite.

" On n'a pas affez cherché les moyens de remedier
" a cet epouvantable defordre ; ce qui deshonorera
" infailliblement nos magiftrats, s'ils ne s'occupent de
" cet objet. On leur a propofé plufieurs plans ega-
" lement bons: ils n'ont plus qu' à choifir.——

* See account of an inftitution at Alet, near Grenoble, in Mrs.
Schimmelpenninck's Tour of Dom Launcelot to the Grande Char-
treufe and Alet, taken in the year 1667.

" On a traité les pauvres en 1679, et dans les
" trois années fuivantes, avec une atrocité une bar-
" barie, qui feront une tache ineffaçable à un fiecle
" qu'on appelle humain et eclairé. On eut dit,
" qu'on a voulu detruire la race entiere tant on mit
" en oubli les preceptes de la charité. Ils moururent
" prefque tous dans les depots, espece de prifons, où
" l'indigence eft punie comme le crime."
    C. 267.   " Mais s'il eft plufieurs mendians que
" la mifere force a tendre la main, et qui affaiffés fous
" le poids de malheur ont dans le gefte l'abbattement
" de la vraie douleur, et dans les yeux le feu fombre
" du defefpoir, il eft auffi un grand nombre de geux
" hypocrites, qui par des gemiffemens impofteurs et
" des infirmités factices furprennent votre liberalité,
" et trompent votre compaffion. D une voix arti-
" ficielle plaintive et monotone, ils articulent en
" trainant le nom de Dieu, et vous pourfuivent dans
" les rues avec ce nom facré ; mais ces miferables ne
" craignent ni fa juftice, ni fa prefence.———
    " Eux ils fe couvrent de plaies hideufes pour
" attendrir le peuple ; mais quand la nuit vient,
" fuivez ces vagabonds dans le cabaret reculé de
" quelque faubourg, lieu de rendezvous ; vous verrez
" toùs ces eftrop és droits et difpos, fe raffembler
" pour leurs bruyantes orgies. Le boiteux a jeté fa
" beguille, l'aveugle fon emplâtre, le boffu fa boffe
" de crin ; le manchot prend un violon ; le muet
" donne le fignal de l'intemperance effrénée.———
    " Ils fe felicitent de fubfifter fans rien faire, de
" partager tous les plaifirs de la fucieté fans en con-
" noitre les charges. Les enfans qui proviennent de
" ces commerces infames et illicites, font adoptés par
" les premiers d'entre eux qui ont befoin d un objet
" innocent pour exciter la pitie publique. Ils dreffent
" leur voix enfantine à l'accent de la mendicité ; et à

" mefure que l'enfant grandit, il transforme en metier
" la funefte education qu'on lui a donnée. Lorfqu'
" ils manquent d'enfans, ces miferables enlevent
" ceux d'autrui : alors ils contournent et disloquent
" leur membres pour leur donner ce qu'ils appellent
" des jambes et des bras de Dieu.——

" Mais comment ofe t'on punir la mendicité, lorfqu'
" on voit celle des ordres religieux revetue d'une
" apparence legale et pour ainfi dire confacrée.——

" Toutes ces filles qui le foir vous offrent leurs
" appas pour une legere retribution, peuvent etre
" confiderées comme de jeunes mendiantes ; ca relles
" font plus affamées que libertines.   Elles vous
" demandent votre argent plutot que vos careffes.

C. 268. " Il n'eft prefque pas poffible dans la
" fituation actuelle de notre gouvernement, qu' il ne fe
" trouve un grand nombre de coupables ; parcequ'il
" y a une foule de neceffiteux qui n'ont qu' une exis-
" tence precaire, et que la premiere loi eft qu'il faut
" vivre.   L'horrible inegalité des fortunes qui va
" toujours en augmentant, un petit nombre ayant
" tout, et la multitude rien ; les peres de famille de-
" pouillés d'argent par la voie trop feduifante de
" loteries," &c.

Dean Swift concludes his ironical epigram on the
place of the damned—

" Then hell, to be fure, is at Paris or Rome,
" And how happy for us that it is *not* at home !"

Chap. 269. " J'irai à l'hopital, s'e crie le pauvre
" Parifien ; mon pere y eft mort ; j'y mourrai auffi;
" et le voila a moitié confolé.—La Maifon de Dieu!
" et l'on ofe l'appeller ainfi! Le mepris de l'humanité
" femble ajouter aux maux qu'on y fouffre.   Le
" medecin, le chirurgien, font payés; d'accord: les
" remedes ne coutent rien: je le fais: mais on
" couchera le malade a coté d'un moribond et d'un

" cadavre ; on lui mettra le fpectacle de la mort fous
" les yeux, lorfque les angoiffes de la terreur pene-
" treront deja fon ame epouvantée. On le plongera
" dans un air rempli de miafmes putrides, &c.———

" L'Hôtel Dieu a été fondé en 660, par Saint
" Landry, et le Comte Archambaud, pour y reçevoir
" les malades de l'un et de l'autre fexe fans exception
" de perfonne. Le Juif, le Turc, *le Proteftant*,
" l'Idolatre, le Chretien, y entrent egalement. Il y
" a douze cents lits, et le nombre des malades fe
" monte a cinq ou fix mille. Comptez pour l'Hôpital
" General dix à douze mille perfonnes, pour Bicêtre
" quatre à cinq mille; vous aurez le denombrement
" des infortunés qui ne favent où pofer leur tête.—Il
" eft prefqu' impoffible de favoir quels font les
" revenus de l'Hôtel Dieu. Ils font immenfes, et
" ce qui le feroit croire, c'eft l'attention que l'on a
" d'en derober la connoiffance au public.———

" On croit pouvoir affurer ici, que le revenu de
" l'Hôtel Dieu eft tel qu'il fuffiroit pour nourrir
" prefque la dixieme partie de la capitale.———

" Rapprochez la Maifon de Charité de Lyon, et
" l'Hôpital de Verfailles, de l'Hôtel-Dieu de Paris ;
" d'un côté, vous apperçevrez un ordre admirable
" une regie digne d'éloges, et qui attendrit le contem-
" plateur, de l'autre, vous verrez tous les vices qui
" affligent l'ame.———

" L'Hôtel Dieu de Paris a tout ce qu'il faut pour
" etre peftilentiel à caufe de fon atmofphere humide
" et peu airée ; les plaies s' y gangrenent plus facile-
" ment, et le fcorbut et la gale n' y font pas moins
" de ravages, pour peu que les malades y fejournent.
" Les maladies les plus fimples dans leur principe
" acquierent des complications graves par une fuite
" inevitable de la contagion de l'air. C'eft par la
" même raifon que les plaies fimples à la tête, et aux

H

" jambes font mortelles dans cet hôpital. Rien ne
" confirme mieux ce que j'avance, que le denombre-
" ment des miferables qui periffent tous les ans a
" l'Hôtel-Dieu de Paris ; et à Bicêtre ; il meurt le
" cinquieme des malades ; calcul effrayant !——

C. 270. " Les corps que l'Hôtel-Dieu vomit
" journellement font portés a Clamart : c'eft un
" vafte cimetiere, dont le gouffre eft toujours ouvert.
" Ces corps n'ont point de bierre: ils font confus
" dans une ferpilliere. On fe depeche de les enlever
" de leur lit ; et plus d'un malade réputé mort s'eft
" reveille fous la main hâtive qui l'enfermoit dans ce
" groffier linceul: d'autres ont criés qu'ils etoient
" vivans, dans le chariot même qui les conduifoit a
" la fepulture !——

C. 271. " L'Hôpital des Enfans trouvés eft un
" autre gouffre. qui ne rend pas la dixieme partie
" de l'efpece humaine qu' on lui confie. Dans la
" province de Normandie, on a calculé d'après l'expe-
" rience de dix ans, qu'il mouroit cent quatre enfans
" fur cent huit.—Sept a huit mille enfans legitimes
" ou illegitimes arrivent tous les ans à l'hôpital de
" Paris, et leur nombre augmente chaque année. Il
" y a donc fept mille peres malheureux, qui renoncent
" au fentiment le plus cher au cœur de l'homme.——

" Le quart de Paris ne fait pas bien furement la
" veille, fi fes travaux lui fourniront de quoi fubfifter
" le lendemain. Faut il etre etonné qu'on fe porte
" au mal moral, quand on ne connoit que le mal
" phyfique? En tout tems, a toutes les heures du
" jour et de la nuit, fans queftion et fans formalité, on
" reçoit tous les enfans nouveaux-nés qu'on prefente
" à cet hôpital.——

" Ce fage etabliffement a prevenu et empeché
" mille crimes fecrets: l'infanticide eft auffi rare, qu'il
" étoit commun autrefois.——

" On avoit propofé de faire de tous ces enfans
" trouvés autant de foldats. Projet barbare !" &c.
[It may be a fad deftiny; but while the fad bufinefs of
war exifts, it may be as well to train infants gradually
to its toils and terrors, as to tear away men, trained
to arts, from their induſtry, and from the bofom of
their families.] " Un grand nombre de ces enfans
" viennent de la province.—Un homme apporte fur
" fon dos les enfans nouveaux-nés dans une boite
" matelaffée, qui peut en contenir trois. Ils font
" debout dans leur maillot, refpirant l'air par en
" haut. L'homme ne s'arrête, que pour prendre fes
" repas, et leur faire fucer un pen de lait. Quand il
" ouvre fa boite, il en trouve fouvent un de mort;
" il acheve le voyage avec les deux autres, impatient
" de fe debarraffer du depôt. Quand il l'a depofé a
" l'hôpital, il repart fur le champ pour recommencer
" le même emploi; qui eft fon gagne-pain. Prefque
" tous les enfans qu'on tranfportent de Lorraine par
" Vitry, periffent dans cette ville. Metz a vu dans
" une feule année neuf cents enfans expofés. Quelle
" matiere à reflexion!" In eftimating the effects of
this vaft and indifcriminate foundling hofpital, this
latter circumftance is a melancholy weight in the
oppofite fcale to the prevention of infanticide alleged
in its favour.

A work of Monf. J. B. S. Salgues, on Paris, its
Manners, Literature, and Philofophy, publifhed 1813,
juft before the great events which have given peace
to Europe, and hopes of extended amelioration
throughout the civilized world, gives the following
comparifon of the ftate of the hofpitals before and
after the Revolution. He refers alfo to a work
publifhed by an intelligent and benevolent phyfician,
M. Duchannoy, on the fame fubject.

" Could the Hôtel Dieu, in the ftate in which we
" remember it, be compared with any thing elfe than
" a common fewer, loaded with the infectious miaf-
" mata of a thoufand different contagions? when the
" fick, heaped together, ferved only to conceal the
" diftinction between the dying and the dead, and
" feemed to meet but in order to fecure the abforp-
" tion of fome fufficient caufe of diffolution. The
" means of cure were often the object of horrid
" fpeculation. It was referved for an adminiftration
" more humane, more principled, and more informed,
" to direct its attention to the condition of the indi-
" gent, and thus to found the pureft pillar of national
" glory. Indeed, the prefent management of the
" hofpitals deferves every praife.

" Before the Revolution, Paris could only boaft
" of three hofpitals, the Hôtel-Dieu, the Charité,
" and the St. Louis; but now four additional build-
" ings have been founded in the fuburbs; with fome
" fpecial hofpitals, (thefe three being opened to the
" difeafed of every defcription,) fuch as the hofpital
" for *maladies honteufes*, for cutaneous diforders, for
" difeafes of children, and for lying-in women. At
" Bicêtre, and at Salpêtriere, are alfo lunatic afylums,
" which are improved, but not new, eftablifhments.

" Firft, it was neceffary to repair the large edi-
" fices applied to thefe purpofes, to provide additional
" conveniences of various kinds, furniture fixed and
" moveable, baths, and beds, the utenfils of the
" apothecary and the kitchen. This has been done
" with judgement. At the Hôtel Dieu the fick were
" mingled and confounded together: all forts of
" difeafes, the moft contagious and the moft offen-
" five, were huddled into the fame apartment; child-
" ren and men, boys and girls, perfons afflicted with
" hideous infirmities, the feverifh, the fcrophulous,

" the epileptic, the infane were ftowed in the fame
" rooms with lying in women and venereal patients,
" three, four, fometimes fix, in a bed. It was Mil-
" ton's lazar-houfe with aggravations. The imagi-
" nation fhudders over the mere picture of thefe
" death breathing apartments, where the fufferer
" was invited but to a fepulchre; yet they had
" continued thus for centuries. Now, thanks to a be-
" neficent philofophy, the fick are infulated; each has
" his bed apart; and the beds are fo conftructed, that
" the old abufe cannot be repeated. The number of
" beds is proportioned to the fize of the apartments;
" which are lighted by larger windows, ventilated
" with thorough drafts, neatly white-wafhed, and
" purified with chemical vapours. This is a fhort
" fketch of what has been done for the indigent
" fick. It was difficult to carry further the amelio-
" rations of every kind. Let us not forget the
" excellent eftablifhment of a central Difpenfary;
" nor the Houfe of Health in the fuburb, where
" perfons able to pay for attendance are admitted
" at a moderate price, and provided with thofe com-
" plex accommodations which cannot be obtained at
" home. Let us add the School for Midwives, and
" the two Hofpitals for Age; that of the men of St.
" Lawrence, and that of the women of St. Sêvres.
" Let us add, alfo, the Refuge for Old Couples;
" where a man and his wife, who have fallen into
" indigence, can live together on public alms. For-
" merly, indigence was a fentence of divorce, which
" drove the hufband to the *Bicêtre*, and the wife to
" the *Salpêtriere*. And the Houfe of Succour, a new
" inftitution, in which (as in a monaftery) elderly men
" are admitted, on providing fecurity for the payment
" of two hundred livres yearly; and the two Orphan
" Houfes, one for children of each fex; and the

" Foundling Hofpital, for thofe whom parental un-
" kindnefs reduces to the ftate of orphans. Here
" children are received without inveftigation, in order
" to prevent the temptations to infanticide, which
" fhame has been known to occafion, as well as
" want. The adminiftration continues to watch
" over thefe little unfortunates, and allows penfions
' for their board until the age of twelve; after
" which mafters will take them for their own earn-
" ings. It has not been reckoned fufficient to or-
" ganize in a new and better fpirit the ancient
" inftitutions, and to found fuch others as were
" wanting; it has alfo been deemed fit to connect
" them under the fuperintendance of a common
" authority, which can prefcribe to each the expe-
" dient limits of its divifion of humane labour. For
" this purpofe, a central committee of the public
" charities has been formed; together with efpecial
" committees for managing the eftablifhments for the
" fick, for the old, and for children.

" Befides the bureaux of thefe four committees
" each eftablifhment keeps acceffible account-books
" with great exactnefs; fo that the central adminiftra-
" tion can readily and weekly afcertain any thing that
" it wants to know concerning the ftate of the feveral
" inftitutions. A certain attention in comparing the
" number of inmates with the habitual outgoings is
" the beft preventive of embezzlement."—Quoted
from *Appendix to v.* 73 *of the Monthly Review, p.* 534.

Among the very few French books which I have
been able to procure on the fubject which engages
my attention, particular notice feems to be due to
Idées d'un Citoyen fur lès befoins, les droits, et les de-
voirs des vrais Pauvres. Amfterdam, 1765.

" ORPHELINS.—Parlons d'abord des befoins phy-
" fiques de l'enfance, proprement dite. L'ancienne

" legiflation Françoife avoit impofé l'obligation d'y
" pourvoir, aux Seigneurs Hauts-Jufticiers: mais
" auffi les enfans illegitimes devenoient leur ferfs,
" c eft à dire a peu pres leur efclaves dans l'ancienne
" rigeur du droit feodal." The author ftrongly
recommends foundling hofpitals, and the training all
the youth to agriculture: this muft manifeftly depend
on the demand for hands. It feems to be a juft
principle, that all who from infancy are reared at the
public expenfe fhould be trained to thofe purfuits
by which the community may be moft benefited;
and if wars muft continue, and fome in all ftates muft
be trained to it, it feems but equitable to train to
the defence of the ftate thofe who have been reared
at the common expenfe. This was the practice
of Athens; and young men thus reared, when able
to bear arms, appeared at the feaft of Bacchus in
their panoply, and declared themfelves ready to devote their ftrength to the fervice of their beneficent
country. Exceptions in fuch cafe might eafily be
made with refpect to the fickly, and to thofe who
might exhibit extraordinary proofs of intellect, and
dexterity in any of the arts.

" DesVieillards.—Les citoyens qui font le meil-
" leur emploi de leurs forces tant qu'ils en ont, font
" le plus communement affiégés de la pauvreté dans
" leur vieilleffe. Les ouvriers devoués aux travaux
" de l'agriculture, et aux arts de premiere neceffié,
" font toujours le plus mal payés. Les befoins de la
" vieilleffe pauvre etoient trop fenfibles dans nos
" villes pour ne pas s'attirer l'attention du gouverne-
" ment : c'éft principalement pour eux qu'on a ima-
" giné de bâtir et de doter les hôpitaux. Le deffein,
" qu'on a fi fagement formé depuis longtems d'abolir
" abfolument la mendicité en France, exigeoit qu'on
" prit les moyens de pourvoir à la fubfiftence des vieil-

" lards invalides de l'un et l'autre fexe : il eft clair qu'ils
" ont droit de l'exiger de la part des adminiftrateurs
" de la republique, des qu'on leur ôte leur feule
" reffource en les empéchant de foliciter la compaffion
" de leurs concitoyens." [Thefe are juft ideas ; and
it may be hoped, that her renovated government, devoting its attention to the arts of peace,
may direct the abundant energies of that ingenious
people to the adoption of inftitutions thus characterifed by wifdom and benevolence. The author generally condemns poor-houfes, as hateful to the
poor, as crowding the vicious and the decent pro-
mifcuoufly together, and partaking too much of the
character of prifons. This is true : it will, however, be neceffary to advert to this fubject more particularly hereafter. Invalids, he obferves, are generally better attended in private houfes, than in hofpitals, &c. This may be true : yet for thofe who
are quite helplefs, alms-houfes may be ufeful, in
which they may be affembled, not crowded, fo that a
few trained attendants may give more effectual aid
than could be procured otherwife ; and in which,
machinery might be conftructed, efpecially adapted
to give eafe, or to amufe, by providing fome flight
occupation to fuch perfons. His remarks, however,
as applied to the generality of poor invalids, appear
to be correct and humane.]

" Pourquoi ne laifferions nous pas ces pauvres
" caducs dans le lieu meme qu'ils habiterent autrefois,
" jouir du droit de domicile, de liberté de citoyen,
" qui plait toujours, et qu'on a toujours le droit de
" revendiquer. La plupart y trouveroient de petits
" fecours d amitié, des confolations, une fociéte dans
" les parents, des amis, des voifins, des anciennes
" connoiffances, qui ne vont point les chercher dans
" les horreurs d'un hôpital.

" *Hôpital des Aveugles, a Paris.*—Nous croyons
" que les aveugles pauvres du royaume doivent etre
" tous alimentés et entretenue dans le lieu même
" de leur domicile ordinaire ; une maifon commune
" leur eft inutile, fur tout une maifon dans la
" capitale ornée comme un des plus beaux palais
" de l'Europe, qui contrafte fi bifarrement avec le
" metier qu'ils exercent dans les eglifes d'une men-
" dicité tres incommode et tres indecente.   Donnez
" leur de quoi vivre chez eux en vrais et bons
" pauvres, fans tourmenter les fideles, &c.—L'au-
" mône publique etant devenu generale pour toute
" efpece des pauvres, et pour tous leur vrais be-
" foins fans exception, la mendicité eft un crime
" qui merite d'etre reprimé fans menagement, et
" punie avec feverité.—En fuppofant ce principe
" comme vrai, politiquement et moralement parlant,
" il ne faut pas croire qu'il foit nuifible à la charité
" chretienne, et que nous pretendions ôter aux
" fideles la refource falutaire de l'aumone, &c.—

" Nous ne condamnons pas les troncs dans les
" eglifes, [or collections at the church door,] a
" Dieu ne plaife. Le commiffaire paroiffial, le Curé,
" les femmes charitables, le juge de la paroiffe,
" auront toujours les mains ouvertes pour reçevoir
" les dons de la pieté.—Nous en concluons, que fi
" c'eft un crime au pauvre entretenu par l'etat de
" mendier, ce feroit une faute, et une efpece de delit
" au citoyen de donner de l'aumone à un mendiant ;
" c'eft un fuperflu qu'il prodigueroit à l'un pour
" priver un autre du neceffaire, et pour mettre les
" autres citoyens dans la neceffité de le fournir à leur
" depens; ce qui forme dans la realité une forte de
" vol fait au public.   La loi donc pourroit pro-
" noncer une amende pour tout diftributeur d'au-
" mônes aux mendians, et meme attacher à cette

"peine une humiliation. C'eſt auſſi le prononcé
" formel d'une de nos anciennes ordonnances, auſſi
" ſage en elle même, mais, malheureuſement, auſſi
" prematurée que tous les autres de ce genre.—
" Nous n' entendons pas prohiber petits preſens
" aux pauvres domiciliés, penſionnés, et non men-
" dians, &c."

This is plain ſenſe, and well worthy of general
attention. Experience proves by far the greater
number of thoſe who beg, to be indolent impoſtors,
or active only in fraud. The worthy and really
diſtreſſed apply to their friends, who can judge of
their worth and their wants, and to the legal ſources
of ſupply, in ſhort, to any legal means of ſuſtenance,
rather to the ſtrange, precarious, immodeſt obtruſion
of their whining, ſervile, or obſtreperous complaints,
on thoſe who are hurrying from place to place, too
much occupied with their own private cares to examine duly into circumſtances ſo ſtated.

Our offices of churchwarden and overſeer of the
poor, being raiſed on an old eccleſiaſtical foundation, are
not without a prototype in the Roman Catholic church.
Marguillier, (*Moreri's Dict.*) " Celui qui a
" l'adminiſtration des affaires temporelles d'une egliſe
" paroiſſiale, qui a ſoin de la fabrique et de l'œuvre.
" L'intendance de la fabrique des egliſes apparte-
" noit anciennement à l'evêque. Les eveques
" s'en dechargent ſur les archidiacres, et les
" archidiacres ſur les curés. L'avarice ou la negli-
" gence des derniers fut cauſe qu'on choiſit des per-
" ſonnes notables et zelées entre les paroiſſiens pour
" prendre la direction des affaires de l'egliſe. Ce-
" pendant les eveques ont pretendus que ces Mar-
" guilliers quoique laics n'étoient point diſpenſés de
" rendre compte de leur adminiſtration devant le
" juge eccleſiaſtique.—Le mot de Marguillier vient

" de Matricularius. La matricule etoit un regiſtre
" public, où l'on enrolloit les pauvres qui deman-
" doient l'aumône à la porte des egliſes ; et les Mar-
" guilliers etoient les gardes de ces regiſtres, et les
" diſtributeurs de ces aumônes. On a confié depuis
" ce ſoin à ceux qui ont la garde du revenu des
" egliſes, et on les a auſſi nommés Marguilliers, &c."
Eariy after the French Revolution, the National
Aſſembly appointed a committee of mendicity. The
projeĉt of eſtabliſhing a poor's rate was diſcuſſed
and rejeĉted. *Quat. Rapport*, 8vo. 1792. *A.
Young's Travels.*

In a report of the proceedings of a Philanthropic
Society in Paris, during the year 1813, publiſhed in
1814, I find the following intereſting notices.
" Dans l'epoque defaſtreuſe, dont le retour de Louis
" XVIII. a marqué la fin, tandis que nos guerriers
" bravoient la mort dans les combats, nous avons vu
" les femmes reſtées dans les villes ſe conſacrer au
" ſoin des bleſſés, et tous les citoyens faire des dons
" volontaires pour leur fournir ce dont ils avoient
" beſoin. Ce n'eſt point le ſuperflu qu'on a offert.
" Les gens les moins riches ſe ſont impoſé des priva-
" tions pour ſoulager les infortunés. Les Chirurgiens,
" les Medecins, les Sœurs de la Charité, ſe ſont de-
" voués ; et pluſieurs ont été viĉtimes de leur zèle.
" —Si les membres de la Société Philanthropique
" ont dans ces circonſtances montré tous individu-
" ellement les ſentimens qui les animent, le comité,
" chargé-de les repreſenter, a dû faire les derniers
" efforts pour ſeconder leurs intentions.—La Societé
" Philanthropique n'eſt point une inſtitution nouvelle ;
" elle avoit été fondée en 1780, ſous la proteĉtion
" de Louis XVI. par des ſouſcripteurs reunis pour
" venir au ſecours des pauvres.*

* " On voit par les rapports faits annuellement à l'ancienne
" Société Philanthropique, qu'elle s'etoit progreſſivement accrue

" Les Princes que la Providence a rendu à nos
" vœux protegeront fon exiftence, et faciliteront fes
" entreprifes. Ou pourroient ils trouver une admi-
" niftration plus capable de remplir leur vues ?
" Tout eft gratuit chez nous ; notre zele n'a d'autre
" but, d'autre aliment, que la charité ; et nous nous
" concertons avec ceux qui dans les villes les plus
" eloignées, font occupés des memes objets, et
" dirigés par les memes motifs."

The Society of Paris has, in fact, extended its
efforts to every object of charity ; to the diftribution
of aid to the diftreffed, to the eftablifhment of Difpenfaries and of Schools, on the plan of Pestalozzi.

" Appelée par le gouvernement à feconder les
" mefures qu'il vouloit prendre contre la difette,
" produite par une mauvaife recolte, et par les mal-
" heurs de la guerre, elle etablit, avec une incroyable
" célérité, et fans aucuns frais d' adminiftration, 42
" fourneaux de foupes qui, dans le courant de l'
" hivèr de 1812 à 1813, diftribuerent aux indigens
" 4,342,600 rations, les unes contre les cartes, les
" autres vendues a un prix fort au-deffous de ce
" qu'elles coutoient ; elle fut fecouru par les hom-
" mes qui occupoient les places les plus eminentes,
" et fe livra à l'efperance d'augmenter le nombre des
" Difpenfaires, de revenir fur les ecoles ; d'etablir,
" dans les divers quartiers, des maifons où les femmes
" chargées d'enfans en bas age pourroient les depo-
" fer pendant qu'elles iroient vaquer à leurs travaux.
" (Il en exifte une de ce genre etablie, depuis plufieurs

" depuis 1780, jufqù, à 1789; qu'elle etoit compofée dé 821 mem-
" bres, au nombre desquels on voyoit avec reconnoiffance *Monfieur*,
" aujourdhui notre Roi ; que fes reçettes avoient plufieurs fois
" excédé la fomme de 120,000 francs, et que pendant dix années de
" fon exiftence les fecours qu'elle avoit diftribués dans la ville de
Paris s'étoient elevés a plus de 1,200,000 francs."

" années, par Madame la Comtesse Pastoret, au fau-
" bourg St. Honore ;) et d'autres où l'on preteroit
" aux ouvriers connus, des outils dont ils paieroient
" peu a peu le prix sur leur salaire."

Poverty and Charity in Russia.*

" In each government" (says Mr. Tooke, *View of the
Russian Empire, during the Reign of Catherine II. &c.
vol. ii. p.* 181, *&c.*) " there is a college of general
" provision, which, besides several other duties, is
" entrusted with the erection and inspection of the
" hospitals and infirmaries. These are instituted for
" a determinate number of patients, (about twenty or
" thirty,) and may not admit any more. They are
" intended for the poor and necessitous, who are
" cured and attended free of all expense. Besides
" these infirmaries, the College of General Provision
" maintains particular houses for incurable patients,
" who have no support, and receptacles for lunatics.
" The design of the former is, that the unhappy ob-
" jects for whom they are destined may not deprive
" the poor, who may be afflicted with curable diseases,
" of a place in the hospitals, and yet not be them-
" selves entirely without relief. The College of
" General Provision is bound to provide them lodg-
" ing, board, nurses, and attendance, that at least
" they may have some mitigation of their sufferings.
" For the erection and regulation of these and other
" institutions for the relief of suffering humanity,
" within the province of the College of General
" Provision, each of them receives, at its opening,
" from the imperial coffers, the sum of 15,000 rubles,

* " Russia is divided into 41 governments, exclusive of Cosacks
" of the Don and the Eaxine, and nine vice-royalties, acquisitions
" since 1783, comprehending 36 millions of persons."

" which in moft of the governments is confiderably
" augmented by the charitable contributions of the
" public. In the capital, and in the generality of
" populous towns, thefe inftitutions are now not only
" upon a much larger fcale than the general precept
" at firft promifed, but they are multiplied in various
" ways by the co-operation of the community at
" large. The town hofpital of St. Peterfburg was
" founded in the year 1784. In one of the fkirts óf
" the city, by the fide of the beautiful and broad
" Fontanka Canal, is a large brick infulated building,
" of handfome but fimple architecture. It receives
" all neceffitous patients, (venereal excepted,) and
" attends their cure without fee or reward : handi-
" craftfmen and gentlemen's fervants pay four rubles
" per month. All patients, on admiffion, are imme-
" diately bathed, and have their heads fhaven. The
" number of beds amounts ufually to 300, but in
" cafes of emergency is increafed to 400. In the
" year 1790, fix contiguous buildings of timber, on
" brick foundations, were erected behind the main
" edifice, by the College of General Provifion, and
" furnifhed with 250 beds. Here the patients, in
" fummer, enjoy the frefh air; and during the interval
" thus procured, the principal building is thoroughly
" cleanfed. In the four years, from 1785 to 1789,
" it had altogether taken in 9427 patients; and the
" number is found annually to increafe. Of thefe,
" 7417 were fent out cured, 1773 died, and 237
" remained at the conclufion of the latter year.———
" The city hofpital of St. Peterfburg, for poor and
" incurable patients, was opened in 1781. The
" indulgence which qualifies for admiffion to it is
" diftinguifhed into degrees which form two claffes,
" one whereof comprifes the completely impotent,
" who have a full claim to the benefit of the houfe:

" to the fecond 'clafs belong thofe who are capable
" of doing fome kind of work. Thefe are employed
" in any adequate occupation about the houfe. The
" expenditure amounts annually (according to the
" eftablifhment) to 15,417 rubles. The City Hos-
" pital at Mofcow, which was endowed in 1775,
" admitted at that time 150 patients, and is com-
" pletely on the fame footing with that of St. Peters-
" burg. Several inftitutions, on a fmaller fcale, are
" proportionably upon as good a footing ; and the
" benefit thus accruing from Catherine's philanthropic
" regulations for the prefervation of her people, and
" for the alleviation of poverty and affliction among
" them, merits the higheft applaufe. There are
" many fimilar inftitutions, partly endowed by the
" Crown, and partly by rich and humane individuals.
" In a hofpital founded at Mofcow 1763, by the
" Grand Duke and heir apparent Paul Petrovitch,
" fifty perfons were maintained and attended gratis.
" The philanthropic Howard, who vifited this hofpital,
" fays, that it would be difficult to find a better fitua-
" tion in the vicinity of the city. He tafted the
" bread and beer, and found both good ; and adds,
" ' on the whole, I muft confefs that this little hofpital
" ' would do honour to any country.'—" Military hof-
" pitals for land forces. Befides the two general land
" hofpitals at St. Peterfburg and Mofcow, there are 14
" large field hofpitals at Aftrakhan, &c. and battalion
" lazarets are every where in great numbers. There
" are, moreover, eleven fea hofpitals, befides one for
" marines. The fea hofpital at Cronftadt, during
" the war with Sweden, was annually obliged to
" admit near 25,000 patients. A new hofpital was
" therefore founded at Oranienbaum." Howard
cenfures the Ruffian field hofpitals, particularly for
want of cleanlinefs, which Mr. Tooke inclines to

vindicate, by fuggefting that Ruffian and Englifh habits and ideas are different in that refpect: and on Howard's cenfure of the bad nourifhment, Mr. Tooke obferves, " here alfo we fhould have regard " to cuftom." He enumerates and defcribes feveral other grand eftablifhments for the poor and infirm, houfes for lying-in women, foundling hofpitals, fmall-pox hofpitals, and peft houfes. The foundling hofpitals are denominated education houfes. " The rooms," fays Mr. Coxe, " are lofty and large; " the dormitories, which are feparate from the work- " rooms, are very airy, and the beds are not crowded; " each foundling, even each infant, has a feparate " bed; the bedfteads are of iron; the fheets are " changed every week, and the linen three times " a week. In going over the rooms, I was par- " ticularly ftruck with their neatnefs; even the " nurferies were uncommonly clean, and without " any unwholefome fmells. I was convinced " from the behaviour of the children, that they " were in general happy and contented, and could " perceive from their looks that they were remark- " ably healthy." A great proportion of thofe brought thither is, however, found to be in a miferable fickly ftate, and the proportion of deaths to the total number reared exceedingly high. It appears from Mr. Tooke's numbers, that hardly more than one in fix is reared. In the Emprefs Catherine's inftructions for framing a code of laws, it is faid, " the boors have, generally fpeaking, from twelve " to twenty children by one marriage, but it rarely " happens that the fourth part of them reach ma- " turity." All who are below the degree of gentry, and who do not refide in towns, appear to be of the generic clafs of boors; of which, however, there are feveral divifions: as, 1. Free.Peafants. 2. Od-

nodvortzi, or one houfe owners. 3. Coffacks:
fome of whom, by military fervice, have become
noble. 4. Tartar tribes. 6. Difbanded foldiers.
7. Emancipated ferfs. 8. Malo-Ruffian boors. 9.
Vaffal boors. Thefe are of three kinds, 1. Crown
boors. 2. Œconomy boors, formerly belonging to
churches and monafteries. 3. Boors of the mines.
4. Noble and private boors. Refpecting thefe laft,
the Emprefs, in her inftructions, &c. declares her
diffatisfaction at the feverity with which this inferior
clafs is treated; a feverity, as fhe fays, readily leading
to refiftance. She difplayed unwearied attention in
ameliorating their condition, and promoting their
welfare, declaring her wifh that vaffalage fhould be
gradually abolifhed.

Amongft the valuable paffages quoted from the
journal of Mr. Reginald Heber, in *Clarke's Travels
in Ruffia*, it is faid, " we obferved a ftriking difference
" between the peafants of the crown and thofe of
" individuals. The former are almoft all in compa-
" ratively eafy circumftances. Their *abrock*, or rent,
" is fixed; and as they are fure it will never be raifed,
" they are more induftrious. The peafants belong-
" ing to the nobles have their rent regulated by their
" means of getting money; thus it becomes, not a
" rent for land, but a downright tax on induftry.
" Each male peafant is obliged to labour three days
" in each week for his proprietor. If a flave exer-
" cifes any trade which brings in more money than
" agricultural labour, he pays a higher *abrock*.
" The aged and infirm are provided with food, and
" raiment, and lodging, at their owner's expenfe.
" Such as prefer cafual charity to the miferable
" pittance they receive from their mafter, are
" frequently furnifhed with paffports, and allowed to
" feek their fortune; but they fometimes pay an

"*abrock* even for this permiffion to beg. The
"number of beggars in Peterfburg is very fmall ;
" as when one is found, he is immediately fent back
" to his owner. In Mofcow, and other towns, beg-
" gars are numerous, though I think lefs fo than in
"London. They beg with great modefty, in an
" humble and low tone of voice, frequently croffing
" themfelves, and are much lefs clamorous and im-
" portunate than London beggars. The mafter has
" the power of correcting his flaves by blows or con-
" finement; but if he is guilty of great cruelty, he
" is amenable to the iaws. Inftances of barbarity
" are, however, by no means rare. Domeftic fer-
" vants, and thofe employed in manufactories, as they
" are more expofed to cruelty, fo they fometimes
" revenge themfelves in a terrible manner. No
" flave can quit his village, or his mafter's family,
" without a paffport. The prifons of Mofcow and
" Koftroma were filled with runaway flaves, who
" were for the moft part in irons. If a mafter is
" difpleafed with his flave, he may at any time
" fend him for a foldier. With regard to the pea-
" fant's comforts, or means of fupporting exiftence,
" I do not think they are deficient," &c.

Thefe extracts, taken in fragments, with a view
to brevity, fhew that a ftate of lordfhip and vaffalage, however galling to the poor, is, probably,
not lefs onerous to the rich than the fyftem of
legal poor's rates, and is furely not more favourable
to general induftry.

Iceland Poor Law.

In the very interefting narrative of Sir George
Stewart Mackenzie's Travels in Iceland, during the
fummer of 1810, &c. we find an account of a regularly eftablifhed law to fecure the maintenance of
the infirm poor. " The Icelandic laws refpecting
" the condition and maintenance of the poor are
" very ftrictly enforced, and become much more
" burthenfome to the farmers and peafants of the
" country than the taxes to which they are fubject.
" With the exception of three fmall buildings for
" the admiffion of a few incurable lepers, there is no
" public eftablifhment in the island which affords a
" permanent abode to the aged and deftitute ; and
" by all fuch the more immediate affiftance of their
" fellow citizens is therefore imperioufly required.
" The laws render it neceffary for every farmer or
" houfeholder to receive into his family, and to give
" fupport to, thofe of his relations, even in the fourth
" degree of kindred, who may be in a deftitute
" condition. If he has no fuch calls made upon
" him by confanguinity, he is ftill required to affift
" in fupport of the poor, either by admitting fome
" orphan or aged perfon into his houfe, or by con-
" tributing an annual fum proportioned to the value
" of his property. It not unfrequently happens, that
" a landed proprietor, who pays little more than two
" rix-dollars to the public revenue, is called upon for
" forty, fifty, or even fixty, as his ratio towards the
" maintenance of the poor in the diftrict, when he
" is unwilling to receive any of thefe into his own
" habitation. The execution of the poor laws is
" committed to the Hreppftiore of each parifh, and
" forms the moft effential part of the duties of his
" office."

State of the Poor, and Charities, in Ireland.

The wealth of Ireland is lefs diffufed than that of England. The great opulent proprietors are rarely refident on their eftates. The middle clafs is proportionably fmall, and ill educated. The poor numerous, ignorant, moft prolific, and moft thoughtlefs. A mixture of popery, with peculiar pagan fuperftition, the prevailing religion. Mendicity univerfal. All the helplefs, infirm, and deftitute, feek fubfiftence from cafual charity. Wretches who cannot walk abroad to beg are carried by their idle neighbours from door to door, and fet down to obftruct the entrance, till they obtain a pittance of meal or money. Police in Dublin, and induftry in Belfaft, however, preferve their ftreets in fome degree from fuch exhibitions.

In an " Account of Ireland, ftatiftical and poli-
" tical, by Edward Wakefield, 1812," it is remarked,
" the mountain tenants of Connaught are *the ' spai-*
" *peens,'* who in fummer travel into Leinfter in fearch
" of work, while the wife and children wander about
" begging, and foliciting charity ' for the honour of
" GOD.' Groupes of thefe poor creatures may be
" feen during the fummer months, from one fhore to
" the other, perambulating the country, in want and
" mifery. One of the children carries a tin kettle :
" others, if ftout enough, have a bundle of bed
" clothes on their backs; and the mother is fre-
" quently loaded with an infant, that peeps over her
" fhoulders out of a blanket in which it is fufpended.
" Their clothes are filthy rags; and although the
" roads are rugged and hard, none of them have
" ftockings or fhoes." The author of the ftatiftical account of the parifh of Inch, in the county of Wigton, complains of its being infefted with Irifh beggars. " This parifh," fays the author,

" is both willing and able to provide for its own
" poor, but the people are greatly oppreſſed by
" inundations of poor vagrants from Ireland. The
" great road from Portpatrick to Dumfries paſſes
" through this pariſh, and is conſtantly ſwarming
" with Iriſh beggars. They turn aſide into the
" country, and either by entreaties, or by threats,
" extort alms from the inhabitants."—*Sir J. Sin-
clair's Statistical Account of Scotland, vol. iii. p.* 139.

I am not willing to extract inſtances of the
wretchedneſs of the Iriſh poor from Mr. Wakefield's
book, (as vol. ii. p. 773,) I hope they are exag-
gerated; if they are not, much of the diſtreſs of
that country is attributable to the barbarous manners
not only of the lower claſs, but of thoſe above them.
The beſt authority relative to the ſtate of the poor
is to be found in the different county ſurveys. "It
" is ſurpriſing," ſays Mr. Tighe, Survey of Kil-
kenny, p. 473, " how, in the cheapeſt times, they
" can ſtruggle for exiſtence, unaided as they are
" by many little helps they meet with in this coun-
" try (England); and, in fact, we feed them on
" ſuch wretched diet, curtailed of that neceſſary
" article milk during great part of the year; ſcantily
" ſupplied with potatoes; clothed with rags; famiſhed
" with cold in their comfortleſs habitations; nor can
" they, though ſober, frugal, and laborious, which
" from my own knowledge I aſſert, provide againſt
" infirmity and old age with any other reſource than
" begging and dependence, than the precarious re-
" lief of charity; extremities to which many are con-
" ſtantly reduced. None can tell better than the
" members of the charitable ſocieties, what numbers
" of miſerable objects depend on the diſtribution of
" their bounty for exiſtence, and how inadequate
" language is to convey a juſt idea of their poverty

" and fuffering. Thefe ftatements may be applied,
" more or lefs, to all parts of the country."

Sir C. Coote gives the following account of the
poor in the King's and Queen's counties. " Candour
" obliges me to acknowledge that they are much
" addicted to theft, which it is no difgrace to them
" to be detected in. The population of the county
" is much increafed of late years; and it is a fad
" reflection, that their miferies are multiplied in the
" fame proportion."

" A faithful but melancholy picture of the mifer-
" able ftate of the poor in Dublin has been given
" by the Rev. James Whitelaw, whofe invaluable
" work fhould be ftudied by every friend of huma-
" nity, and of the Irifh in particular."—*Wakefield, p.* 790—791.

" In the ancient parts of this city, with few
" exceptions, the ftreets are generally narrow, the
" houfes crowded together, and the rears or back-
" yards of very fmall extent. Of thefe ftreets, a
" few are the refidence of the upper clafs of fhop-
" keepers, and others engaged in trade; but a far
" greater proportion of them, with their numerous
" lanes and alleys, are occupied by working manu-
" facturers, by petty fhopkeepers, the labouring poor,
" and beggars, crowded together, diftreffing to
" humanity. A fingle apartment in one of thefe
" truly-wretched habitations rates from one to two
" fhillings per week; and to lighten this rent, two,
" three, or even four families become joint tenants.
" As I was ufually out at very early hours on the
" furvey, I have frequently furprized from ten to
" fixteen perfons, of all ages and fexes, in a room
" not fifteen feet fquare, ftretched on a wad of
" filthy ftraw, fwarming with vermin, and without
" any covering, fave the wretched rags that confti-
" tuted their wearing-apparel. Under fuch cir-

" cumftances, it is not extraordinary that I fhould
" have frequently found from thirty to fifty indi-
" viduals in a houfe. An intelligent clergyman of
" the Church of Rome affured me, that No. 6,
" Braithwaite ftreet, fome years fince, contained 108
" fouls. This crowded population, wherever it
" obtains, is almoft univerfally accompanied by a
" very ferious evil, a degree of filth and ftench in-
" conceivable, except by fuch as have vifited thefe
" fcenes of wretchednefs. Into the back yard of
" each houfe, frequently not ten feet deep, is flung
" from the windows of each apartment the ordure
" and other filth of its numerous inhabitants; from
" whence it is fo feldom removed, that I have feen
" it nearly on a level with the windows of the firft
" floor; and the moifture that after heavy rains flows
" from this heap, having frequently no fewer to
" carry it off, runs into the ftreet by the entry leading
" to the ftaircafe. One inftance out of a thoufand
" that might be given will be fufficient. When I
" attempted, in the fummer of 1796, to take the
" population of a ruinous houfe in Jofeph's-lane,
" near Caftle market, I was interrupted in my pro-
" grefs by an inundation of putrid blood, alive with
" maggots, which had from an adjacent flaughter-
" yard burft the door, and filled the hall to the depth
" of feveral inches; by the help of a plank and
" fome ftepping-ftones, which I provided for the
" purpofe, (for the inhabitants without any concern
" waded through it,) I reached the ftaircafe; it had
" rained violently, and from the fhattered ftate of
" the roof a torrent of water made its way through
" every floor, from the garret to the ground. The
" fallow looks, and filth and ftench, of the poor
" wretches who crowded round me, indicated their
" fituation. In the garret I found the entire family of

" a poor working fhoemaker, feven in number, lying
" in a fever, without a human being to adminifter to
" their wants. On obferving that his apartment had
" had not a door, he informed me that his landlord,
" finding him not able to pay————. I will not
" difguft my reader with any farther detail, and only
" obferve, that I generally found poor room-keepers
" of this defcription, notwithftanding fo many caufes
" of wretchednefs, apparently at eafe, and perfectly
" affimilated to their habitations. Filth and ftench
" feemed congenial to their nature ; they never made
" the fmalleft effort to remove them ; and if they
" could anfwer the calls of hunger, they felt, or
" feemed to feel, nothing elfe of inconvenience. How
" far it is the duty of the magiftrate to interfere
" in the removal and prevention of fuch dreadful
" nuifances, or how far he is enabled to do fo by the
" exifting laws, I fhall not prefume to determine. I
" am certain that every friend to decency and clean-
" linefs, any perfon who is anxious to promote the
" comforts of the poor, will join me in opinion, that
" a police which attends to our ftreets and lanes only,
" and that but partially, while it never beftows a
" thought on the back yards of the poor, performs
" only half its duty. The more effential part, per-
" haps, is neglected. The ftench of filth in the open
" ftreet may be diffipated by an unobftructed current
" of air ; but that arifing from human excrement in
" narrow yards, enclofed by lofty buildings, muft
" operate with unchecked malignity. In the courfe
" of the furvey, I frequently remonftrated with the
" inhabitants, and particularly when I found them
" unemployed and idle, on their not attempting to
" remove their dirt ; but their univerfal anfwer was,
" ' It is not my bufinefs; if I remove it, who will
" ' pay me ?'

The Irish are a warm-hearted people. No one who knows them will accuse them of wanting charity: but Ireland wants, more than any other country, at least than the other divisions of the British empire, an enlightened middle clafs, to whose refpectability and comfort thofe of the lowest may hope to raife themfelves by industry and good character: and, perhaps, rather more than their neighbours, a general difpofition in the superior clafs to devote a considerable portion, not of their money, but of their time and their intellect, to the improvement of the condition of the poor. To this remark, however, it were eafy to name many brilliant exceptions, both among the Irish resident in England, and among those in Ireland. In the foremost rank of thofe in England, it may fuffice to name the EARL OF MOIRA, and his fister LADY FITZGERALD; and LADY ISABELLA KING, the benevolent foundrefs of several ufeful establifhments in Bath, viz. the Houfe of Protection, in which poor orphans are trained to good principles, and every art which may render them ufeful as domestic fervants: and the Society for Suppreffion of Mendicity, and Encouragement of Industry, which has induced a body of refpectable gentlemen and ladies, to affociate and devote themfelves to the investigation of all cafes of alleged distrefs, with a view of directing charity into its proper channel. The Irish county furveys bear honourable testimony to the humane exertions of many of the resident gentry. I take particular pleafure in here naming Mr. and Mrs. GREENE, of Kilranelagh, in the county of Wicklow, and their neighbour Mr. SAUNDERS, of Saunders' Grove; whofe exertions for the benefit of the lower orders afford an example, which, if duly followed, might make Ireland a paradife, blest in itfelf, and diffusing bleffings to the rest of the united kingdom. The name of LA TOUCHE appears prominent among thofe of the fupporters of all the Dublin charities; but the fame of the many great and bright characters, whofe titles and names decorate thofe lifts, and do honour to human nature, needs not to be declared in thefe pages.

There are in Dublin at leaft fifty public charities, extending to every human want and infirmity, bodily or mental. I take the enumeration from the Treble Almanack, Regiftry, and Directory, for the year 1814.

Societies, &c. for the promotion of Religion and Morals.—1. For the Suppreffion of Vice.—2. Hibernian Bible Society.—3 Sunday School Society. It is noted, that, being eftablifhed in 1809, it has given affiftance to 167 Sunday-fchools, confifting of at leaft 19,000 children —4. Society for promoting the Education of the Poor.—5. Blue Coat Hofpital, containing 150 boys, to be maintained, educated, clothed, and apprenticed.—6. Incorporated Society for Proteftant Schools.—7. Hibernian Society, for maintaining and educating, apprenticing, or placing in the army, orphans and children of foldiers.—8. Hibernian Marine Society, for orphans and children of feamen.—9. Dublin Weekly Schools. 10. Sunday and Daily Schools —11. Freemafon's Orphan School.—12. Orphan Houfe for deftitute female children.—13. Foundling Hofpital. There are 1032 children in the houfe, who are, when qualified, to be apprenticed to eligible mafters; and above 5000 with nurfes in the country.—14. Houfe of Induftry.—15. Houfe of Refuge, for the reception of young women out of employment, who can bring full teftimonials of good character, &c.— 16. Richmond National Inftitution for the inftruction of the induftrious blind.—17. Board of Education

Societies for the Sick-Hofpitals.—1. Royal Hofpital, néar Kilmainham, for ancient and maimed officers and foldiers of the army in Ireland.—2. Royal Military Infirmary.—3. The Charitable Infirmary.—4. Dr. Stevens's General Hospital for 300 patients.—5. Mercer's Hofpital for the fick poor, containing about 50 beds.—6. Hofpital for Incurables, containing 60, clothed, fed, and fupplied with nurfes and medical attendance.—7. St. Patrick's Hofpital, founded by Dean Swift, for lunatics and ideots.—8. Hofpital for poor lying-in women. 9. The Meath Hofpital —10. Weftmoreland Lock Hofpital.—11. Fever Hofpital. This inftitution embraces two objects; the immediate removal of the difeafed perfon from his own dwelling-place, and the adoption of meafures for counteracting the progrefs of infection in the habitations of the poor. The hofpital was opened in May 1804, from which time to October 1813, 13,607 were admitted, of whom near 12,500 were difcharged cured.—12. Sir Patrick Dun's Hofpital.—13. Difpenfary for St. Mary's and St. Thomas's parifhes.—14. The Dublin General Difpenfary.—15. St. George's Difpenfary and Fever Hofpital.—16. Northweft Difpenfary. 17. United Hofpital of St. Mark and St. Anne.— 18. Difpenfary for Infant Poor.—19. Cow-Pock Inftitution.—19. Sick Poor Inftitution, Meath-ftreet. 20. Eftablifhment for relief of the ruptured poor.

Alms-Houfes and Societies, for exploring and relieving general diftrefs.—1. Simpfon's Hofpital for the reception of poor, decayed, blind, and gouty men.—2. Stranger's Friend Society.—3. Old Men's Afylum, intended to receive forty —4. Afylum for aged and infirm female fervants.—5 The Charitable Loan. The governors of the Charitable Mufical Society, incorporated by Act of Parliament

in 1780, for lending out money, interest free, to
indigent tradesmen, meet monthly to lend not less
than two pounds, nor more than five pounds, to any
one person at one time, which sums are to be repaid
at sixpence in the pound weekly. Since March
1781, 3267 persons have been relieved; the sum
lent £12,469.—6. Meath Charitable Loan.—7.
Charitable Society for the relief of sick and indigent
room-keepers. This admirable institution, if it be,
and while it shall be, sustained in all its departments
with a zeal, assiduity, and sagacity, in any degree com-
parable to that of its indefatigable and most worthy
treasurer, Mr. Samuel Rosborough, a name to be
classed with those of Curl and Coram, perhaps of
Hanway and of Howard, must possess most of the
advantages, free from many of the defects, of the
English system of poor's law.

It resembles in many respects the institution at
Bath, before mentioned, which I shall hereafter find
occasion to describe more fully. The plan of the
Dublin Society is thus concisely detailed at the back
of the half-sheet containing the report of receipts
and expenditure during the year 1809. The receipts of that year are stated to have been
2218l. 11s. 11d. chiefly from voluntary contribution. Balance in the treasurer's hands at the
year's end 9l. 6s. 5¼d.

" The institution is conducted by the general
" monthly meeting of subscribers for superintending
" and controuling the receipts and expenditures, and
" the description of persons relieved, during the preced-
" ing month :—The committee of trustees delegated by
" divisional meetings, and approved by the general meet-
" ing, to arrange all business, and act as circumstances
" may require during the intervals of general meetings:
" —The local or divisional meetings of the resident

" members of each divifion, and fuch other members
" as choofe to attend. At thefe meetings all applica-
" tions for relief are received, and given out for ex-
" amination to members, not being the recommenders,
" and received back with the neceffary reports, and
" then finally difpofed of. Every furgeon, phyfician,
" and clergyman, refident in town, has a power to
" recommend objects. A weekly allowance for a
" month is the ufual mode of relief, with an immediate
" advance of money in urgent cafes; but frequently a
" fum is given to releafe fome indifpenfable articles of
" clothing, or implements of trade, (often unavoidably
" pawned during ficknefs, or occafional want of employ-
" ment), or to aid in fome induftrious purfuit, fuited
" to the abilities or opportunities of the petitioner.

" The objects of the inftitution are fuch poor per-
" fons of all religious perfuafions as have never pub-
" licly begged, and are in diftrefs from ficknefs, want
" of employment, or other caufe; and the relief ad-
" miniftered is always with a view to reftore them to
" their ufual means of fupporting themfelves; it being
" the uniform practice to extend *temporary* relief to
" as many as poffible, and not to give to any fuch
" permanent affiftance as might tend to prevent in-
" duftry, or alienate the funds from their proper
" objects. Thofe who are found to have been for-
" merly in better circumftances, and to have preferved
" a good character, are confidered as the moft de-
" ferving. Whenever impofitions are difcovered, the
" recommenders are apprifed of the deceit, and the
" impoftors are rejected and regiftered. The fociety,
" however, obferve that inftances have occurred of
" perfons in the receipt of the public bounty, who have
" denied their having received any relief, in order to
" obtain fome from thofe who recommeuded them :
" they, therefore, think it right to caution the public

" againſt giving credit to the reports of petitioners,
" without making further enquiry."

No perſon engaged in the conduct of the inſtitution receives any compenſation for his trouble, except the ſecretary and collectors.

Penitentiaries.—1. Dublin Female Penitentiary.
—2. General Magdalen Aſylum.—3. Magdalen
Aſylum, Leeſon-ſtreet.—4. Lock Penitentiary.—5.
Kilmainham Gaol Penitentiary.†

At Belfaſt is a poor-houſe and infirmary on ſo
extenſive a ſcale, as probably to provide no leſs aid
to the poor than would be ſupplied by the poor's
rate in any Engliſh town of equal population.
The ſtatement of the year 1809 ſhews an expenditure of 2706*l.* 2*s.* 3*d.* It appears to be conducted
with great prudence, and equal attention to the
morals and comforts of the poor. The ſums collected are, by donations, by bequeſts, by ſermons; by
fines and penalties, paid by order of magiſtrates;
by collections at places of worſhip, amounting, in
1809, to 414*l.* 3*s.* 2*d.*; by annual ſubſcriptions
amounting, in 1809, to 876*l.* 3*s.* 6½*d.*; by burying-
ground fees; by ſmall rents of fields and tenements;
and by ſale of pigs. I find no account of profit by
ſale of manufacture; which probably, as in other
places of the kind, is very contracted, and conducted
with loſs. Belfaſt contained, in 1791, 18,320 inhabitants.

* In the Houſe of Commons, Thurſday June 8, 1815, in a de-
bate on a motion by Mr. Roſe, for the appointment of a Committee to enquire into the ſtate of mendicity in the metropolis,
Mr. Peele ſaid, " he doubted whether it would be politic to
" extend an eſtabliſhment like the Houſe of Induſtry in Ireland
" to this country. It coſts £50,000 a year, and relief was given to
" all who applied, becauſe there were no poor rates; but if he were
" to judge of its efficacy from the ſtate of induſtry in Dublin, his
" opinion would be far from favourable, as there was no city
" in which mendicity prevailed to ſuch a degree as in the Iriſh
" capital."—*Courier Newspaper.*

Poverty, and Charity, in Scotland.

" The poor of Scotland (fays Mr. Malthus, c. viii.
" v. ii.) are in general fupported by voluntary con-
" tributions, diftributed under the infpection of the
" minifter of the parifh; and it appears upon the
" whole, that they have been conducted with confi-
" derable judgment. Having no claim* of right to
" relief, and the fupplies, from the mode of their
" collection, being neceffarily uncertain, and never
" abundant, the poor have confidered them merely
" as a laft refource in cafes of extreme diftrefs, and
" not as a fund on which they might fafely rely,
" and an adequate portion of which belonged to
" them, by the laws of their country, in all difficulties.
The confequence of this is, that the common
people make very confiderable exertions to avoid
the neceffity of applying for fuch a fcanty and
precarious relief. It is obferved, in many of the
accounts, (ftatiftical, of Scotland,) that they feldom
fail of making a provifion for ficknefs and for age;
and in general the grown-up children and relations
of perfons who are in danger of falling upon the
parifh ftep forward, if they be in any way able, to
prevent fuch a degradation, which is univerfally
confidered as a difgrace to the family.
" The writers of the accounts of the different
" parifhes frequently reprobate, in very ftrong terms,
" the fyftem of Englifh affeffments for the poor, and
" give a decded preference to the Scotch mode of
" relief." In the account of Caerlaverock, v. vi.
p. 21, in anfwer to the queftion, How ought the
poor to be fupplied? it is moft judicioufly remarked,

* Mr. Rofe, in a late pamphlet, has controverted this obfervation;
but whatever may be the law on the fubject, the practice is certainly
as here reprefented.

that " diftrefs and poverty multiply in proportion to
" the funds created to relieve them : that the meafures
" of charity ought to remain invifible till the moment
" when it is neceffary that they fhould be diftributed:
" that in the country parifhes of Scotland, in general,
" fmall occafional voluntary collections are fufficient:
" that the legiflature has no occafion to interfere to
" augment the ftream, which is already copious
" enough : in fine, that the eftablifhment of a poor's
" rate would not only be unneceffary but hurtful,
" as it would tend to opprefs the landholder, without
" bringing relief to the poor. Thefe, upon the
" whole, appear to be the prevailing opinions of the
" clergy of Scotland."

It appears, however, that epidemic difeafes are
extremely frequent and fatal. Scurvy, low nervous
fevers, rheumatifms, and confumptions, are attributed
to the common refidence of the poor, who are chiefly
affected by them in cold and wet fituations ; to fcanty
and unwholefome food ; to impure air from damp
and crowded houfes, indolent habits, and inattention
to cleanlinefs. " Scotland has at all times been
" fubject to years of fcarcity, and occafionally even
" to dreadful famines." It is faid, that in 1783
Scotland was faved from famine by the ceffation of
the American war, and the confequent opening of
the magazines, particularly of peafe, provided for the
navy. " Many fimilar defcriptions occur in different
" parts of the ftatiftical account ; but thefe will
" fufficiently fhew the nature and intenfity of diftrefs
" which has been occafionally felt from want." Yet,
" it has been calculated, that half of the furplus of
" births in Scotland is drawn off by emigrations;
" and it cannot be doubted that this drain tends
" greatly to relieve the country, and to improve the
" condition of thofe that remain." Ch. x. v. 1.

The neceffity of this drain for fuperabundant population is found to exift, although the population is
not forced by the operation of poor's rate. Emigration, alternately acting as caufe and effect of
augmented population, feems to have been the ef-
fective fubftitute for the general enforcement of the
poor law. Such a law, however, exifts, and is enforced for the maintenance of the fyftem of general
education, by which the condition of the poor in
Scotland has been greatly improved. " An Act,
" paffed in 1646, obliges the heritors and minifter of
" each parifh to meet and affefs the feveral heritors
" with the requifite fum for building a fchool-houfe,
" and to elect a fchoolmafter, and modify a falary
" for him in all time to come. The Society for
" promoting Chriftian Knowledge, incorporated in
" 1709, have applied a large part of their fund for
" the fame purpofe. By their report, 1ft May 1795,
" the annual fum employed by them in fupporting
" their fchools in the Highlands and Iflands was
" 3913l. 19s. 10d. The influence of the fchool
" eftablifhment in Scotland cn the peafantry of that
" country feems to have decided by experience a
" queftion of legiflation of the utmoft importance—
" whether a fyftem of national inftruction for the
" poor be favourable to morals and good govern-
" ment." In the year 1698, Fletcher of Saltoun
declared as follows: " There are at this day in Scot-
" land 200,000 people begging from door to door.
" And though the number of them be, perhaps,
" double to what it was formerly, by reafon of this
" prefent great diftrefs, (a famine then prevailed,)
" yet in all times there have been about 100,000 of
" thofe vagabonds, who have lived without any regard
" or fubjection either to the laws of the land, or even
" thofe of GOD and nature." He accufes them as

K

frequently guilty of robbery, and fometimes of mur-
der. "In years of plenty," fays he, "many thou-
"fands of them meet together in the mountains,
"where they feaft and riot for many days ; and at
"country weddings, markets, burials, and other
"public occafions, they are to be feen, both men and
"women, perpetually drunk, curfing, blafpheming,
"and fighting together." This high-minded ftatesman, of whom it is faid by a cotemporary, "that
"he would lofe his life readily to fave his country,
"and would not do a bafe thing to ferve it," thought
the evil fo great, that he propofed as a remedy the
revival of domeftic flavery, according to the practice
of his adored republics. "A better remedy has
"been found, which, in the filent lapfe of a century,
"has proved effectual. The ftatute of 1696, the
"noble legacy of the Scottifh Parliament to their
"country, began foon after this to operate : and
"happily as the minds of the poor received inftruction,
"the Union opened new channels of induftry, and
"new fields of action to their view." *Account of
Parifh Schools in Scotland. by James Currie, M. D.
27th Report of the Society for bettering the Condition
of the Poor, vol. v.*

A moft interefting picture of the ancient Highlanders is drawn by Lord Selkirk, on Emigration
and the State of the Highlands, p. 20 and 21, with
a pen manifeftly guided by the pureft benevolence,
and impelled by a manly ardour in the caufe of truth.
"Their lands afforded few objects of commerce : the
"only article of which they ever had any confider-
"able fuperfluity was cattle ; and from the turbulent
"ftate of the country, thefe could not be brought to
"market without the utmoft difficulty. The defire
"of accumulating was checked by the infecurity of
"property: thofe, indeed, who derive their acqui-

" fitions from the fword, are feldom in the habit of
" hoarding them with care: what may next day be
" replaced by the plunder of an enemy, they are
" difpofed to lavifh with carelefs profufion. Thus
" among the ancient Highlanders, the fame men who
" made a glory of pillage and rapine, carried the
" fentiments of hofpitality and generofity to a ro-
" mantic excefs. The devoted attachment of the
" common people to their chiefs, though defcribed
" in terms of aftonifhment by contemporary writers,
" was an effect eafily deducible from the general
" principles of human nature. Among the poor in
" civilized countries, there is, perhaps, no circum-
" ftance more feverely felt, than the neglect they meet
" with from perfons of fuperior condition, and which
" appears to ftigmatife them as of an inferior fpecies:
" and if in the hour of diftrefs they meet with an
" unexpected degree of fympathy, the attention be-
" ftowed on their fituation is often more foothing
" than direct benefits conferred without any ap-
" pearance of fenfibility or concern. When a perfon
" of rank treats his inferiors with cordiality, and
" fhews an intereft in their welfare, it is feldom that
" in any country this behaviour is not repaid by
" gratitude and affection. This was particularly
" to be expected among the Highlanders, a peo-
" ple naturally of acute feelings, habituated to
" fentiments of a romantic and poetical caft: in
" them the condefcending manners and kindnefs
" of their chiefs excited an attachment bordering
" on enthufiafm." This did not efcape the ob-
fervant eye of Dr. Johnfon, who, in fpeaking
of his refidence in the houfe of Mr. M'Lean, of
Col, (*Journey to the Weftern Iflands, page* 297,)
fays, " Wherever we roved, we were pleafed to fee
" the reverence with which his fubjects regarded

" him. He did not endeavour to dazzle them by
" any magnificence of drefs; his only diftinction was
" a feather in his bonnet; but as foon as he ap·
" peared, they forfook their work, and cluftered
" about him; he took them by the hand, and they
" feemed mutually delighted." Nothing can be
more juft than Lord Selkirk's obfervation; no
object more interefting than that commerce of
good fympathy, which arrefted Dr. Johnfon's attention. The moft baleful effect of luxury is that
felfifhnefs, indolent as to all that concerns the welfare of others, and active only in purfuit of particular and immediate gratification, which wholly
alienates the rich from the poor. Surely to the
reaction of this want of fympathy, arifing from
luxurious habits, from the perverfion of religion, and
the wreck of morals, is to be attributed much of the
atrocity which cafts fo deep a ftain of horror over the
fourth and fifth years of the French Revolution.

In Lord Kaimes's Sketches of the Hiftory of Man,
(properly called fketches, from the frequent marks of
hafte) are fome juft reflections on the poor. He is
incorrect in ftating, that an Englifh labourer " dares
" not remove from a parifh in which he has gained
" a fettlement to another where wages are higher,
" from fear of being cut out of a fettlement al-
" together." P. 70. Sk. 10. But he anticipates
the conclufions of Mr. Malthus, in declaring refolutely againft a perpetual tax for the poor. " If
" there muft be fuch a tax, I know of none lefs
" fubverfive of induftry and morals, than that efta-
" blifhed in Scotland, obliging the landholders in
" every parifh to meet at ftated times in order to
" provide a fund for the poor; but leaving the ob-
" jects of their charity, and the meafure, to their own
" humanity and difcretion." In this plan there is

no encroachment on the natural duty of charity, but only it is provided that the minority muſt ſubmit to the opinion of the majority.

In large towns, where the character and circumſtances of the poor are not ſo well known as in country pariſhes, the following variation is propoſed. " Inſtead of landholders, who are proper in country " pariſhes, let there be in each town pariſh a " ſtanding committee, choſen by the proprietors of " houſes, the third part to be changed annually. " Let this committee, with the miniſter, make up a " liſt of ſuch as deſerve charity, adding an eſtimate " of what, with their own labour, may be ſufficient " for each of them. Let the miniſter, with one or " two of the committee, carry about this liſt to " every family that can afford charity, ſuggeſting " what may be proper for each to contribute. This " liſt, with the addition of the ſum contributed by " each houſholder, ſhould be affixed on the principal " door of the pariſh church, to honour the contri- " butors, and to inform the poor of the proviſion " made for them. Some ſuch mode may probably " be effectual, without tranſgreſſing the bounds of " voluntary charity. *But if any one obſtinately* " *refuſe to contribute, after ſeveral applications, the* " *committee at their diſcretion may tax him.*" The committee will, in effect, be a veſtry ; the collection, a poor's rate ; and the diſtribution judicious or otherwiſe, according to the intelligence or activity of thoſe who ſhall at any time compoſe it. In fact, the Scotch poor law differs little from that of England. The habits of the Highlands make it needleſs amongſt the mountaineers : in the great towns, the difficulty of raiſing a ſupply for the infirm poor, rapidly increaſing in number, according to the advances of wealth and luxury, has occaſioned its partial enforcement,

In Erſkine's Inſtitute of the Law of Scotland,
fol. ed. b. i. tit 7. *par.* 63. *p.* 148, it is obſerved,
" The poor may be divided into thoſe nuiſances to
" ſociety, who, though they are able, are not willing
" to work ; and ſuch indigent perſons as, from age
" or bodily infirmities, cannot earn a ſufficient live-
" lihood by labour. The puniſhments inflicted by
" law on the firſt ſort ſhall be explained." *B. iv.*
t. 4. " The poor who are aged, or diſabled from
" work, were appointed to be maintained by a tax, to
" be levied upon the pariſhes where they were ſeve-
" rally born. 1535. *c.* 22. (Boyd, office, power, and
" juriſdiction of his Majeſty's juſtices of the peace,
" and commiſſioners of ſupply, obſerves, that this
" was the firſt ſtatutary maintenance appointed by
" the legiſlature of Scotland for the poor. *b. i. p.*
" 192.) This tax was to be proportioned among
" the inhabitants of boroughs, by the magiſtrates ;
" and in landward pariſhes, by judges named by the
" king. 1579. *c.* 74. By a poſterior Act, 1663—16,
" a power is given to the landholders in landward pa-
" riſhes to aſſeſs themſelves for the maintenance of ſuch
" of the poor, as cannot fully maintain themſelves by
" labour, in the manner ſpecially deſcribed in that Act,
" and to demand relief of half of the ſum ſo raiſed from
" their tenants. Where the place of a poor man's
" nativity is not known, the burthen of his mainte-
" nance falls on the pariſh where he has had his moſt
" common reſort for the three years immediately pre-
" ceding his being taken up, or his applying for the
" public charity. 1663, *c.* 16. 1698, *c.* 21. *See*
" *New Col. ii.* 19. And in a late caſe, Aug. 7, 1767,
" Baxter, it was adjudged, that the maintenance of
" indigent or poor perſons ought to fall on the pariſh
" of their laſt three years reſidence, even preferably to
" the pariſh of their birth, though that ſhould be

" known. In parishes where a sufficient fund cannot
" be raised for all the poor, either by taxation, or
" by voluntary contribution at the church doors, the
" magistrates of the borough, or the kirk-session, are
" authorised to give them badges, as a sufficient war-
" rant to them to ask alms at the houses of the inha-
" bitants; but they must neither beg at churches, nor
" where there is any public meeting, nor without the
" limits of their own parish. 1579, c. 74. 1672, c. 18.
" The execution of these regulations, so charitably
" intended for the relief of the poor, is attended with
" so much difficulty in most of our parishes, especially
" those which border upon the Highlands, that it is
" in few places only it has been attempted."

The Act of 1663 was confirmed and enlarged by
that of 1672, which states, in preamble, that the
vagabonds, beggars, and idle persons, are a great
burthen and reproach to the kingdom ; and for the
most part live without law or rule, sacred or civil.
And to remedy these defects, enacts that the magistrates of several boroughs mentioned in the Act shall
provide correction-houses for receiving and entertaining of the beggars, &c. within their boroughs.

The Act of James VIth, entitled *Anent the Poor*,
enacts, that poor and indigent children may be bound
as servants to those who will receive and maintain
them, their heirs and assignees, till such children shall
attain the age of thirty years; and they are to be
subject to the correction of their masters in all
manner and sort of punishment, says the Act, life and
torture excepted. The 10th Act of 22d Parliament,
Boyd, p. 197.

I had proceeded thus far, before I was enabled to
procure Dr. Macferlan's enquiries concerning the
poor, whose collections on this subject would have
saved me much trouble ; I shall now content myself

with referring for farther information to page 44 of his useful book.

Edinburgh abounds in charitable establishments, some of which it may be interesting to enumerate, with a view of considering how large a sum they supply toward the aid of the poor.

Heriot's Hospital, the funds of which are applied to the education, and placing out in various ways, of boys, of whom above 100 are in the house.

Watson's Hospital, for the same purposes.

Merchants' Maiden Hospital, for girls.

Trades' Maiden Hospital, on a similar plan to the preceding.

Orphan Hospital maintains above 150; empowered to hold real property of 1000l. per ann.; supported by charitable contributions.

Gillespie's Hospital, for old men and women, and for the education of 100 boys.

Trinity Hospital, for the reception of poor aged burgesses, their widows and daughters, maintains about fifty.

Asylum for the blind, supported by charitable contributions, and the sale of their manufactures.

The Charity Workhouse, maintaining commonly about 700 persons of both sexes, including children; there are besides, 300 out-pensioners. The only permanent fund for defraying this expense is a tax of two per cent. on the valued rents of the city, about 600l. annually; other funds yield about 400l. The rest is derived from collections at church doors, and voluntary contributions; but these fall short of the requisite supply, and recourse is had to extraordinary collections. The sum arising from the rents of the city is constantly increasing; but *the members of the College of Justice are exempted.* The expense of this inftitution is fuppofed to be annually not lefs than 4000*l.*

There are two other Charity Work-houfes, one in Canongate, the other in St. Cuthbert's or Weft-kirk parifh.

Captain William Horn's charity, 3500l. invefted, that the intereft may be divided, on Chriftmas day, to poor out day-labourers, who muft at that feafon want employment, 5l. to thofe who have large families, one half to thofe who have fmaller.

Robert Johnfton's charity, 3000l. to the poor, 1000l. to be employed in materials, for work, &c. 1000l. to clothe boys in Heriot's Hofpital.

Mr. John Strachan's charity, in truft to the Prefbytery of Edinburgh, to be difpofed of in fmall fums to poor old people, not under 65 years of age, and to orphans not above 12.

Magdalen Afylum.

Society for the Sons of the Clergy.

Deftitute Sick Society.

Royal Infirmary.

Public Difpenfary.

Vaccine Eftablifhment.

Lying-in Hofpital.

Truftees for Minifters' Widows.

Friendly Society of Diffenting Minifters, for relief of Widows and Orphans.

Deaf and Dumb Inftitution.

Lunatic Afylum.

Gratis Sabbath School Society.

Society for Suppreffion of Beggars, for the relief of Occafional Diftrefs, and for the encouragement of Induftry among the Poor. Inftituted January 25, 1813. This Society is founded on fimilar principles and plan to one previoufly eftablifhed in Bath, which will be hereafter defcribed. *Guide to Edinburgh*, 1807.

To thefe may be added the parochial inftitutions for religious education of children of the poor, and Society for promoting Religious Knowledge among the Poor ; but perhaps as thefe are wholly of a fpiritual nature, their revenue is not to be added to the above account.

The conclufion of the report of the Society for Suppreffion of Beggars, (the writer of which feems to have had the Bath reports in his eye,) defcribes correctly the beft objects of charity as the aim of the inftitution. "Inveftigation is the bafis of their "fyftem. True charity looks beyond the mere "giving of alms. It aims at the amendment of the "poor : it directs its efforts to the education of the "young; to the recovery of the fick; the reforma-"tion of the diffolute ; the employment of the idle "and unoccupied ; the comfort of the aged, helplefs, "and afflicted. Thefe duties, the fociety, as far "as in their power, attempt to fulfil." What heart, in any quarter, wherefoever humanity exifts, would not prompt a prayer for their fuccefs.

The population of Edinburgh is faid to be near 90,000. That of Glafgow is faid, in the Picture or Stranger's Guide, to be 110,000.

The charities of Glafgow appear to bear a due proportion to thofe of Edinburgh. There is, however, a toll levied on the trades' incorporations, which appears to be peculiar to Glafgow incorporations.

Hammermen pay annually to the poor	£250
Tailors	570
Cordiners	250
Maltfters	300
Weavers	480
Bakers	250
Skinners	65
Wrights	440

Coopers	-	-	-	-	-	£ 40
Flefhers	-	-	-	-	-	200
Mafons	-	-	-	-	-	105
Gardeners	-	-	-	-	-	60
Barbers	-	-	-	-	-	130
Dyers	-	-	-	-	-	40
						3180

Befides above 8o*l.* paid to the Trades-houfe School, in different proportions.

The amount of collections at places of worfhip is to be added to the above amount of contributions for the poor in Edinburgh.

From the beft account of each, which I have been able to procure, the total amount of charities in Edinburgh equals at leaft 40,000*l.* per annum.

Let us compare the revenue fo dedicated, with that of Liverpool. Edinburgh, inhabitants, 90,000. Charities, &c. 40,000*l.*—Liverpool ditto, 94,000. Poor-rate expenditure for the poor, 1803, 23,119*l.*

Liverpool has many fplendid eftablifhments of a charitable nature, hofpitals, afylums, difpenfaries, fchools for the poor ; yet, probably, not amounting, in total expenditure, to more than 24,000*l.* per ann. ; fo that Liverpool will not appear to apply to the fupport of its poor, even with its very high poor-rate, a much greater fum, in proportion to its population, than Edinburgh.

The public charities of Milan (*A. Young,* before quoted) are faid to amount to 87,500l. fterling : the population to 116,000.

English Poor Law.

We have feen the rudiments of a poor law, in the allotment of a portion of tithe to this object, by the law of Mofes. We have found that the neceffity of fome continued provifion for the poor has been recognized by moft of the civilized ftates ancient and modern; and that the mifchievous tendency of habitual mendicity has been generally and duly reprobated, and marked out for fuppreffion; except only where the human mind itfelf has been generally degraded by the groffeft fuperftition. England, in the different periods of its hiftory, prefents an epitome of almoft all other nations. The Jewifh law naturally influenced the ordinances of the Catholic church. The common law of England, compounded of Jewifh, Greek, Roman, Papiftical, Br tifh, Saxon, Danifh, and Norman, laws and cuftoms, ordained generally, that the poor were to be fuftained, fo that none die for want of fuftenance. Yet till the time of Henry VIIIth, the means of providing fuch fuftenance appear to have been left principally to the care of the church.

" The clergy moft affuredly, from the nature of
" the ecclefiaftical eftablifhment, and the eleemofy-
" nary principles upon which every donation to
" religious bodies was conferred, were confidered as
" the peculiar and official guardians of the poor;
" and whatever doubts may be now entertained of
" any legal claim that the indigent claffes of the
" community have on the much reduced revenues
" of the church, it feems clear, from the unequivocal
" expreffions of the Legiflature in 1391, that a
" certain portion of tithe, when appropriated to

" monaſtic inſtitutions, was ſet apart for purpoſes of
" charity." St. xv. R. II. c. 6, confirmed by 4. H.
" IV. c. 12. In this (the former) ſtatute, and in the
" 12th of Richard II. we may obſerve the great out-
" lines of a ſyſtem of compulſory maintenance, which
" is commonly imagined to have originated in conſe-
" quence of the Reformation. I ſhall, however, ſhew
" that the 43d of Elizabeth, however highly praiſed
" for its originality, is nothing more than a deve-
" lopement of an ancient ſyſtem, and a more perfect
" organization of legal regulations, that, from lapſe of
" time, had become either impolitic or impracticable."
Sir F. M. Eden, v. i. p. 62, 63.

" It is juſtly obſerved, that, among other bad
" effects which attended the monaſtic inſtitutions;
" it was not perhaps one of the leaſt (though fre-
" quently eſteemed quite otherwiſe) that they ſup-
" ported and fed a very numerous and very idle poor,
" whoſe ſuſtenance depended upon what was daily
" diſtributed in alms at the gates of the religious
" houſes. But upon the total diſſolution of theſe,
" the inconvenience of thus encouraging the poor in
" habits of indolence and beggary was quickly felt
" throughout the kingdom; and abundance of
" ſtatutes were made, in the reign of King Henry
" the VIIIth, for providing for the poor and impo-
" tent ; which, as the preambles to ſome of them
" recite, had of late years ſtrangely increaſed. Not-
" withſtanding this opinion and expreſſion in the
" ſtatutes, I very much doubt, however, whether the
" monaſteries generally and greatly troubled them-
" ſelves with relieving the poor that did not imme-
" diately belong to their own demeſnes. The ſame
" ſort of charity was practiſed by the nobility on
" their eſtates. The ſtatutes before this period often
" mention the great increaſe of the poor." *Id. p.* 95.

" To the introduction of manufactures, and the
" consequent emancipation of those who were dif-
" miffed by mafters, and those who ran away from
" them, with the adventurous project of trying their
" fortunes in the lottery of trade, I aſcribe the in-
" troduction of a new claſs of men, thenceforward
" deſcribed by the legiſlature under the denomina-
" tion of *poor*; by which term, I conceive, they
" meant to ſignify freemen, who being either inca-
" pacitated by ſickneſs or old age, or prevented by
" other cauſes, from getting work, were obliged to
" have recourſe to the charitable for their ſubſiſtence.
" It is impoſſible that the term could have been
" applicable to thoſe who ſtill continued in a ſtate
" of ſervitude; ſince the obligation to ſerve another
" for life, according to the definition of Grotius,
" imports a reciprocal obligation in the mafter to
" provide his ſlave with, at leaſt, the bare neceſſa-
" ries of life; and indeed, in the early periods of
" our hiſtory, this muſt of neceſſity have been the
" caſe; for with the exception of thoſe who were
" engaged in trade and manufacture, who formed
" a very inconſiderable portion of the nation, the
" people in general muſt have ſubſiſted by agri-
" culture: and as the land was poſſeſſed by a few
" great proprietors, and cultivated by their ſervile
" dependents, it was only to territorial lords that,
" in periods of diſtreſs, a bankrupt tenant, or an
" aged bondſman, could look for ſuccour." *Id. p.* 57.
" When, by flow degrees, a new race of men aroſe
" in the country, and manufactures became firmly
" eſtabliſhed, it is remarkable that the exiſtence of
" poor as firſt noticed by the legiſlature. The
" decreaſe of villenage ſeems neceſſarily to have been
" the era of the origin of the *poor*. Manufactures,
" though they added to the capital ſtock of the

" nation, yet by creating a neceffity for free hands,
"; and confequently enabling men to make ufe of the
" moft valuable of all property, their own induftry,
" fubjected thofe who were any ways incapacitated
" from availing themfelves of that fund, to the mifer-
" able alternative of ftarving independently.

" Without the moft diftant idea of difparaging
" the numberlefs benefits derived to this country
" from manufactures and commerce, we are led to
" the inevitable conclufion, that thefe are the true
" parents of our national poor. To complain, how-
" ever, that they have, by the inequality which in-
" duftry muft ever occafion, been the fource of mifery
" to fome members of the community, is to complain
" of the caufes which have raifed us to an unexampled
" pitch of national profperity, and of the confequences
" which are neceffarily attached to it.

" A new clafs being thus infenfibly created, they
" very foon, from their numbers, their vices, and
" their miferies, rofe into notoriety. In the year
" 1376, they are firft noticed by the legiflature, under
" the denomination of beggars, ftaff-ftrikers, and
" fturdy rogues; and from the language of a fubfe-
" quent ftatute I fhould infer, that the diftrict where
" impotent beggars were directed to refide was bound
" to maintain them; and that the juftices of peace,
" who had a confiderable latitude of difcretionary
" power, in fome cafes regulated both the place of
" their abode, and the amount of the alms they were
" to receive." *Id. p.* 61.

In citing the Statute of Labourers, however, paffed
23 Ed. III. 1349, he obferves, " It is remarkable
" that the firft public information we have that la-
" bourers ' were rather willing to beg in idlenefs
" than by labour to get their living,' was at a pe-
" riod when there was a fcarcity of fervants; and

" that plenty of work feems to have (if not created)
" certainly increafed the number of beggars. The
" ftatute, in order to compel able men to labour for
" the neceffaries of life, impofed the penalty of im-
" prifonment on all perfons who, giving alms through
" pretence of piety or charity, fhould encourage the
" idlenefs of fturdy labourers."—*Id. p.* 34.

But even in the laws of our Saxon Monarchs
vagabonds are noticed, and means of affigning a
fettlement decreed. " Leges Æthelftani 2. De
" hominibus domino carentibus. Statuimus de ho-
" minibus domino carentibus, a quibus nullus jus fuum
" obtinere poteft, ut oretur cognatio ecrum ut eos
" ad jus gentium adducant et dominum iis inve-
" niant in conventu populi; et fi hoc tunc requirere
" nolint vel non poffint ad hunc terminum, tunc fit
" poftea fugitivus, et pro fure eum capiat quisquis in
" eum inciderit, &c."

The ftatutes, regulating wages of labourers, and
appointing punifhments for vagrants, between 23
Ed. III. and the end of the reign of Henry VIII. are
numerous; and duly noticed by Sir F. Eden. In
22 H. VIII. c. 12, it is faid, that throughout the
realm vagabonds and beggars have of long time increafed, and daily do increafe in great and exceffive numbers.

" Very early in Edward 6th's reign, the legis-
" lature reiterated the old complaints againft 'idle-
" nefs and vagabondrie.' They conceived " that
" the godly Acts which had hitherto been framed on
" the fubject, had not had the fuccefs which might
" have been wifhed;' that it was partly afcribable
" to the ' foolifh pitie and mercie of thofe who
" fhould have feene the faid godly lawes executed;'
" and partly owing to the ' perverfe nature and
" long-accuftomed idleneffe of the perfons given to

" loytering ;' and they thought that 'if the vaga-
" bonds who were unprofitable members, or rather
" enemies, of the commonwealth, were punifhed by
" death, whipping, imprifonment, and with other
" corporall pains, it were not without their deferts;'
" it was therefore enacted, that if any man or
" woman, able to work, fhould refufe to labour,
" and live idly for three days, that he or fhe fhould
" be branded with a red hot iron on the breaft
" with the letter V. and fhould be adjudged the
" flave, for two years, of any perfon who fhould
" inform againft fuch idler, &c."—*Sir F. E.* 101.

This is coarfe and clumfy legislation; expreffing
anger againft a manifeft evil; imperfectly and partially confidering the caufe; and directing immoderate penalties, without clearly defining the objects
againft whom fuch penalties are enacted.

Under Philip and Mary thefe fevere ftatutes were
enforced ; yet juftices were allowed to grant licenfes
to the poor to go abroad and beg, and receive alms,
out of their refpective parifhes.

Dr. Burn, in his Hiftory of the Poor Laws, remarks, " it is curious to obferve the progrefs by
" what natural fteps and advances the compulfatory
" maintenance became eftablifhed Firft, the poor
" were reftrained from begging at large, and were
" confined within certain diftricts. Next the fe-
" veral hundreds, towns corporate, parifhes, hamlets,
" or other like divifions, were required to fuftain
" them with fuch charitable and voluntary alms, as
" that none of them of neceffity might be compelled
" to go openly a begging; and the churchwardens or
" other fubftantial inhabitants were to make collec-
" tions for them, with boxes, on Sundays, and other-
" wife, by their difcretions. And the minifter was
" to take all opportunities to exhort and ftir up the

L

" people to be liberal and bountiful. (St. 27 Hen.
" VIII. and Canon 84.) Next, houſes were to be
" provided for them by the devotion of good people,
" and materials to ſet them on ſuch work as they
" were able to perform : then the miniſter, after the
" goſpel, every Sunday, was ſpecially to exhort the
" pariſhioners to a liberal contribution. Next, the
" collectors for the poor, on a certain Sunday in
" every year, immediately after divine ſervice, were
" to take down in writing what every perſon was
" willing to give weekly for the enſuing year; and if
" any ſhould be obſtinate, and refuſe to give, the
" miniſter was gently to exhort him; if he ſtill re-
" fuſed, the miniſter was to certify ſuch refuſal to
" the biſhop of the dioceſe, and the biſhop was to
" ſend for and exhort him in like manner. If he
" ſtood out againſt the biſhop's exhortation, then
" the biſhop was to certify the ſame to the juſtices
" in ſeſſions, and bind him over to appear there; and
" the juſtices of the ſeſſion were again gently to move
" and perſuade him. And finally, if he would not
" be perſuaded, then they were to aſſeſs him what
" they thought reaſonable towards the relief of the
" poor ; and this brought on the general aſſeſſment
" of the 14th year of Queen Elizabeth."—P. 105.
During the reign of Elizabeth numerous Acts were
paſſed for ſuppreſſion of mendicity, for compelling
the idle to labour, for ſuſtaining the infirm poor.
Mr. Ruggles *(Hiſtory of the Poor)* obſerves, " The
" wiſdom and humanity of government, during this
" long and proſperous reign, engrafted by degrees
" ſome of the beſt moral principles of the Chriſtian
" religion into the ſtatute law. Our Saviour, in
" his converſations with his diſciples, lays great
" ſtreſs on the duty of giving to the poor, &c.
" *Matt. xxv.* By the 14th Eliz. chap. 5, aſſeſs-

" ments are directed to be made in every parifh for
" relief of the poor of the fame parifh.   The par-
" liament of this wife and happy æra were as pro-
" greffive in improving the fituation of the poor,
" and in laws replete with tendernefs and humanity
" affecting the lower claffes of the ftate, as were the
" parliaments under the two preceding reigns retro-
" greffive and deficient.   The 35th Eliz. repeals that
" part of the ftatute law which contained unneceffary,
" and therefore improper, feverity, regulating the
" management of thofe poor and impotent perfons
" who are compelled to live by alms; and practical
" experience being called in aid of theoretic legif-
" lation, we find, towards the end of the fixteenth
" century, and in the beginning of the 39th year
" of this reign, thefe various matters and important
" regulations taking fomewhat the appearance of a
" code or fyftem.   Hence it appears, that the 43d
" of Eliz. which is confidered by many as the foun-
" tain and origin of the poor's rate, is in fact not fo;
" but is the refult of the collected wifdom, obferva-
" tion, and experience of the fame, or nearly the fame,
" individual ftatefmen, and thofe men of acknow-
" ledged wifdom and prudence, attending to the fame
" object, the general good of fociety, in this moft
" important article of police, during the term of
" almoft half a century."—*Vol. i. p.* 76, 79, 80.
     " The following are the great outlines of the
" 43d of Elizabeth.
     1. " Setting the children of the poor to work,
" when their parents cannot maintain them.
     2. " Putting poor children out apprentices.
     3. " Setting the idle to work.
     4. " Purchafing raw materials for that purpofe.
     5. " Raifing, by affeffment, a fum of money, for
" the fupport of the old, lame, impotent, blind, and

" fuch as are unable to work, from infancy, or other
" caufes.

6. " Appointing two overfeers, in addition to the
" churchwardens, to carry the Act into execution.

7. " Authorizing juftices to appoint the overfeers,
" and to infpect the proceedings of the parifh officers."

Between fifty and fixty ftatutes of different reigns
are recited as now in force, relating to the poor, in
the Digeft prefixed to Bott's Poor Laws, edited by
Mr. Conft; and between 15 and 1600 adjudged
cafes, explanatory of the law. Two fubftantial
houfholders are to be appointed yearly, on 25th of
March, or within a month after it, to be overfeers of
the poor in each parifh, under the hands and feals of
two juftices of the county.

The churchwardens and overfeers, or the greater
part of them, with confent of two juftices, are by
taxation of every inhabitant of their refpective parifhes,
to raife competent fums of money to fet the poor to
work; to relieve the lame, impotent, &c.; and to
put out poor children apprentices.

Overfeers, within four days after the end of each
year, muft render true accounts, to two juftices, of all
affeffments, receipts, and expenditure by them. They
muft hold monthly meetings on a Sunday, in the
parifh church, to confider of their various duties.

The poor's-rate, affeffed by churchwardens and
overfeers, muft be allowed by two juftices; and may
be enforced by diftrefs and fale of goods of thofe
who withhold payment. Perfons aggrieved may appeal
to quarter-feffions.

Two juftices may rate one parifh within the hundred in aid of another parifh; averring on their order
that the poor parifh was not able to pay fufficient fums.

The father, grandfather, mother, and grandmother,
and children, of every poor and impotent perfon,

muſt relieve and maintain ſuch poor relatives, according to the rate which the juſtices in ſeſſions ſhall aſſeſs; the order ſtating that the perſon on whom it is made is of ſufficient ability. 43d Elizabeth.

Two juſtices may alſo make an order for the maintenance of a baſtard child, by charging the mother or reputed father with a weekly payment, and may make an order for the puniſhment of the mother and reputed father.

To aſcertain the particular pariſh by which a poor and helpleſs perſon is to be relieved, is often a point of conſiderable difficulty.

The ſettlement or pariſh of an illegitimate child is the place of his birth, except in caſes of fraudulent removal, of births in priſons and hoſpitals, and where the mother is in ſtate of vagrancy, wandering and begging.

Legitimate children belong to the ſettlement of their father; but after the age of ſeven years may gain another ſettlement. If the father and mother be both foreigners, the child is to be maintained where found. But if the father only has no ſettlement, the children have that of the mother.

The ſettlement of a huſband is by marriage immediately communicated to his wife; and this ſettlement ſhe retains after his death; but if ſhe marry for the firſt time a man who has no ſettlement, her maiden ſettlement remains unaltered.

Churchwardens and overſeers may apply to a juſtice for an order to remove any perſon ſettling in a tenement under the yearly value of 1ol. and actually become chargeable to the pariſh; but perſons who rent and reſide forty days on a tenement of the yearly value of 1ol. obtain a ſettlement.

Any perfon inhabiting in any parifh, and paying a fhare towards the public rates or levies of the parifh, thereby gains a fettlement.

The act of ferving any public annual office in the parifh has the fame effect.

Unmarried perfons, having no children under feven years, hired into any parifh for a year, and continuing a whole year in fuch fervice, are fo fettled.

A perfon bound apprentice to another gains a fettlement by fuch binding and inhabitation in his mafter's parifh.

Alfo, the purchafer of an eftate, the price of which amounts to, at the leaft, 30l.; and an eftate for life or inheritance, though under 10l. a year; will, by refidence thereon of forty days, gain a fettlement.

The poor wanting work muft apply for employment to the churchwardens and overfeers; and the lame, blind, and helplefs, for aid.

The poor refufing to work may be fent, by the order of one or two juftices, to the houfe of correction.

Overfeers may erect habitations for the poor, and contract for their maintenance; but juftices of peace may vifit parifh workhoufes, and fee that proper care be taken of the poor.

A book is to be kept in every parifh, to regifter the names of all who receive collection out of the poor-houfe; and parifhioners fhould meet yearly in Eafter week, (or as often as fhall be thought convenient,) in the veftry, or other ufual place, to examine the book, and make a new lift, if requifite.

But a poor perfon having applied for relief at the veftry, or to two overfeers, and being rejected by them without aid, may apply to a juftice refiding in the parifh, (or if none be there dwelling to a juftice in the neareft parifh,) and make oath of his matter of complaint; and if the juftice fhall deem the ftatement

on oath to be a reasonable ground of relief, he shall
summon the overseers; and if they do not disprove
the statement, or if they make default, and do not
appear, the justice may make an order for relief.
And the person whom such justice shall order to be
relieved must be entered in the parish books, as one
of those who is to receive collection, as long as
the cause for such relief continues, and no longer.
The order for relief may be made either by one justice,
or by the court of quarter-sessions, and it must be
obeyed, without delay for appeal; for it is humanely
decided, K. v. N. Shields, Hil. 20, Geo. III. " No
" appeal lies from an order of maintenance, left,
" while the point is litigating, the poor starve."

But if a poor person seek relief in one parish,
whose legal settlement is in another, it is lawful for
two justices, upon complaint being made by the
churchwardens or overseers, to make an order for the
removal, by the parish officers, of such person, not
being too sick to be removed without danger, to his
or her place of legal settlement; and if those who
have been so removed return to the place from whence
they were sent, they may be committed as vagrants
to the house of correction. The removal of the
poor to their place of settlement must be by order of
justices, and not by a pass given as to vagrants.

The justices cannot order the officers of the parish,
where a pauper is legally settled, to send relief in
consequence of the poor person being too ill to be
removed; but aid must be given by the parish in
which he is resident.

But by 35th Geo. III. justices may make an order,
and suspend its operation by indorsing a memorandum,
that the pauper is too ill to be removed, and then
charging the parish to which the removal is directed
with the expense of maintenance from the date of

the order; and the fufpended order may extend to others, as the wife or children of the fick pauper, in order to prevent the cruel feparation of a family.

Baftard children remaining with their mother for nurture, are to be relieved by the parifh where they were born, in the parifh where the mother is fettled and refides.

On receipt of an order for maintenance, overfeers may require the pauper to go into the poorhoufe; and on his refufal to do fo, may decline any other compliance with the juftices' order ; but if a mother feek relief for her child, and not for herfelf, the parifh officers cannot compel her to go into the workhoufe, nor, on her refufal, can they legally with-hold the allowance from the child. But juftices may make a fpecial order for relief to paupers at their homes, for a period not exceeding one month, affign-ing the caufe in writing on the order; and two juftices may extend fuch order from time to time. This power, however, is not to extend to places where houfes of induftry are eftablifhed, under the authority of 22 Geo. III. c. 83.

Appeals againft orders of removal lie to the court of quarter-feffions.

Mr. Colquhoun, after a concife view of the nu-merous fevere ftatutes againft vagrants, from the year 1383, in the reign of Richard the Second, to 1744, the feventeenth year of George the Second, gives the following abftract of the ftatute of the latter year, by which the former Vagrant Acts were confo-lidated: to which the only additions have been in the 23d, 29th, and 32d years of his prefent Majefty, extending the provfions of that Act to fufpicious perfons having picklock keys and to lolling offenders, and fpecifying the punifhment to be inflicted on va-grants previous to their being paffed to their parifhes.

" The Act of 17th Geo. II. creates three feparate
" offences under the general term vagrancy ; namely,

I. " Idle and diforderly perfons to be committed
" to the houfe of correction, not exceeding one
" month, thus defcribed :

1. " Perfons who threaten to run away, and leave
" their families on the parifh.

2. " Perfons returning to parifhes from whence
" they have been legally removed.

3. " Perfons without property, who live idly, and
" refufe to work.

4. " Perfons begging in parifhes or places where
" they dwell.

5. " Perfons, (by 32 Geo. III. c. 45,) who, being
" able, yet neglect to work, fpend their money in
" alehoufes, &c. and do not employ a portion of
" their earnings for the fupport of their families, by
" which they come upon the parifh.

II. " Rogues and vagabonds, who on conviction
" are to be whipped, (if not females,) or imprifoned
" until the feffions, or a fhorter period. The feffions
" may order a further imprifonment of fix months at
" hard labour, thus defcribed :

1. " Perfons gathering alms on pretence of lofs
" by fire, or other cafualty ; and patent gatherers.

2. " Perfons going about as collectors for prifons
" and hofpitals.

3. " Fencers, (not defined.)

4. " Bearwards, (not defined.)

5. " Players of interludes, without being autho-
" rized by law.

6. " Minftrels, (except the heirs and affigns of
" John Dutton, late of Chefter.)

7. " Jugglers, (not defined.)

8. " Gypfies, or perfons wandering as fuch.

9. " Fortune-tellers.

10. " Perſons uſing any ſubtle craft to deceive,
" (not clearly defined.)

11. " Perſons playing and betting at unlawful
" games.

12. " Perſons who run away, and abandon their
" families to the pariſh.

13. " Pedlars wandering abroad without licenſe.

14. " Perſons wandering, ſleeping in the open air,
" and *lodging in alehouſes*, barns, and outhouſes, and
" not giving a good account of themſelves.

15. " Perſons wandering abroad, and begging,
" on pretence of being ſoldiers, marines, or ſeafaring
" men.

16. " Perſons wandering on pretence of going
" to work in harveſt, without a certificate from the
" miniſter or churchwarden.

17. " Perſons wandering abroad, and begging.

18. " Perſons (by 23 Geo. III. c. 88) apprehended
" with picklock keys, crows, or implements of houſe-
" breaking; or with arms with an intent to aſſault;
" or found in any houſe, outhouſe, &c. with intent
" to ſteal.

III. " Incorrigible rogues and vagabonds, puniſhed
" by impriſonment till the ſeſſions, when the juſtices
" may extend it to two years, and not leſs than ſix
" months; and may order the offender to be whipped
" during impriſonment; or may be tranſported, if
" they break out of priſon; thus deſcribed:

1. " End gatherers, offending againſt ſtat. 13 Geo. I.

2. " Perſons apprehended as rogues and vaga-
" bonds, and who eſcaped; refuſing to go before a
" juſtice, or to be conveyed by a·paſs, or giving a
" falſe account of themſelves.

3. " Perſons impriſoned as rogues and vaga-
" bonds, who ſhall break priſon and eſcape before
" their time expires.

4. " Perfons, who, after being punifhed as rogues " and vagabonds, fhall again commit the fame " offence."

" The ftat. 17. G. II. (obferves Mr. C.) cer- " tainly removed much that was objectionable in " former ftatutes ; but it ftill left the fyftem extremely " imperfect; and can be confidered only as a fabric " erected by ufing many of the ufelefs and old ma- " terials and machinery of former Acts, generally ill " adapted to the prefent ftate of fociety ; fince offen- " ces (moft of them ill defined) are ftill fubject to " very fevere punifhments, to which the human mind " can fcarcely annex any adequate degree of moral " turpitude, &c." *Treatife on Indigence*, p. 70.

Any perfon may apprehend a vagrant, and carry him to a conftable or to a juftice ; and the juftice, by warrant under his, hand and feal, may order the overfeer to pay five fhillings to the apprehender of fuch perfon, going about from door to door, or placing himfelf in ftreets, highways, or paffages, to beg alms in the parifh where he dwells ; and to any perfon conveying in like manner a rogue and vaga- bond, wandering abroad and begging out of his own parifh, the juftice may make an order on the high conftable to pay ten fhillings, to be reimburfed by the treafurer of the county.

By 13 and 14. C. 2. juftices in feffions may tranfport vagabonds, and fturdy beggars, adjudged to be incorrigible.

A vagrant, after imprifonment, is to be conveyed by pafs to his legal fettlement, if it can be found ; and the pafs muft certify the imprifonment or whip- ping. The pafs ought to certify how they are to be conveyed, and what allowance the conftable is to have for conveying them. The pafs may be fuf- pended during ficknefs.

Scottifh vagrants are to be conveyed to the neareſt adjoining fhire of Scotland, and delivered to a conftable.

Every mafter of a veſſel bound for Ireland, the ifles of Guernfey, Jerfey, or Scilly, fhall, on receipt of a warrant from a juftice of the place where fuch veſſel fh ll lie, take on board fuch vagrant as fhall be expreſſed in the warrant, to be paid at fuch rate per head as the juftices in feſſions fhall appoint.

Lunatic vagrants to be in cuftody of conftables, churchwardens, and overfeers; and all charges, during reftraint, to be paid by parifhes to which they belong.

Perfons knowingly giving lodging and fhelter to rogues and vagabonds, convicted, on oath of one witnefs, before a juftice, forfeit from ten fhillings to forty fhillings.

Thofe who impede officers in their duty, under the Act 17 G. II. are liable to forfeiture from ten fhillings to five pounds.

Statutes 22, 33, 36, 41, 43, 49, 50, and 52, of his prefent Majefty, authorize and regulate contracts and agreements for the maintenance of the poor, in an efpecial manner, by incorporated focieties, by appointment of guardians of the poor, governors of the poor-houfe, and vifitors, &c. Thefe guardians, &c. are in fact efpecially invefted with the full power of overfeers.

This imperfect fketch is an attempt to exprefs, by a bare outline, the principles of that fyftem of the poor's law, which has long been the important fubject of ferious controverfy, having engaged the minds and pens of moft able writers on both fides: fome extolling it as charity and policy, combined and fyftematized, as equally beneficial to the rich and to the poor, and as a great fource of the general profperity of the nation. Others confidering it as evil from its commencement, continually advancing in augmentation of mifchief, like a cancer or wen, threatening fpeedy deftruction to the body on which it grows.

Mr. Colquhoun obferves, (*Treatife on Indigence*, *p.* 53,) " Nothing can appear more excellent in " theory than the fyftem thus eftablifhed ; and had " it been ftrictly carried into effect, the nation, for " the two laft centuries, could only have been bur- " thened with the fupport of infants, and aged or " infirm perfons, reduced to a ftate of indigence " from inability to labour. But experience has " fhewn, that no part of this ftatute has been exe- " cuted, either in its letter or fpirit, fave and except " the raifing of money by affeffments ; which has " been moft accurately carried into effect from year " to year, until the burthen has increafed (as is " fuppofed) from 200,000l. in the year 1601, " when the Act commenced, and when the popula- " tion of the country was eftimated at about " 5,000,000, to 4,267,965l. on a population amount- " ing to 8,872,980, in the year 1803."

Mr. Ruggles, in his *Letters on the Hiftory of the Poor*, cites a pamphlet of Mr. Hay, a member of Parliament, publifhed in 1735. "It is certain, " that the obligation of every parifh to maintain its " own poor, and the confequence of that, a diftinct " intereft, are the roots from which every evil relating " to the poor hath fprung, and which muft ever " grow up, till they are eradicated. Every parifh is " in a ftate of expenfive war with all the reft of the " nation, regards the poor of all other places as " aliens, and cares not what becomes of them, if it " can but banifh them from its own fociety. No " good is therefore ever to be expected, till parochial " intereft is deftroyed ; till the poor are taken out of

" the hands of overſeers, and put under the ma-
" nagement of perſons wiſer and more diſintereſted;
" and until they be ſet to work on a national or at
" leaſt a provincial fund, to ariſe from benefactions,
" and the labour of the poor, as far as theſe will
" go; and what more is wanting, to be levied by an
" equal (*perhaps univerſal*) tax."

Theſe remarks contain a defect, of exceedingly
common kind, in the complaints of well-meaning perſons reſpecting acknowledged grievances; namely,
an aſſumption that the ſubject of complaint has been
overlooked or diſregarded by thoſe, whoſe duty it
was to provide a remedy. This warfare of pariſhes
is certainly a melancholy fact, and wiſer perſons
might be named in moſt pariſhes than the perſons
appointed to be overſeers. But it is the intereſt of
the wealthy part of all pariſhioners, that the moſt
fit men amongſt them ſhould be appointed: they
may themſelves legally promote ſuch appointment.
They may themſelves engage in the office. If they
are too indolent to undertake ſuch duty, or to attend
the veſtry, can they juſtly complain?

Mr. Colquhoun remarks, " Many eminent writers
" of the two laſt centuries violently declaim againſt
" the conduct of parochial officers appointed to exe-
" cute the poor laws, and impute the whole blame to
" a claſs of men, who, however well qualified at
" the beginning, are now, from their rank in ſociety,
" and often deficient education, unequal to details
" of ſuch extreme difficulty, &c."

Fielding writes, in 1753, " Every man who hath
" any property, muſt feel the weight of this tax; and
" every man who hath any underſtanding, muſt ſee how
" abſurdiy is applied." Fielding perhaps erred even
in his time, when groſſer manners prevailed, and
juſtice of all kinds, eſpecially in its lower departments,

appears to have been much worfe adminiftered, than
at prefent ; he attributes, univerfally, to this fource,
the mifconduct which he noticed in the overpeopled,
corrupt, and tumultuous parifhes of London. He,
however, moft energetically calls on the wealthy and
enlightened to attend to their duties and their interefts united, on behalf of the poor.   " So wretched
" is the difpofition of this heavy tax, (fays he,) that
" it is a queftion, whether the poor or the rich are
" actually more diffatisfied, or have indeed greater
" reafon to be fo ; fince the plunder of one ferves fo
" little for the real advantage of the other.   The
" fufferings of the poor are indeed lefs known
" than their mifdeeds, and therefore we are lefs apt
" to pity them.   They ftarve, and freeze, and rot,
" among themfelves ; but they beg, and fteal, and
" rob, among their betters."   All this is true, in a
limited degree.   Habit, however, not only reconciles
the poor to many privations which the rich might
regard with terror, but makes them delight in objects
and conditions affociated with the abodes of their
youth, and in articles of food, and perhaps in odours,
from which their wealthier neighbours would turn
away with naufea and difguft.   Their fufferings, ne-
verthelefs, continually demand the humane attention
of their wealthy neighbours ; and the poor-rate,
however, profufely diftibuted, can never fuperfede the
duty of charity, for the exercife of which grief and
ficknefs will ever provide copious occafion.
   It appears, that in 1776, the net expenfes folely
applied to relief of the poor were 1,529,780l ; the
medium of the years 1783-4 and 5, 2,167,749l.
in 1803, the amount was about 4,200,000l. : but it
will be found that the price of labour, and of moft
of the neceffaries and comforts of life, had advanced
in an equal proportion ; that, in fact, the circulating

med'um bore a reduced value in proportion to all articles for which it was employed in payment ; and that with reference to the returns of the revenue, and the advancement of all prices, 4,000,000l. in 1800, muft have been nearly equivalent to 2,000,000l., in 1780. See *Enquiry into the Policy and Humanity of the Poor Laws*, p. 304.

The queftion refpecting the good or evil refulting from our fyftem of poor-law has of late been fo powerfully agitated by two difputants of eminent fagacity, that I fhall content myfelf with producing a characteriftic fpecimen from each, to fhew that the views of both accord with the principle for which alone I am defirous to contend; namely, that whether the poor-law fyftem be maintained or abolifhed, it is equally the duty and the interefts of the rich to be the patrons, protectors, guardians, friends of the poor ; to cultivate their refpect, their gratitude, their affection ; to guide them, to fuftain them, to cheer them, as officers their men by the endearing term of fellow foldiers, equalizing to the ear, but not deceptive, not deftructive of fubordination ; to regard them as a charge, for whofe fecurity they are refponfible to an unerring Commander, from whofe almighty fiat they hold their facred commiffion. But I am far from intending to affirm that this duty is well performed by large rates or almsgiving ; it may be as confcientioufly executed by thofe who fully accede to the theory of Mr. Malthus, as by thofe who adopt the fyftem of his adverfary.

Much blame is thrown on overfeers, who, as Mr. Colquhoun fays, " are from their rank in fociety, " and deficient education, unequal to details of fuch " difficulty." But why are fuch men alone chofen to fill fuch powerful and highly refponfible offices ? An important reply to this queftion is given by a

a gentleman, who, that he might be a mafter of the
fubjeƈt, aƈted for a long time in the office of overfeer,
and has publifhed the refults of his experience.
" Obfervations on the Prefent State and Influence of
" the Poor Laws, founded on experience, and a
" Plan for Improvement, &c. by Robert Saunders,
" efq; of Lewifham. 1799.

  " The whole bufinefs of the poor hinges on the
" duties of the overfeers, and the manner in which
" they are executed ; for (except the right of appeaĺ,
" on the part of the pauper, to the bench of juftices)
" there is hardly any check on their conduƈt ; and
" the powers with which they are invefted are im-
" menfe, which I confider as the foundation of all
" the evils that attend the fyftem. It is a medley of
" confidence, and of menial duty, which has done
" the mifchief. The overfeers, in the firft place,
" have the purfe of the parifh fo completely put
" into their hands, that the Statute authorifes their
" calling weekly, if they fee proper, for a rate, and
" without the leaft limitation with refpeƈt to its
" quantum ; and in this refpeƈt, the concurrence of
" the inhabitants in making a rate is not neceffary.
" Two of his Majefty's juftices of peace *muft* confirm
" the rate, by figning the fame. I fay muft, for this
" is fo perfeƈtly a minifterial duty on their part, that
" if they refufe, the Court of King's Bench would grant
" a mandamus to compel them. Here is unbounded con-
" fidence on the part of the legiflature. We might ex-
" peƈt, that when the legiflature placed fuch powers in
" the hands of individuals, care would have been taken
" that thofe invefted with fuch powers were, from fitu-
" ation and refpeƈtability, above the temptation of
" mifapplying them ; but we fhall foon fee that the
" duties impofed on overfeers, in a manner, exclude
" every perfon of refpeƈtability and independence from

M

" executing the office. The overfeer, in the firft place,
" is to be his own tax gatherer or colle&or ; he is
" the perfon who muft fummons defaulters, and he
" muft in perfon fue for a warrant, and a& the part
" of a fheriff's officer, by giving his perfonal atten-
" dance, in levying by diftrefs, &c. The bufinefs
" of colle&ing has been affigned by the overfeers (as
" in my own cafe) to another ; but the veftry could
" not exonerate the overfeer from the rifk and re-
" fponfibility of appointing another to colle& ; and
" when a fummons or warrant was to be executed,
" none but the overfeer could do it. If a pauper is
" to be removed to a diftant part of the kingdom,
" he muft be conveyed by an overfeer ; and without
" a&ual delivery by his own hands, there is no ob-
" ligation on the part of the parifh to which he is
" removed to receive him. In fhort, as the law now
" ftands, there is not a duty, be it ever fo menial
" and degrading, which relates to the poor, that is
" not to be performed perfonally by the overfeer.
" I have, therefore, no hefitation in faying, that the
" office of overfeer is fo conftituted, that no perfon
" of refpe&ability and independence can accept it,
" to execute literally all that the law dire&s him to
" do ; and that it is, on the other hand, fo confti-
" tuted, as to make it highly hazardous both for
" the good of fociety, and the moral habits of indi-
" viduals, to place fo much confidence and pro-
" perty in the hands of people, whofe occupation or
" conne&ion expofe them to the temptation of
" abufing a fund appointed to the relief of the
" indigent ; the proper and honourable management
" of which is fo peculiarly facred a duty, and on
" which the general habits and difpofitions of the
" lower clafs of people in this country fo entirely
" depend. To complete the defcription of this

" abfurd fyftem, the parifh that is fortunate enough
" to meet with an overfeer who executes the duty
" in a rigid and confcientious manner, cannot continue
" to avail itfelf of his fervices, but muft change him
" every other, if not every, year. He has not the
" fmalleft temptation, from fee, reward, or future
" credit, to execute the truft with attention ; for he
" is not allowed to receive any compenfation for his
" fervices, and the public are feldom fufficiently ac-
" quainted with the detail of parochial management
" to give credit where it is due."

The overfeers, however, of large and very populous parifhes in great towns have adopted a practice,
with confent of the veftry, perceiving that fome contingent evil is overbalanced by manifeft advantage,
of appointing a permanent affiftant overfeer, or
contractor for the poor, according to 9 Geo. I. c. 7;
who acts with all the overfeer's authority, and being
commonly a perfon felected for fagacity and firmnefs,
and not much engaged in any fort of bufinefs, can
devote his fteady attention to all the details of the
office. This perfon receives, and, if he acts up-
rightly, well earns, a high falary. He collects rates,
and accounts to the overfeer. He receives and re-
gifters all applications; inquires into the actual circumftances of all applicants, who are too commonly
difpofed to exaggerate ftatements of diftrefs, and to
fupprefs accounts of their means of fubfiftence. He
decides arbitrarily on the merits of each cafe. To
the friendlefs and helplefs, who feek for entire fupport, he offers the fhelter of the poor-houfe. To
thofe who can do any thing for themfelves, he gives
a weekly allowance out of the houfe. He lives,
indeed, in a ftate of continual warfare with the poor;
and from thence, probably, too often acquires an air
of feverity and impatience of manner, of which moft
who apply to him find occafion to complain. But

his fixed ftation renders his perfon and refidence well
known. He is commonly fyftematic; and all may
know, or divine with correctnefs, what will be the
refult of any application. His credit with the veftry
depends greatly on his prevention of the advance,
and yet more on his reduction, of the rates. Thofe
who look to this object more than to any other, form
the vaft and refiftlefs majority of the veftry in the
parifhes of all great towns: the few, therefore, who
might be occafionally willing to encreafe the rates,
for the fake of ameliorating the condition of their
poorer neighbours, find it vain to contend againft
any of his decifions, fupported by the interefted majority. Hence the veftry is abandoned by perfons of
fuperior education and refined manners. This mode
of proceeding has certainly harfhnefs in its principle,
and is vexatious in its refult; yet it has an admixture
of good, which much diminifhes its peculiar evil, by
operating as a remedy for evil of an oppofite defcription. The fevere parfimony with which the rates
are thus diftributed, the rigorous and perhaps in-
fulting fcrutiny with which the claims of applicants
are canvaffed, ferve to deter indolent impoftors from
feeking a maintenance in idlenefs from the refource
of the parochial fund. It, therefore, much leffens
the principal weight of objection ordinarily advanced
againft the fyftem of relief by poor's rates; and
while it leaves much fcope for difcriminating charity,
may poffibly be ufefully employed in defining its
objects, and affifting its exertions. A modification
of this arrangement, in fome degree correfponding
with Mr. Saunders's fuggeftions, by legiflative regulation, would, probably, meet with the limited approbation of Mr. Malthus, and not be difapproved by
his antagonifts.

Mr. M. thus ftrongly fums up his objection to the
laws of rates and fettlements.

"The poor laws may be faid to diminifh both the
" power and the will to fave among common people,
" and thus weaken one of the ftrongeft incentives
" to fobriety and induftry, and confequently to
" happinefs.

" It is a general complaint among mafter manu-
" facturers, that high wages ruin all their workmen ;
" but it is difficult to conceive that thefe men would
" not fave a part of their high wages for the future
" fupport of their families, inftead of fpending it in
" drunkennefs and diffipation, if they did not rely on
" parifh affiftance for fupport in cafe of accidents.
" A man, who might not be deterred from going to
" the alehoufe by the confideration, that on his
" death or ficknefs he fhould leave his wife and
" family upon the parifh, might yet hefitate in thus
" diffipating his earnings, if he were affured that in
" either of thefe cafes his family muft ftarve, or be
" left to the fupport of cafual bounty.

" The mafs of happinefs among the common
" people cannot but be diminifhed, when one of the
" ftrongeft checks to idlenefs and diffipation is thus
" removed; and pofitive inftitutions, which render
" dependent poverty fo general, weaken that dif-
" grace, which for the beft and moft humane reafons
" ought to be attached to it.

" The poor laws of England were, undoubtedly,
" inftituted for the moft benevolent purpofe; but it
" is evident that they have failed in attaining it.
" They certainly mitigate fome cafes of fevere dif-
" trefs, which might otherwife occur, though the
" ftate of the poor who are fupported by parifhes,
" confidered in all its circumftances, is very miferable.
" But one of the principal objections to the fyftem
" is, that for the affiftance which fome of the poor
" receive, in itfelf almoft a doubtful bleffing, the

" *whole class* of common people of England is fub-
" jected to a fet of grating, inconvenient, and tyran-
" nical laws, totally inconfiftent with the genuine
" fpirit of the Conftitution." This objection has
loft much of its force by ftat. 35 Geo. III. as none
now but thofe who become *actually* chargeable to
parifhes are affected by thefe laws ; and according to
Mr. M.'s own principles, (which I am not difpofed to
controvert, but which I think may be more conve-
niently applied to modify than to abolifh the poor
laws,) the more the inducements to feek for parifh
aid are obftructed and diminifhed, in fuch degree
will the evils of which he complains be alfo leffened.]
" I feel perfuaded," he adds, " that if the poor
" laws had never exifted in this country, though
" there might have been a few more inftances of
" very fevere diftrefs, the aggregate mafs of happi-
" nefs among the common people would have been
" much greater than it is at prefent. The radical
" defect of all fyftems of the kind is, that of tending
" to increafe population, without increafing the means
" for its fupport ; and by thus depreffing the con-
" dition of thofe that are not relieved by parifhes, to
" create more poor."

The principal and (as far as I have been able to
difcover) the only well-informed and rational adverfary of Mr. Malthus, after expreffing the higheft
refpect for his good intentions and ability, and
making grateful acknowledgement for the ftock of
ufeful information found in his effay, obferves,
" His general principles feem juft, and their applica-
" tion in many cafes might, no doubt, be extremely
" beneficial. They are, moreover, fortified and
" illuftrated with a body of ufeful and entertaining
" information, applicable to the purpofes of the po-
" litical œconomift in all ages, &c. That his fyftem

" would lead a country, under certain circumſtances,
" from a ſtate of nature to a higher degree of mora-
" lity and happineſs than has ever yet exiſted in the
" world, ſeems not improbable. And if the appli-
" cation of it to this country is refiſted, it is only
" becauſe, in the eſtimation of the author of this
" *inquiry*, England has already advanced ſo far in an
" artificial ſyſtem of ſociety, and its exiſtence depends
" ſo much upon a continuance of that ſyſtem, that
" any attempt to alter it, according to the principles
" laid down in the *eſſay*, muſt immediately produce
" greater evils than could be compenſated even by
" the full enjoyment of thoſe advantages, of which
" ſuch attempt would only hold out a diſtant proſ-
" pect."—*A Short Inquiry into the Policy, Humanity,
&c. of the Poor Laws, by one of his Majeſty's Juſtices
of the Peace for three inland Counties.* The author
ſhews by a table, comparing the advance of the
poor's rate, from 1776 to 1803, to the advance in
the value of ſhipping, of imports, of exports, of income from funds, and of income from land, that
the total of the latter advance, conſidered as the
means or ability of the nation to pay the rates,
is, on an average, much more than equal to the advance of the rates themſelves. " All arguments,
" therefore, reſting upon the aſſumption that they
" are a great and growing burthen upon the com-
" munity, interfering with its proſperity, and gra-
" dually eating up its profits, muſt fall to the ground;
" or at leaſt muſt change their foundation from the
" *amount* of the rates, to the unfair manner of their
" *diſtribution* among the perſons poſſeſſing property."
P. 306. This author ſhews, by reference to proof
from experience, that the effect of the poor law is to
advance population only in proportion as its fund
enables its conductors to find means of employment

for the poor; that by lowering wages, it has enabled
England to enter into fuccefsful competition with
richer and more populous countries in manufactures
and commerce, and to fuftain the affaults and repel
the machinations of powerful enemies, efpecially directed againft thofe fources of its profperity. " If
" a high price of labour be neceffary to encourage
" population, and a low one to fecure fuch means of
" employment as can alone render the people ufeful,
" we feem to be reduced to this dilemma; that by
" granting either propofition, the other muft appa-
" rently be renounced; that unlefs the increafe of
" people can be encouraged by high wages, and a
" vent for manufactures fecured by low ones; that
" is, unlefs this feeming contradiction can be recon-
" ciled, the national profperity muft fuffer." But
" the poor laws may be confidered as a premium,
" given in lieu of high wages, at once to encourage
" population, and to enable the manufacturer to
" work cheap; confequently, to find a market for
" commodities." This enlightened author would,
however, introduce various alterations of the exifting fyftem. He wifhes for a more equal levying
of the rates upon the general profits of the aggregate of land and labour, and then would fix them to
a certain average in the pound fterling. " We have
" feen that the amount of the rates has in no period
" kept pace with the ability of the country to pay
" them; and from the improvements in the conftruc-
" tion of machinery, we have reafon to hope this
" difproportion will beftill morefavourable."—P. 350.

An examination of Mr. Malthus's work in the
Britifh Review is faid to have been written by the
author of the *Inquiry*, and is certainly compofed in
the fame fpirit of candour which becomes the gentleman, and benefits the caufe of truth in charity.

Alas, how rare! Αληθευειν εν Αγαπη! Another
article in the 5th number of the fame Review, reported to have proceeded from the fame pen, contains a paffage fo well expreffed and fo fully accordant with the principal deduction which I find
continually urged upon my mind by every fact of
the preceding furvey of the relative condition of the
poor, at various periods and in different countries,
that I cannot hefitate to cite it.

"*Article, Increafe of the Poor. No. 4 and 5.*
" It may be admitted as a general axiom in the
" politics of a free and extenfive country, that when
" once a ftrong bond of reciprocal intereft is efta-
" blifhed between the higher and lower orders of the
" community, the ftatesman's tafk is half performed
" to his hand , and that fuch a people, by their native
" energy, and internal refources, will not only pre-
" ferve the integrity of their own empire, but muft,
" by the force of their inftitutions, gradually triumph
" over their enemies.   In Scotland, the feudal fyftem
" prevented the introduction of a ftate of degeneracy
" fimilar to that in Ireland; and as poor laws have
" for a very long time fubfifted in Scotland, poor's
" rates have been regularly called into operation, in
" proportion as the feudal fyftem has worn away ;
" and commerce, manufactures, and tillage ufurped
" the feats of baronial fplendour, and encroached
" upon the idle hofpitality of the lords of the wafte.
" An inftitution which produces fuch phænomena in
" fociety, muft neceffarily reft on grounds of deep
" moral and political expediency.   It has been af-
" ferted by fome, particularly by foreign writers,
" to be the millftone around the neck of England,
" which muft at length engulf her in a fea of ruin :
" and we are willing to admit that it is, in the fpirit
" of our other inftitutions, calculated for a ftate of

" progreffive profperity ; but that it may accelerate
" our downfall, fhould the circumftances of the coun-
" try begin to decline.   But to compenfate this evil,
" we think it will appear, that, under Providence,
" fo long as the feveral ranks of the people are true
" to themfelves and to each other, fuch a ftate of de-
" clenfion is not within the fcope of probability.
" And we have yet to learn that a law or inftitution
" is objectionable, becaufe it is inconfiftent with a
" felfifh neglect of duty in thofe for whofe govern-
" ment it is intended."*

It has been obferved by Judge Blackftone, " that
" the farther all fubfequent plans for maintaining
" the poor have departed from the original defign,
" the more impracticable, and even pernicious, thofe
" vifionary attempts have proved."   Some attempts,
however, have been made in Parliament to produce
great changes in the fyftem.   Numerous ufeful mo-
difications have been introduced from time to time.
But a fcheme of moft extenfive character was brought
forward by Mr. Pitt in 1796.   His mind, occupied
with balancing the relations of all the ftates of the
civilized world, with new modifying thofe of the
Britifh empire, with foreign war, with domeftic tur-
moil, with national finances, and parliamentary controul, could never have poffeffed adequate leifure to
give due confideration to the various minute details
of this fubject.   Such a mind, however, could not
have contemplated with approbation any project, of

* In Mr. Birkbeck's notes on a *Journey through France*, 1815,
it is obferved, " the labourer is paid in kind for the two principal
" operations of hufbandry, harvefting and threfhing, *one sixth* of
" the grofs produce, or three bufhels on a crop of eighteen.   The
" Englifh labourer receives about a tenth, at the prefent prices of
" corn and labour, when he is beft paid.   The Englifh labourer re-
" ceives two bufhels (I fuppofe in twenty), the French labourer
" three bufhels and one third.   Money wages are nearly in the
" fame proportion.   The difference we pay in poor rates."

which fome prominent features had not borne the ftamp of important utility   Mr. Saunders, (in *Obfervations on the ftate of the Poor Laws*, before quoted,) amongft many ufeful obfeavations on that bill, notices efpecially an article which was to have regulated the voting in veftries, with a view to have given greater weight to property in fuch meetings. The eftablifhment of a parochial fund to encourage economy among the poor was alfo an excellent fuggeftion of this bill: but upon the whole Mr. S. appears to agree with Mr Belfham, that Mr. Pitt's plan was objectionable, becaufe, inftead of fimplifying a fyftem already over complex, it made, " by engrafting " a heap of new on the exifting ftock of old provi- " fions, the entire aggregate or code of poor laws " infinitely more *operofe*, confufed, and intricate, than " before." This opinion may have occurred, perhaps, during the argument, to Mr. Pitt himfelf; as the bill, though introduced in the plenitude of his power, was finally abandoned.   In 1807, Mr. Whitbread introduced a bill for promoting induftry among the labouring claffes, and for the relief and regulation of the neceffitous and criminal poor.   The objections to this bill were the fame as thofe applied to that of Mr. Pitt, namely, that it aimed at too much, was therefore complicated and impracticable.   Like that of Mr. Pitt, it fuggefted a general favings bank or fund for the poor, to enable depofitors of very fmall fums to poffefs fhares of government ftock, that the facility of obtaining intereft on fmall fums might operate as an encouragement to induftry and economy.   This plan (however difficult, when attempted to be adapted to the nation) might, no doubt, fucceed within a fingle town or fmall diftrict; and an inftitution founded at Bath on this principle is at prefent profperous.   Mr. W. propofes to bring

county rates largely in aid of parifhes ; and to give
bounties to thofe who have reared families independent of parochial relief. It allowed a fettlement to
be gained by refidence for five years, without having
received aid from any parifh during fuch time. An
Aft of Parliament, which fhould allow a fettlement
to be gained by fuch refidence during ten years,
would probably pafs without objeftion, as the period
exceeds the average period of the probable life of any
individual ; and the hardfhip of removing to diftant
fettlements aged perfons of good charafter from
places where they have lived for the greater part of
their lives, and which they have benefited by their
labour, and in which they have formed every endearing conneftion, to parifhes in which they are
wholly unknown, and where their arrival is confidered as a baneful intrufion, is univerfally acknowledged. This objeft has been aimed at in a bill
brought forward lately by Sir E. Brydges. The
term of refidence propofed by him was feven years.
The bill, however, is not paffed. The multitude
of objefts in Mr. Whitbread's bill occafioned the
defirable to be facrificed to the objeftionable. It
would, doubtlefs, be the moft likely method to en-
fure fuccefs to any fyftem of improvement, to attempt
the eftablifhment of only one objeft at a time; and
when the firft fhould be accomplifhed, and approved
upon experience, to bring forward the next in fucceffion, fo that all might be prepared for its adoption
by perception of its natural conneftion with the
former. This mode of proceeding, indeed, is neceffarily flow, and rather unfuited to minds exalted
by the ardent defire of brilliant achievement. On
the other hand, minds wholly · devoid of fome fuch
ardour might, perhaps, reft in perpetual inaftion.
The true ftimulus to fuch exertion, however, that

which admits of no change, no fluctuation, no uncertainty, is not the emulation which feeks for man's applaufe, nor even that love of glorious improvement which feeks to render'the men of one period or country fuperior to thofe of another; but that fteady conviction of duty, which never lofes fight of its relations to GOD, while it contemplates thofe to man; nor in its devotion to GOD, overlooks its relations to friends, to kindred, to country, to mankind.

For an abftract of the returns to Parliament relative to the expenfe and maintenance of the poor in 1803, fee Appendix.

English Charities.

It has been fhewn that the charities of periods and countries in which a fyftematifed poor's law did not exift, have fupplied its place very imperfectly, and by no means œconomically. Mr. Arthur Young, in his Agricultural Tour, ftates the population of Milan to be 116,000; and the amount of the public charities to be £87,500. The aggregate amount of the poor's rates and public charities in Liverpool have been faid but little to exceed that of the public charities in Edinburgh. 1. The Difpenfary.—2. The Infirmary.—3. Lunatic Afylum.—4. Blue Coat Hofpital.—5. Ladies' Charity for lying-in cafes.—6. Ladies' Benevolent Society for vifiting the poor, &c.—7. School for the Blind.—8. Female Penitentiary.—9. Stranger's Friend.—10. Benevolent Society of St. Patrick.—11. Sunday and Daily Charity School.—12. St. James's School.—13. Manefty's-lane School.—14. Welfh Charity School.—15. Methodift Charity School.—16. Methodift Female Clothing Society.—17. Circus Free School.—18. Catholic Charity School.—19. Society for bettering

condition, &c. Thefe charities in Liverpool appear
by their reports to have actually expended about
24.000*l.* in the year 1813. The amount of rates
actually applied to the relief of the poor in 1803 was
about 23,000*l.* The total fomewhat exceeds the
probable proportionate amount of the Edinburgh
charities; but the fhare of the amount raifed by
the contributions of voluntary benevolence fufficiently evinces that the preffure of the poor's law,
and the knowledge of its extenfive applicability to
fuccour the diftreffed, has not, even in this city of
commercial activity, and eager purfuit of worldly intereft, operated to check the impulfe of charity;
and that the ample relief afforded by means of the
rates to the poor and infirm, has not fuperfeded
the neceffity for extenfive beneficent exertions.

   It is difficult to collect either an exact ftatement
of the population, of the amount of the rates, or of
the charities, in the metropolis; becaufe it is not
clear what parifhes different ftatements include in
the term. From Kentifh-Town, north, to Camber-
well, fouth, inclufive, and from Kenfington, weft, to
Limehoufe, eaft, inclufive, may be all confidered as
London. The number of inhabitants within thefe
limits, according to the population returns made in
1803, exceeded a million. The number of parifhioners relieved by the poors-rate was found to be
about 8 in 100. The ratio to the total population
in England and Wales is faid to be higher, namely,
12 in 100. Although the average number of perfons
relieved in London falls fhort of the general ratio
of relief to population, yet the amount of the rates
exceeds the general proportion. In the abftract of
returns to Parliament 1803, the poor of the kingdom
in and out of workhoufes are faid to be relieved at
the rate of 3*l.* 17*s.* 9½*d.* per head; but fuppofing

the number relieved in London, 8 in 100, to amount
to 80,000, taking the inhabitants as 1,000,000, and
raising the rate to 4*l*. per head, the amount will be
only 320,000*l.* : whereas by the returns, the expenditure of rate, in the metropolis on account of the
poor, in 1803, appears to have been nearly 348,000*l.*
from which fum, if 16,000*l.* the amount of law
expenfes, &c. omitting a fraction, be deducted, the
remainder may be ftated at 332,000*l.*: (by the returns it is 332,624*l.* and a fraction.) Now if, with
a view to clearnefs, we make a rough eftimate,
calling Liverpool a population of 100,000, and the
rates 20,000; and London 1,000,000, and its rates
300,000*l.* the excefs of expenditure for an equal
number of poor in London, above that in Liverpool,
will be one-third. This may, perhaps, be attributed
to the greater dearnefs of many of the neceffaries of
life in London, and partly to the greater facility of
raifing money, than of fuperintending fuch enormous
diftribution. But the charities of London appear to
exceed thofe of all other Britifh cities, and indeed of
all cities in the world in a much greater proportion.
The charities of Edinburgh approximate to the aggregate of rates and charities in Liverpool, but thofe
of Milan appear to be double of the aggregate amount
in Liverpool. The principal charities of London,
however, can hardly be confidered as ftrictly local,
as many extend their munificence to the whole of
the Britifh dominions, and fome are wholly beneficial
to foreigners. The enumeration of thefe charities,
with a flight memoir refpecting each, fills a thick
octavo volume, publifhed by Mr. Highmore 1810 ;
which concludes by extracting a fummary view of the
whole from another publication, entitled the Picture
of London, which the author of *Pietas Londinenfis*

quotes, with approbation of the writer's induſtry and
correctneſs.

 " Among the moral features of the metropolis
" is the multitude of its nſtitutions for the relief of
" the indigent and the diſeaſed. Beſide two hoſpitals
" ſupported at the public charge, one for the main-
" tenance of invalid ſeamen at Greenwich, and
" the other for invalid ſoldiers at Chelſea, London
" has twenty-two hoſpitals or aſylums for the ſick
" and lame, and pregnant women; one hundred and
" ſeven alms-houſes for the maintenance of old men
" and women; eighteen inſtitutions for indigent per-
" ſons of various other deſcriptions; ſeventeen dif-
" penſaries, for gratuitouſly ſupplying the poor with
" medicine and medical aid at their own dwellings;
" forty-one free ſchools, with perpetual endowments
" for educating and maintaining 3500 children of
" both ſexes; ſeventeen other public ſchools for
" deſerted and poor children; 165 pariſh ſchools,
" ſupported by their reſpective pariſhes, with the aid
" of occaſional voluntary contributions, which on an
" average clothe and educate 6000 boys and girls;
" and in each pariſh a workhouſe for maintaining
" its own helpleſs poor. In the city, belonging to
" the Corporation, there are ninety-four public com-
" panies, who diſtribute above 7500l. annually in
" charity. The ſums annually expended in the
" metropolis in charitable purpoſes, independently
" of private relief to individuals, has been eſtimated
" at 850,000l. Moſt of the hoſpitals and aſylums
" were founded by private munificence. Of theſe,
" ſome are endowed with perpetual revenues, and
" others ſupported by annual or occaſional and vo-
" luntary contributions." Perhaps, as workhouſes
are here mentioned, the whole amount of the poor's-
rate may be included in the ſum of 850,000l.: and

if the revenues of Greenwich and Chelſea hoſpitals, and ſome others of deſcription far from local, be deduĉted, the amount of London charities may be found not ſo much to exceed the proportionate amount of thoſe in ſome other great towns, as at firſt ſight it may appear to do.

If it be true, as I am perſuaded it will certainly be found, that the charities of other countries have never at any period been ſo conducted as to relieve the poor, of an equal population, ſo adequately as the poor's-law, with leſs encouragement of idleneſs, or with better ſtimulus to induſtry; it may be intereſting farther to enquire, whether any experiment has ever been made to act upon a plan which may poſſeſs the good properties of both, without the miſchiefs of either; to ſteer between the extremes of almſgiving without ſyſtem, and with ſmall probability of diſcretion, and of taxation operating in part as a ſubſtitute for wages, and in part for charity. I ſpeak of the practical conduct of theſe ſyſtems, rather than of their theoretic principles: for, without admitting the axiom, that " whate'er is beſt adminiſter'd is " beſt," I think the converſe of the propoſition may be found nearer to the truth, ' whate'er is worſt ' adminiſter'd is worſt,' for even *optimi corruptio fit peſſima.* The objections, in fact, urged with truth on both ſides, by their mutual advocates, againſt each ſyſtem, are reſolvable into this common argument; that both are liable to much miſconduct, and both have accordingly been miſconducted. Miſconduct in both ſyſtems has been juſtly attributable to a want of zealous, active, perſevering, and enlightened men, who ſhould conſtantly keep watch over the whole detail, and engage in the execution; when benevolence and judgment, with equally balanced forces, ſhould ſtimulate and ſhould controul.

N

Several experiments have been made, in Bath, to form inftitutions, which may fix the attention of the wealthy on the concerns of the poor, and make out practicable limits of time and exertion, within which thofe of the higher clafs may occupy themfelves in promoting, fubftantially, the welfare and happinefs of the inferior ; without romantic or fanatical neglect of ordinary duties, or inconvenient abandonment of the comforts and elegancies of their ftation.

Such may indeed be faid to be the object of the more extended plans for National Education, by the advocates of the methods of Dr. Bell and Mr. Lancafter, or the improved fcheme of Mr. Poole ; alfo of the Society for promoting Chriftian Knowledge, and of the Bible Society. But the object of the promoters of thefe inftitutions is fpiritual good, neceffary, undoubtedly, to temporal as well as to eternal welfare, but not providing means for the immediate relief of bodily wants.

It is moft agreeable to ftate, that the foremoft, in point of time, of thefe inftitutions, in Bath, have been founded by ladies of rank ; and fupported with zeal by gentlemen, not generally acquainted with the foundreffes, from full conviction of their utility.

An anxious wifh to induce the lower orders to benefit themfelves, independently of parochial affiftance, by cultivation of fyftematic œconomy, induced Lady Ifabella Douglas, in the year 1808, to propofe the formation of a *Fund to give Intereft on fmall Savings, to perfons of good character.* It was thought important to intereft the truftees in confidering the good character of the depofitors, and to give an additional impreffion, on the minds of the depofitors, of the benefit to be obtained by the prefervation of fuch character : that while the pleafure of conferring a benefit was felt on one fide, the

conviction that the rich and the refined were difinterestedly devoting their labours to the substantial benefit of their poorer compatriots, might be duly impressed on the other. After much deliberation, it was resolved, to contract the plan for a time, and to extend the benefit of the fund only to domestic servants. Four ladies, and as many gentlemen, agreed to become jointly bound to the depositors of sums, amounting at the least to twenty-five shillings, and under 50l. to give half-yearly interest on such deposits at the rate of 4 per cent. The fund was limited to the amount of 2000l. and it was agreed, that when the deposits should equal such amount, no more should be received, except as vacancies might occur. Prejudice against a novelty may have operated for a few months to delay the influx of deposits, but before the end of the first year, the full sum of 2000l. was collected. It was wished, that as for prudential reasons the fund was limited, the benefits might be extended only to the most worthy of its peculiar objects; that the admission should be considered by the depositors as effected by the kindness of their masters or mistresses, rather than by the bounty of the managing trustees; that mutual good-will might be thus promoted in every family, to which each depositor was attached; a detailed good character from the head of each family was therefore made an indispensable condition of the reception of a depositor. A late Advertisement of the Trustees, states, " The books of the fund are, in a moral view,
" peculiarly satisfactory. As none have been ad-
" mitted to the benefit of the fund, except those
" who have brought recommendatory characters
" from the masters and mistresses in whose service
" they were engaged, a record has been kept, for
" nearly seven years, of the continual good characters

N 2

" of above 212 domeftic fervants." A circumftance
which might poffibly be productive of utility to a
fervant, when the family in which he has lived has
been fuddenly broken up and difperfed by misfortune,
or in confequence of the deaths of the principals.
It is added, " As the Truftees have refolved not
" to hold a depofit belonging to any one fervant, ex-
" ceeding 45*l.* and have conftantly, on repayment of
" fums to that amount, recommended their immediate
" inveftment in the public funds, they are gratified
" (in the year 1815) in obferving an eafy oppor-
" tunity of making fuch inveftment afforded by the
" *Provident Inftitution*, recently eftablifhed in this
" city ; the fundamental principle of which is a
" pledge, on the part of the truftees and managers,
" that each depofitor of 1*l.* and upwards, fhall be-
" come proprietor of five per cent. ftock, according
" to the price of fuch ftock at the time in which fuch
" fum fhall be found to be depofited." This arrangement, fuggefted perhaps by claufes in Mr. Pitt's and
Mr. Whitbread's bills before mentioned, was with
great credit to themfelves, and with great benefit to
the public, brought forward by Mr. Enfor, and Dr.
Haygarth, of Bath. The extenfive advantages
which may be expected to refult from the eftablifhment of fimilar inftitutions in the feveral counties, or
generally in great towns, fuperintended by the refident gentry, are too numerous to be here detailed.
It may fuffice to obferve, that, independently of their
tendency to promote and fuftain a laudable fpirit of
œconomy, they may operate with no fmall political
good, in giving to the lower claffes an extended
intereft in the ftability of the government funds ; and
ufefully correct many erroneous apprehenfions, and
idle jealous feelings, refpecting that important portion
of the ftate's machinery.

Prior, in point of time, to thefe inftitutions, was founded another, which I mention laft, becaufe it falls within my prefent view to detail its principles fomewhat more minutely : I mean the *Bath Society for the Inveftigation and Relief of Occafional Diftrefs, Encouragement of Induftry, and Suppreffion of Va-grants, Street-beggars, and Impoftors, inftituted Jan. 1805, at the fuggeftion of Lady Ifabella King.**

This charity makes no pretence to novelty of principle ; but it attempts to combine together, and to extend in application, what was deemed to be moft ufeful and practicable in fome projected, and in fome exifting, eftablifhments. Previous to the inftitution of this fociety, M. Martin, efq; of Poet's corner, Weftminfter, had publifhed a letter to Lord Pelham, on the ftate of mendicity in the metropolis, March 1803, defcribing the progrefs of an enquiry, com-menced in 1796, into the circumftances of the beg-gars; being led, as he fays, to fuppofe that the general obloquy paffed on this defpifed though nu-merous clafs of fociety, was in many inftances unjuft. He ftates, that he received a grant of 500*l.* from the Treafury, to enable him to profecute the enquiry; that " about 6000 tickets were printed, and fold at " the price of threepence each, for the purpofe of " being diftributed to beggars, who were admitted " to the office in confequence of their fhewing fuch " tickets, and received the value, and frequently more." He obferves, " It is not furprifing that fome of " the parochial beggars fhould have been difap-" pointed in their expectations. Thofe of home " parifhes were not ftrictly confidered as proper " objects for a diftinct provifion. With refpect to " parochial beggars of diftant parifhes, refident in " London or its neighbourhood, it was utterly out

* See Appendix, No. 2.

" of my power to fecure a general reimburfement
" of advances to them, however neceffary, if I had
" made them, and to have made fuch advances in
" any proportion'to their wants, without profpect
" of return, would have borne too hard upon, or
" rather exhaufted, my limited funds. With confi-
" derable regret, therefore, I was conftrained to leave
" thefe objects nearly as I found them. It was a
" forrowful circumftance, but it {was unavoidable."
The profpectus, indeed, publifhed towards the clofe
of the year 1800, particularly ftated, that " the
" acquifition of information, rather than the relief
" of diftrefs, was the primary object of the enquiry."

Although in the courfe of his enquiry, Mr. M.
was enabled to afford occafional affiftance, yet his plan
confeffedly had no tendency to diminifh the exifting
fyftem of mendicity prevalent within the compafs of
his labours. He propofes, however, that a public
board fhould be appointed, with a prefident, and four
other commiffioners ; that the metropolis be divided
into five diftricts, and that each commiffioner have
the charge of a feparate diftrict; to whofe care
fhould be confided the difpofal of beggars of diftant
parifhes; who fhould be authorifed to advance aid to
thofe who fhould have obtained written permiffions
from magiftrates, "approving the caufes and mo-
" tives for their non-refidence within their own
" parifhes." He propofes, alfo, that the commiffioners fhould have power to fupply raw materials,
and provide employment, for fuch as fhould be able
to work.

On confidering the effect of Mr. Martin's tickets,
in checking the importunity of beggars, and inducing
them to apply to a public office, it occurred to Lady
I. King and her friends, that if fuch office fhould be
attended by a number of enlightened perfons, pof-

fefling fufficient means of affording temporary relief
to all who fhould be deemed deferving of it, and by
magiftrates ready, after due notice, to exert the authority with which the law already invefts them ;
if the gentlemen fo affembled fhould be fufficiently
numerous and active duly to inveftigate every cafe
that fhould be prefented for enquiry within the
whole diftrict which might be fixed on as the fphere
of their exertions ; and if all ftreet almsgiving
fhould be then fufpended, and nothing fhould in
future be given to ftreet beggars but tickets of reference to the office ; the chief inducement to ordinary mendicity, ftiled by the old ftatute of Edward
VI. " foolifh pitie," ceafing to fuftain it, the mifchievous practice would foon wholly ceafe. The
morafs might be drained by cutting off the fpring ;
and as water, which, when diffufed, reared only
rufhes, and exhaled putrid miafmata, when confined
and conducted in channels, may educe fertility, and
promote various induftry and happinefs ; fo charity,
which, when blindly fcattered with indifcriminate
profufion, ferved only to cherifh idlenefs, and give
activity to fraud, when directed by fkilful and fteady
inveftigation, would convey due comfort to worth
in affliction, and give wholefome encouragement to
honeft induftry.*

* An ancient and a modern anecdote are earneftly recommended
to the attention of thofe whofe obftinate and ' foolifh pitie' oppofes, undoubtedly, a principal obftacle to the fuppreffion of idle
mendicity. " A Lacedæmonian faid to a beggar, if I fhould give
" thee any thing, I fhould but make thee a greater beggar; for
" he that firft gave to thee made thee idle ; and fo determined thee
" to this bafe way of living." *Plutarch's Laconick Apophthems.*—
A lady paffed refolutely by a melancholy whining beggar, and
heard him mutter in a tone of defpair, " I muft then ! I will do it!"
Thinking to avert fome terrible refolve, fhe turned back ',and gave
him money, and then tenderly enquired what was his defperate
determination. " O my dear, good lady," he replied, " but for
" vour timely charity, I had almoft refolved to go to work."

Societies called Samaritan, or Strangers Friend Societies, exifted in London, at Bath, and in many large towns, inftituted for the occafional relief of diftreffed perfons, without legal fettlement in the places in which calamity had befallen them. The conductors, however, of thefe inftitutions were, it is believed, almoft without exception, although perfectly refpectable, both in underftanding and principles, yet inferior in education and property to thofe who are commonly called gentry; and almoft wholly confifted of diffenters from the ceremonies or doctrines of the church.* The committee of fubfcribers to the plan for fuppreffion of mendicity perceived, that if ftreet begging were univerfally repreffed, the inveftigation undertaken by them would bring under their notice all cafes of real unfeigned fuffering, together with extenfive information relative to the moral character, merits, or demerits of fufferers. They perceived numerous and great advantages, which would not fail to refult from fuch efforts and enquiries, not merely to the objects of their inveftigation, but to themfelves, from the very nature of their occupations, tending to ftrengthen refolution, patience, and benevolence, by habitual exertions. They perceived benefits to their diftricts and parifhes, from the improvement of character to be expected among the poor, when it fhould be found that it was attended with fubftantial advantages; to the fuperior claffes of fociety, when it fhould be duly apprehended by the inferior, that many amongft the wealthy and refined were ready to renounce luxury and eafe, and to devote their furplus of riches and leifure, and their exalted talents, to the alleviation of the diftreffes, and advancement of the

* See Appendix, No. 3.

welfare, of their poorer fellow citizens; and to the community at large, from the combined operation of the former refults. They accordingly refolved to engage in continual inveftigation of all cafes of alleged diftrefs, relieving, according to the extent of their fund, fuch cafes as fhould appear in any way incapable of obtaining adequate relief from the parifh rates, or other legal fources.

It was at firft refolved to extend limited relief. only to cafes of a temporary nature. Thefe perfons were to be affifted with donations of food or money, during ficknefs; or with fmall loans, payable by in-ftalments of one fhilling in the week, without intereft; the repayments to be guaranteed by the fecurity of competent neighbours, being houfekeepers. Many cafes, however, having been obferved of decent perfons labouring with permanent calamity, a fub-fcription was folicited for the formation of a fund, to fupply fmall additional comforts during life, above the bare pittance of neceffaries yielded from other quarters.

Great part of the Annual Report of this Society, publifhed in the beginning of the year 1815, ten years after its inftitution, is here fubjoined; with a perfuafion, that it will be found to exhibit an ufeful middle courfe between the advocates and adverfaries of the poor's law; thofe who are anxious for its utter abolition, and thofe who conceive it to poffefs a degree of excellence not requiring any attempt at meliorative modification.

" The Inftitution was not formed for the purpofe " of collecting money to be diftributed indifcrimi- " nately to any applicants, whom fubfcribers, anxious " to be rid of importunity, might fend to the office; ' but for the purpofe of fuppreffing that fwarm of " audacious impoftors which had formerly made

" this city the fubject of a contemptuous proverb:
" and for the further purpofe of affifting thofe who
" fhould be defirous of affording aid to real diftrefs,
" in exploring the retreats of the humble, the inob-
" trufive, the friendlefs, the helplefs, the hopelefs.
" INVESTIGATION IS THE BASIS OF THEIR SYSTEM.
" The co-operation of the benevolent, both in the
" labour of inveftigating, and in relieving, the
" diftreffes of the indigent, is at all times defirable;
" but the various occupations and engagements of
" moft perfons prevent them from engaging in fuch
" inquiry, and fyftem and habit can alone induce
" correctnefs in this as in other exertions. The
" members of the committee, not limited in number,
" and always rejoicing in the acceffion of refpectable
" affociates, offer their time and labour to the public
" to conduct fuch inveftigation. They are willing
" to become the almoners of others, but not anxious
" to be the fole diftributors of charity; they are
" ever ready and defirous to communicate the refult
" of their refearch, that thofe at whofe requeft fuch
" inquiry fhall have been inftituted, may themfelves
" give the requifite fupply, according to their means
" and difcretion. But they again earneftly exhort
" their fellow-citizens to abftain from indifcriminate
" almsgiving; well knowing, from many years atten-
" tive obfervation, that the extravagant tales of
" ftreet-beggars and petitioners are framed by traders
" in impofture; that the fums gained by low cunning
" from indolent credulity are expended in profligacy;
" and that the channel of benevolence is thus diverted
" from its due courfe of conveying fuccour to worth
" in affliction, to fofter idlenefs and fraud. It cannot
" be too often repeated, that mere giving is not cha-
" rity. It is often an act of vanity; often a paltry
" price paid for the ear's eafe, to filence clamour;

" and often a no lefs paltry device to compound for
" petty fins. To give indeed is lovely, when fym-
" pathy prompts, and a fenfe of duty to God
" guides the act. But true fympathy will not yield
" a pittance to ftifle the cry of affliction ; it will
" anxioufly fearch out the fource of want, and the
" beft method of adminiftering fuccour. A fenfe
" of duty to God will give energy to our exertion,
" will make us advance, without naufea or difdain,
" amidft rags, dirt, and darknefs, and without fear,
" to the chamber of difeafe.

" It is particularly defirable, that the public fhould
" clearly underftand, that the Society does not
" pledge itfelf to afford relief to the poor parifhioners
" of Bath in *all* cafes of alleged diftrefs. Many are
" continually fent to the Society, manifeftly much
" diftreffed by their own imprudence, which has
" induced them to expend their earnings, without
" laying by any portion for payment of their rent.
" If the arrear has accrued during ficknefs, charity
" may be ufefully extended in fuch cafes ; but other-
" wife the removal of inconvenience or even diftrefs
" would but augment the evil, by making fuch im-
" prudence habitual in the individual, and general
" throughout the place.

" Very many are fent in full health and vigour of
" limb, ftrongly recommended to the charitable aid
" of the Society on account of alleged want of
" work ; and ftill more with ftatements of inability
" to maintain large and increafing families.

" The Committee requeft the benevolent recom-
" menders of fuch cafes to confider, that nearly
" 12,000l. per annum is raifed by the poor's-rates in
" Bath, for the exprefs purpofe of providing that
" none fhall ftarve from the want of bare neceffaries
" of life. The demands on this vaft fund in fevere

" feafons are neceffarily large and numerous. But
" the annual fubfcription entrufted to the Society
" not exceeding on an average one-twentieth part of
" the poor's-rate, is neceffarily limited in its appli-
" cation. The aid of the Inftitution for the Relief
" of Occafional Diftrefs is therefore generally con-
" fined to cafes of ficknefs, or of peculiar and fudden
" calamity : but as many applicants, enfeebled by
" age, though not labouring under the preffure of
" temporary ficknefs, are, after long refidence in
" Bath, at a great diftance from their places of legal
" fettlement, and unable to procure immediate aid
" from fuch fources ; to thefe temporary affiftance
" is afforded during fuch time as is deemed requifite
" for making due application to the parifh officers or
" magiftrates ; and affiftance is given towards making
" fuch applications, by letter, from the Vifitors or
" the Secretary of the Society, or otherwife, as
" occafion may be found.

" It may not be improper here to obferve, that
" during ten years of continued attention to the wants
" of the poor, the number of applicants at the
" office of the Society has amounted to about
" 11,000. If we add to thefe the number of per-
" fons vifited after the floods, in two of thefe years,
" above 1500, we. may fay, that individuals of
" above 12,000 families have engaged the attention
" of the Society. Of thefe about one-third is to
" be claffed feparately as travellers, many of whom
" have been attended with wives and children.
" Taking the average, however, as low as three to a
" family, on account of the number of fingle tra-
" vellers, the numbers benefited at different times
" will appear to be not lefs than 36,000.* The

* Perhaps it may convey an incorrect idea to ftate, that fo many
as 12,000 feparate families have engaged the attention of the

" calculation does not include cafes of permanent
" diftrefs, relieved by a fund fet apart for the purpofe
" of fuftaining thofe who, from age and infirmity,
" are no longer capable of earning their fubfiftence,
" and who often require aid, diverfified with care,
" and leniently adminiftered, in addition to the bare
" fupply of neceffaries from the parifh rate. The
" comfort extended to this clafs of applicants has
" been a fource of much gratification to the Com-
" mittee : and they take this occafion to exhort the
" benevolent public to the fupport of the general
" fund, that it may be better enabled to fpare the
" allotted fupply, without injury to other branches of
" the inftitution. The number of permanently
" infirm, aged, and difeafed perfons receiving penfions,
" generally amounting to 2l. 12s.. per annum,* is,
" at the clofe of 1814, ninety-fix. The average
" age of the penfioners (with the exception of one
" nearly blind, two paralytic, and one confumptive)
" exceeds 75. About two-thirds are females. The
" characters of all are excellent, and well authenti-
" cated. Very many have experienced the comforts
" of decent circumftances, and the affliction of a
" painful reverfe. Moft are thus barely preferved
" from the neceffity of feeking a refuge in a crowded
" poor-houfe, and exprefs the moft affecting gratitude
" for the aid which is attended with fuch refult.

" We are happy in an opportunity to ftate, that
" the members of our Ladies' Committee have en-
" gaged to vifit the female penfioners of the Perma-
" nent Fund, and report their obfervations, from time
" to time, to the General Committee. There cannot

Society; as probably the fame refidents have on an average been
twice vifited and affifted in different years.

* The total penfions at prefent amount to 249l. 12s. per ann.

" be a doubt, that the confoling attention fo beftowed
" will be received by the fufferers vifited with delight
" and correfponding gratitude, equal if not fuperior
" to that produced by the pecuniary fupply. It is
" hoped, however, that a fimilar affiftance to the
" charity may be afforded in fucceeding years, as
" the penfions to the objects of the charity amount
" at prefent to the fum of 4l. 16s. weekly ; and to
" the greater number the diftributors would be moft
" happy to be enabled to augment the allowance.

" It is requifite to remind the friends of the Infti-
" tution, that the vifitors to the different dwellings
" of the poor, throughout the diftant parts and fub-
" urbs of Bath, and the fearch after perfons to
" whom they refer for teftimony and for general
" character, occupy a great portion of time ; and
" that it is therefore abfolutely requifite to limit the
" inveftigation to ten cafes in the week. If a greater
" number fhould be fent by fubfcribers, who have
" not leifure to aid enquiry by any previous exami-
" nation on their own parts, it muft unavoidably
" happen that fome will experience the delay of one
" or two weeks before they can get a full hearing.
" Great pains, however, are taken that no cafe of
" extreme urgency fhould ever be difmiffed without
" immediate affiftance ; for after the full weekly
" number of cafes has been taken down for invefti-
" gation, every perfon attending at the regular hours
" is heard. And notice is given to all, of the time
" in which they may expect to be admitted as ob-
" jects of enquiry.

" By the judicious and humane exertions of the
" Ladies' Committee, 76 women have been affifted,
" in the courfe of this year, during the period of
" their lying-in, with the comforts which fuch cafes
" peculiarly require.

" The fuccefs of the Loan fyftem, under ftrictly
" judicious management, has been gratifying beyond
" the moft fanguine expectations, from the manifeft
" promotion of regular habits of œconomy, from
" gratitude frequently expreffed, and from the clearly
" improved condition of thofe who have been fo
" affifted.

" The Committee feel the moft complete confi-
" dence, that by a general co-operation of the inha-
" bitants and vifitors with the views of the Society,
" the moft urgent diftreffes of the induftrious poor
" will not fail to be promptly and properly relieved,
" idlenefs and vice to be detected and difcouraged,
" and the general peace, comfort, and fecurity of
" the town, to be ftrengthened and preferved.

" Perfons defirous of obtaining correct information
" of the real character of any applicant, to whom
" they may be difpofed to give private relief, may
" receive it by calling at the Office, on any day
" between the hours of 12 and 2; or if a written
" requeft be fent, with an addrefs, to the Regiftrar,
" at the Office of Inveftigation, No. 6, Pierrepont-
" place, an extract from the Journals will be returned."

" *Number of Cases registered during the Year.*

" Book 14. Cafes of Refidents - - 521
       " Cafes of Travellers - - 2121
       " Lying-in Cafes - - - 76
       " Permanent Cafes - - - 96
                       2814

" The Members of the Committee have perfon-
" ally vifited all the ground floors and inhabited

" cellars in the lower part of the town, and diftri-
" buted coals to the poor refidents diftreffed by the
" late flood.

" The Committee has obferved, with great
" pleafure, that fimilar Inftitutions have been efta-
" blifhed in Edinburgh, at Briftol, and at Oxford.
" It muft inevitably happen, that the fuppreffion of
" idlenefs and impofture, the extenfion of active
" charity and virtuous fympathy, will prove be-
" neficial, not merely to towns in which fuch affocia-
" tions have been formed, but to the rich and poor
" throughout the kingdom, by the influence of
" ufeful example."

It will, probably, occur to many, that the veftry
of every parifh is almoft at prefent, or might become,
by adjournments from day to day, a fociety of this
kind; deriving peculiar advantage from the power
of the overfeers, and the ample fupply of the poor's
rate. But it muft be obferved, that in fmall country parifhes in which any refpectable gentleman's
family is generally refident, the diftrefs which makes
inveftigation laborious, and aid difficult, is hardly to
be found; and in large towns, where the evil is at its
height, the gentry, as I have before obferved, too
generally fhun the veftry meeting. I am told, however, that an exception exifts in the parifh of St.
George's, Weftminfter, moft honourable to the nobility and gentry, whofe exertions are equally beneficial to all orders of the community in that vaftly
populous diftrict.† It is undoubtedly highly to be

* The Profpectus preceding the regulations and the rules of
the Edinburgh, as well as of the Oxford Society, well deferve
the attention of the inquirer into this fubject.

† Thefe gentlemen form a felect veftry. I cannot conceive any
reafon why felect veftries fhould not be generally formed in the

wifhed that the objects of the Bath Society fhould be adopted by the members of every veftry; that feveral of the principal refidents of every parifh being, of courfe, members of the veftries, fhould devote a confiderable portion of their time and attention to the promotion of fuch purpofes, acting in the veftry, and, as far as poffible, in their capacities as members of the veftry; but alfo wherever fuch mode of acting fhould be found impracticable or inconvenient, as members of a charitable affociation, prepared with ready benevolence to afford aid in all fuch omitted cafes.

I think, however, that it will be found that an ex-tenfive charitable affociation, acting in concurrence with magiftrates, overfeers, and a veftry, may poffefs many advantages, which a veftry, confined to its legal functions, would not attain.

The parifhioners merely affembled in the veftry cannot make adequate enquiry into the numerous cafes which may be prefented for infertion in the lift for relief out of the poor-houfe. A fociety devoted to inveftigation, and regularly allotting to each mem-ber in fucceffion a definite portion of time for fuch purpofe, will not vacillate, and paufe to fee by whom it fhall be undertaken. Each perfon will know his defined duty. The inquiry, which even the moft fagacious might purfue with difficulty when newly engaged, will become eafy from habit. The occupa-tion will benefit the man of leifure by diffipating the ficknefs of *ennui*, and the languid fhame of ufelefsnefs; to the man of bufinefs it will afford the relaxation of

---

parifhes of all great towns except the difficulty of procuring mem-bers; but, quere, what is requifite to eftablifh a *cuftom* in fuch cafe? " By cuftom there may be felect veftries of a certain number of " perfons elected yearly to make rates, and manage the concerns of " the parifh for that year; and fuch cuftom is a good cuftom."— *Burn's Juftice, vol. i. p. 396.*

eafy effort, and the gratifying occafion of doing good without rifk; of indulging the feelings of kindnefs, unalloyed by nicely calculating felfifhnefs. It has been frequently objected againft all inquiry into the circumftances of the pcor, that all the knowledge fo obtained has a tendency to harden the heart; that it is merely a knowledge of folly, and felfifhnefs, and vice, in its groffeft and meaneft forms, calculated to excite difguft and contempt, to deaden fympathy, and to avert charity. Such objectors may rave in praife of the

" Pity which gave, ere Charity began;"

but the objection is founded in falfehood, and the verfe is at the beft mifapplied. It is an amiable character, which in childhood difplays lively fenfibilities at a period when experience cannot poffibly have been acquired to control them ; but manhood is difgraced by the abandonment of reafon, either in refpect to religion or to morals: and the advocates of fuch abandonment may be fairly fufpected, in either cafe, of wifhing to fubftitute formal jargon and oftentation in place of the foul's ftruggle and the body's toil. In fact, the higher faculties of the mind, like thofe of the body, are notorioufly ftrengthened by continual exertions, and become torpid from inaction. Benevolence expands in proportion as it extends the fphere of its regards. The continued contemplation of its exalted relation to the everlafting Fountain of Mercy cannot fail to exalt its affections; the high and folemn thought that the Eternal Spirit in whom all light, all life, all goodnefs, are inherent and effential, beholds each conception as it rifes in the heart, each action throughout all its progrefs, muft furely awaken all the energies of zeal, and inveft charity with the radiant dignity of holinefs.

But the knowledge of the poor is not fo degrading to humanity, in its difplay or in its operation, as the objection ventures to affume. Ignorance muft, perhaps, in equal circumftances of temptation, be more liable to error than wifdom. But the temptations of poverty are mercifully modified to the condition of the poor. If they often are defective in prudence, in neatnefs, and politenefs, they poffefs many qualities which the more refined claffes might do well to copy. They are commonly, to an exemplary degree, patient under affliction, and calm at the approach of death. If the greater number of criminals who fuffer the penalties of the law be found amongft them, it muft be remembered that they are the moft numerous clafs, and that the culture which fhould teach the control of the paffions has been rarely and fcantily imparted to them; and although of late a wholefome emulation (not to fay rivalry) has arifen in extending education, yet many ftill avow a wifh to fee them excluded from fuch, which they deem dubious, advantages. They are, as far as my experience extends, as honeft as their betters. A comparative eftimate of the virtues and vices of different claffes is, however, not eafily made, and it might appear invidious to ftate a balance upon either fide. The poor are moft certainly at the leaft as prompt as the rich in all acts of humanity, according to their means. In all fituations of hazard, inftances continually occur of danger to limbs and to life braved and encountered to convey fuccour to fuffering fellow-creatures. They have, indeed, little to give; but the fhelter of their dwellings is afforded to the wanderer, often with too little caution; and amongft the female poor I have delighted in obferving a magnanimous perfeverance in humane attentions to their fick neighbours, undeterred by naufeating horrors, and undifmayed by the peril of infection. They are accufed of wanting gratitude. This accufation, were it true, would not juftify, in any inftance, the flighteft diminution of charity; a principle not liable to vary with the eddies of temper, caprice, and conjuncture; a combination of elevated intellect, and of purified fenfibility, fixed on the law of GOD, which it delights to contemplate, eternal as the Great Spirit of eternal mercy from whence it draws its birth, afcending ever from height to height of goodnefs, advancing, linked with piety, as " cherub with cherub joined," under the banner of the Moft High, in ftrict and glorious union. But the accufation is not generally true. They may, indeed, be found to be but flightly affected by benefits manifeftly not flowing from fympathy, not afforded with kindnefs, extorted by painful importunity, or fcattered with difdainful carelefsnefs; but let thofe who vifit them in ficknefs, who cheer them in affliction, who, condefcending to conceive that they have hearts to feel, fpeak to thofe hearts with the voice of tendernefs; let thefe fay, whether thofe whom they have thus addreffed have wanted the eloquence of fobs and tears in aid of their unpolifhed language; have foon forgotten the genuine benefactor; have not, even at remoteft periods, rejoiced in opportunities not to difcharge obligation, but to find expanfe in action for the high fwelling flood of affection, which lifts the foul towards the level of that fpring which gave the impulfe to its energies. No. Their feelings are abundantly refponfive to real fympathy, but they have the fagacity to diftinguifh between oftentation and charity.

CONCLUSION.

IN feveral parts of this imperfect furvey of the conduct of different ftates, and the opinions of certain divines, philofophers, and legiflators, relative to the poor, I have in fome degree anticipated inferences, which are yet more ftrongly impreffed by a review of the whole.

The poor have exifted in all periods. The infpired legiflator of the Jews tells them, " the poor fhall " never ceafe out of the land." The fagacious philofopher fays, " All cannot fhare alike the bounties " of nature. Were there no eftablifhed adminiftration " of property, every man would be obliged to guard " with force his little ftore. Selfifhnefs would be " triumphant. The fubjects of contention would be " perpetual. Every individual would be under a " conftant anxiety about corporal fupport; and not " a fingle intellect would be left free to expatiate in " the field of thought." *Malthus, vol. ii. p.* 102.

As the poor have ever exifted, fo the efforts of the rich have ever been directed, fometimes more and fometimes lefs fyftematically, to the alleviation of their wants and diftreffes. The ancient fyftem of flavery was, however odious and degrading, a fyftem of fure fuftenance for the poor. The military arrangement of the feudal fyftem brought the vaffals continually under the notice of their fuperiors and their lords, who were duly prepared to fuftain their human property, and encourage the devotion of their adherents, generally ready to repay kindnefs with the facrifice of life in the lords' quarrel.

When nations are farther advanced in general opulence, and arts and trade have introduced focial gradations; have greatly extended population; have affembled multitudes in fplendid cities; have advanced luxury to its height; the occafions which bring the loweft into contaét with the higheft claffes, are fo rare, that the poor would be in danger of being wholly forgotten, had not the intermediate claffes various urgent motives to prefs the claims of the neceffitous on their attention, that the onus of the fuftenance of the poor may not be unfairly fhifted from thofe who are beft able to contribute to it, on thofe whofe means are much lefs adequate.

Writers on the evil effeéts of exceffive luxury have ufually expatiated on the enervating effeéts, both to the mind ·and the body, of a general difpofition to immoderate fenfual indulgence, to indolent habits, and to the abandonment of hardy exercifes; and have attributed chiefly to thefe circumftances the decline of the profperity of nations. But the moft luxurious people, the moft effeminate in habits, and depraved in morals, have difplayed every diverfity of brilliant talents, and have been equal to the moft arduous and terrific military achievements; witnefs Greece, and Rome, and France: yet luxury, and that criminal excefs of felfifhnefs, which is its great charaéteriftic, has furely brought on revolutions, and anarchy, and all the inevitable train of miferies, the monfters of political difeafe and diffolution, by fapping the great pillars of the political fabric,—morals and religion. Luxury cherifhes fuperftition, which flourifhes like a gaudy weed on the ruins of rational religion; but it engenders indignant contempt, which, with blind rage, has aimed deftruétion at the rubbifh which difgraced the fhrine, and endangered the fanétuary itfelf. Luxury diffufes through all claffes an intemperate defire

of felf-indulgence, what wonder, then, that each, ab-
forbed wholly in felfifhnefs, is neglectful of the focial
duties which are neceffary to the welfare of all.

The weaknefs, then, of corrupt, luxurious, and
vicious ftates, appears to me to arife from an abfence
of that mutual fympathy, refpect, and love, between
the feveral claffes, which are the natural fources of
political ftrength.   Thank GOD! this moral *lues* is
not yet our condition; this tendency to a morbid
folution of political continuity, which endangers the
feparation of the flefh and bone of the ftate, raifing
foul and falfe notions of oppofing interefts between
the rich and the poor, the burning and burfting
tumours of anarchy, inducing the marafmus, the
atrophy of defpotifm.

Piety, however varioufly expreffed, ftill glows
generally and copioufly in Englifh bofoms; and
Charity, its hallowed affociate, abounds amongft us.
The plan, and conduct, and the voluminous Reports,
of that valuable inftitution, *the Society for bettering
the Condition of the Poor*, &c. (too generally known
and refpected to need my mite of applaufe,) give
ample proof to this effect: and no doubt can be
entertained, that thefe bleffings, and fources of innumerable bleffings, are to be traced to the comparative
freedom and purity of our political and religious
fyftems, which allow the energies of intellect, and
the beft feelings of the heart, to expand, free from
thofe bonds of fuperftition and fervility which have
proved fatal to many other nations.

" The apparent end of the impulfe of benevolence
(fays Mr. Malthus, vol. ii. p. 425) " is to draw the
" whole human race together, but more particularly
" that part of it which is of our own nation and
" kindred, in the bonds of brotherly love; and by
" giving men an intereft in the happinefs and mifery

" of their fellow-creatures, to prompt them, as they
" have power, to mitigate the partial evils arifing
" from general laws, and thus to increafe the fum of
" human happinefs. But if our benevolence be in-
" difcriminate, and the degree of apparent diftrefs be
" made the fole meafure of our liberality, it is evident
" that it will be exercifed almoft exclufively upon
" common beggars; while modeft, unobtrufive merit,
" ftruggling with unavoidable difficulties, yet ftill
" maintaining fome flight appearances of decency
" and cleanlinefs, will be totally neglected. We
" fhall raife the worthlefs above the worthy ; we
" fhall encourage indolence, and check induftry ; and,
" in the moft marked manner, fubtract from the fum
" of human happinefs."*

Thofe who afpire to effect the good here pointed
out, and to avoid the evil, muft be efpecially careful
in beftowing benefits, fo as not to excite a general
reftlefsnefs for continual change of condition. Great
judgment is requifite, both in fpeaking to the poor,
and to others in their prefence, refpecting their
condition, their general or their particular circumftances. It is to be remembered, that, though not
refined in their manners, they can diftinguifh real
kindnefs from affectation ; that they can feel infult
from fupercilious airs, and from the grimace of pre-
tended condefcenfion, though not acute in difcrimination ; they can fee the ridiculous in pompous for-
mality, and often guefs pretty fhrewdly at the
diftinction between the cant of hypocrify, obtru-
ding admonition, and the zeal of kindnefs, which
points out what is plainly and practically beneficial.
Nothing fhould ever be even remotely fuggefted or
uttered before them, or expreffed by gefture, which
may excite difcontent with a ftate which cannot be

* See Appendix, No. IV.

amended. It is to be remembered, that they are not neceffarily wretched, becaufe they are comparatively poor, becaufe they are coarfely fed and clothed, becaufe their houfes are mean and fcanty, their apartments crowded and dirty. Cuftom cannot merely reconcile, but can give endearment to all thefe. In fpeaking to the poor, many employ a rhetorical phrafeology, which they cannot underftand, and which excites their ridicule; fome affect to mimic their dialect a ftill greater error, for the awkward abfurdity is obvious, and it may poffibly give pain, from wearing a doubtful air of mockery.

The manners, the habits, the minds, and the feelings of the poor muft then be ftudied with attentive obfervation, not merely cafual but fyftematic, by thofe who wifh to do permanent, fubftantial good to them, or to themfelves, by engaging in fuch occupation.

The vifitor of the poor fhould be attentive not to exhibit ignorance of what belongs to their condition : fhould, in addreffing them, preferve a medium between formal politenefs and free familiarity. Expreffions of levity will at all times be avoided in the prefence of the afflicted, but fhould be efpecially fhunned before the poor. The language, the tone, the gefture of anger fhould be ftudioufly repreffed; fufpicion of falfhood fhould be carefully concealed. Benevolence would rather be for ever duped, than once confent to wound honeft feelings with unjuft doubt. Allowance muft be made for exaggeration in complaint, for great flownefs in apprehenfion of queftions, for confufion in narrative, for mutual mifconception of pronunciation. In fhort, every method fhould be fought, and cultivated with anxiety, which may enhance, every act and expreffion muft be avoided which can tend to leffen, the refpect and affection of the poor towards thofe who vifit them. The fulleft proof fhould be eftablifhed of any attempt to deceive, and the completely expofed fraud fhould be repelled with dignity of grave indignation.

A habit of afking queftions fyftematically will give to an enquirer a facility in difcovering truth, and in developing obfcure meanings; and may prove beneficial to both parties, in giving order to a perplexed, and brevity to a long-tending and wide-wandering, ftory.

The vifitor of the poor fhould be acquainted with the means of relief afforded by law, and with thofe which may be obtained from the eftablifhed public charities; and fhould inculcate economy, by example, as well as precept. He fhould ever bear in mind, that giving is not the only charity. Advifing is often of much greater importance; and a patient, kind hearing frequently is an act of the higheft beneficence, with patience and long-fuffering aiding an over-burthened heart to throw off its load, and fuftaining from defpair a foul, which was funken from long hopeleffnefs of fympathy.

In diftribution of alms, the greateft care is to be taken not to encourage indolence by exceffive, and jealoufies by partial, and envy by publicly-difplayed, donations. It is a foolifh vanity, which feeks to furprize the poor with unexpected magnitude of largefs. Travellers fhould be aided with a much more cautious and fparing hand than refidents, as their ftories have neceffarily very fcanty evidence; as in every town they have equal opportunities of gaining aid, and great numbers fubfift in a wandering way of life, feeking fupport from alms, impofing by fictitious ftories on the carelefs or the credulous.

I know not any way in which men poffeffing wealth and leifure can poffibly be more profitably occupied,

than in the ftudies which tend to the beneficial direction of charity in all its branches, and in the
practical exertions which it requires; and which, if
ftudy does not promote, it is, as Milton fays, no better
than the bufy idlenefs " of children, gathering peb-
" bles on the fhore."

Every great town of the kingdom poffeffes charitable eftablifhments, in the active promotion of which
the rich may be ufefully engaged.   And a catalogue
of thofe noblemen, gentlemen, and ladies, who have
long devoted, not only great part of their income, but
their time and talents, to the fuperintendance of fuch
charities, might confer no lefs honour on the nation,
and might contribute no lefs to account for the bleffings which it has pleafed Almighty GOD to fhower
upon us, than the prowefs of our dauntlefs army and
navy, the fkill and gallantry of their dignified com-
manders.   Glorious is the age and nation, which has
produced a HOWE, a NELSON, a MOORE, a WEL-
LINGTON; and bleffed the country and period, which
could boaft a HOWARD, a HANWAY, a PUSAY, a
BERNARD, a BARRINGTON, a WILBERFORCE, and
fuch females as a TRIMMER and a MORE.   Charity
is a difpofition to place our chief intereft in life, to
feek for our principal enjoyment, in doing all poffible
good to others; and to look up to GOD with love and
gratitude for the bleffed, felicitous emotions which
are the neceffary, the heaven-appointed confequences
of fuch habits and fuch exertions.

I am tempted again to adorn my collection with
a fentence from that admirable ninth chapter of the
fecond volume of Mr. Malthus's effay " on the di-
" rection of our charity."

    " One of the moft valuable parts of charity is its
" effect upon the giver.   It is more bleffed to give
" than to receive.   Suppofing it to be allowed that

" the exercife of our benevolence in acts of charity is
" not upon the whole really beneficial to the poor,
" yet we could never fanction any endeavour to ex-
" tinguifh an impulfe, the proper gratification of
" which has fo evident a tendency to purify and to
" exalt the human mind. But it is particularly fa-
" tisfactory and pleafing to find, that the mode of
" exercifing our charity, which, when brought to the
" teft of utility, will appear to be moft beneficial to
" the poor, is precifely that which will have the
" beft and moft improving effect on the mind of the
" donor."

In an extended view of charity, the fincere diffufer
of religious truth and love, the active magiftrate,
the ftrenuous and upright patriot, the philanthropic
advocate of the oppreffed Africans, as well as the
vifitor of the poor, the fick, and the afflicted, are all
feverally engaged in different branches of the fame
great work; in which, as in arts and manufactures, a
divifion of labour and a devotion of certain perfons
to definite parts of the general undertaking, is the
only fure method of advancement toward perfection.‡
It is vain, therefore, in any cafe to fpeak of charity
as compatible with vice, with a felfifh purfuit of
individual gratification, regardlefs of the mifery which
is inevitably brought on others. The perfection of
Charity is the perfection of man's ftate on earth;
the higheft end and aim of man on this fide of
heaven; of the philofopher, the philanthropift,
and the patriot: yet by the eternal law, which
has ordered both the heaven and the earth, and

‡ It is wholly irreconcileable with all experience to conceive the
poffible compatibility of a general laxity of morals with the permanent welfare or comfort of individuals or of nations. He muft have
obferved little, and thought lefs, who could fail to perceive that
goodnefs and happinefs are reciprocal.

linked the corruptible with the incorruptible,
the mortal with immortality, it is fo involved with
our beſt hopes of a bleſſed and glorious hereafter,
that it is impoſſible for any to feel truly conſcious
of a genuine reſolute devotion to promote peace and
goodwill amongſt men, without a neceſſarily affociated conſciouſneſs of his progreſs toward the blef-
ſing and glory of God on high. The heavenly book
of CHRIST, which in every ſentence blends charity
with holineſs, will cheer through life the labourer in
this purſuit, and elevate his foul in death with the
ſalutation of eternal love, " Enter thou into the joy
" of thy Lord."

APPENDIX.

Abstract of the Returns relative to the
Expense and Maintenance of the Poor.

[43 GEO. III. A. 1803.]

ENGLAND AND WALES.

Observations.

No. I.

I. RETURNS from fourteen thoufand fix hundred
and eleven parifhes or places in England
and Wales have been received, and are entered in
this Abftract. Returns from fourteen thoufand two
hundred and forty parifhes or places are entered in
the Abftract of the Returns of 1785; fourteen
thoufand one hundred and thirteen in the Abftract
of the Returns of 1776.

II. Three thoufand feven hundred and fixty-five
parifhes or places maintain all or part of their
poor *in* workhoufes. The number of perfons fo
maintained, *during the year ending Eafter* 1803, was

83,468 ; and the expenfe incurred therein amounted to 1,016,445l. 15s. 3d. ; being at the rate of 12l. 3s. 6³d. for each perfon maintained in that manner. It appears from the Abſtract of the Returns of 1776, that there were then 1970 workhoufes, "capable of accommodating" 89,775 perfons.

III. The number of perfons relieved *out* of workhoufes was 956,248, (col. x. p. 1. col. 2. and col. 12.) befides 194,052, (col. 14.) who were not parifhioners. The expenfe incurred in the relief of the poor *not in* workhoufes amounted to 3,061,446l. 16s. 10¼d. A large proportion of thofe " who " were not parifhioners," appears to have been vagrants ; and therefore it is probable, that the relief given to this clafs of poor could not exceed two fhillings each, amounting to 19,405l. 4s. This fum being deducted from the above 3,061,446l. 16s. 10¼d. leaves 3,042,041l. 12s. 10¼d. ; being at the rate of 3l. 3s. 7¼d. for each " parifhioner re-" lieved" *out* of any workhoufe.

IV. The number of perfons relieved *in* and *out* of workhoufes was 1,039,716 ; befides thofe " who " were not parifhioners." Excluding the expenfe fuppofed to be incurred in the relief of this clafs of poor, all the expenfes relative to the maintenance of the poor (col. 4 and 5.) amounted to 4,093,758l. 19s. 6¼d. ; being at the rate of 3l. 17s. 9½d. for each parifhioner relieved.

V. The refident population in England and Wales, in the year 1801, appears, from the Population Abſtract, to have been 8,872,980, fo that the number of parifhioners relieved from the poors' rate appears to be twelve in a hundred of the refident population.

The number of perfons belonging to Friendly Societies appears to be eight in a hundred of the refident population.

The amount of " the total money raifed by rates,"
appears to average at 12s. o¾d. per head, on the
population.

The amount of the whole experditure on
account of the poor appears to average at 9s. 7¼d.
per head, on the population.

VI. The expenditure in fuits of law, removal of
paupers, and expenfes of overfeers and other officers,
according to the prefent abftract, amounts to
190,072l. 17s. o½d. The amount of fuch expenditure, according to the Abftract of the Returns of
1785, (comprifed in cols. 11, 12, and 13, of that
Abftract,) was then 91,998l. 1s. 9d.

VII. The expenditure in purchafing materials
for employing the poor, according to the prefent
Abftract, amounts to 47,523l. 11s. 4¼d. The
amount of fuch expenditure, according to the Abftract of the Returns of 1785, was then 15,892l.
8s. 10d.

VIII. The poor of two hundred and ninety-three
parifhes or places in England and Wales are ftated
in the returns to be farmed or maintained under
contract.

IX. The poor of feven hundred and fixty-four
parifhes or places in England and Wales are maintained and employed under the regulations of fpecial
Acts of Parliament.

X. Five thoufand four hundred and twenty-eight
Friendly Societies have been enrolled at the Quarter-
Seffions of the feveral counties in England and
Wales, purfuant to the Acts of 33d Geo. III. c. 54,
and 35th Geo. III. c. 3.; but in this number, are not
included the Friendly Societies which have been enrolled in the county of *Devon*, the *Holland* divifion of
the county of *Lincoln*, and the county of *Carnarvon* ,
the clerks of the peace of thofe places not having

returned any anfwer to the application, requefting
them to fpecify the number of Friendly Societies
which may have been enrolled purfuant to the
faid Act.

XI. Application having been made to the feveral
clerks of the peace, requefting them to fpecify
" the ufual proportion of the rated rental to the
" rack rental;" it appears that, according to the
anfwers received, the rated rental amounts on an
average to about *three-fourths* of the rack rental;
but many of the clerks of the peace have not been
able to ftate any thing fatisfactory in their anfwers to
the above queftion.

The rated rental of each county having been
obtained by calculation from the rates in the pound
returned, and for the amount of money then raifed,
the total rated rental of England and Wales appears
to amount to 24,129,134l.; on which the average
rate in the pound is 4s. 5¼d. equal to 3s. 4d. on the
rack rental, eftimated according to the anfwers received from the clerks of the peace.

In the returns from three hundred and eighty-
feven parifhes or places in England and Wales, the
rate in the pound is ftated on the rack rental. The
amount of money raifed by rates in thofe parifhes
or places is 268,381l. 2s. 9½d. The amount of the
rack rental, as computed therefrom, is 1,679,716l.
10s. 4½d. confequently the average rate in the
pound, on this rental, amounts to 3s. 2¼d.

It appears, however, from the returns made to the
Tax-office for the year ending April 1804, that the
rental of real property in England and Wales
amounts to 34,000,000l.; not including mines,
ca als, and fome other kind of real property, which,
with an allowance for the deficiencies incident to taxation, cannot be eftimated at lefs than 4,000,000l.

per annum. Including this fum, the rack rental of
England and Wales, liable to affeffment, amounts to
38,000,000l.; on which (the amount of the parifh
rates being 5,348,205l.) the actual rate in the pound
averages at 2s. 10d. or nearly *one feventh* part.

XII. The area of England and Wales (according to the lateft autherities) appears to be 58,335
fquare ftatute miles, equal to 37,334.400 ftatute
acres. Wherefore the number of inhabitants in
each fquare mile (containing 640 acres) averages at
152 perfons.

No. II.

THE Houfe of Protection, inftituted, in 1805, by
Lady I. King, has been flightly noticed, page 121.
It is eftablifhed for the reception and inftruction of
young girls of good character, who, from the death
or abfence of their parents, or any other misfortune,
are in want of a fafe afylum, until they can be placed
out as fervants. The charity is under the management of eight ladies; who " take it in turns to vifit
" the houfe daily, to hear the girls read, examine
" their work, and give any directions that may be
" neceffary to the matron." Orphans are admitted
at the age of ten, others not under thirteen. The
Report for the year 1813 ftates, " The object is to
" afford protection to the friendlefs, and at the fame
" time to give them fuch inftruction as may render
" them ufeful in the ftations which perfons of their
" clafs are likely to obtain ; namely, thofe of under
" fervants, or maids of all work in fmall families.
" Their accommodation and relief in the Houfe of
" Protection are inferior to what they probably will
" have when at fervice: they are employed in

P 2

" houfhold work; in wafhing and ironing : they are
" taught to make and mend their own clothes ; and
" particular care is taken to correct the love of drefs
" now fo prevalent among the lower claffes."

The benevolent zeal of this Lady has alfo given
the firft impulfe to an Inftitution of a higher defcription, powerfully fupported by the Queen and Prin-
ceffes, as well as by many of the principal female
nobility, *for improving the fituation of Ladies of
refpectable character and fmall fortune.* The plan is
thus announced.

" It has long been anxioufly wifhed, that a plan
" could be effectively brought forward, which fhould
" induce ladies of rank and refpectability through-
" out the kingdom to unite, for the purpofe of
" affording affiftance and protection to females of
" good families, who are, by the death of parents, or
" by other calamities, much reduced below the ftate
" of comfort to which they have been accuftomed.

" The frequency of fuch afflictive cafes muft have
" brought fome within the range of every one's
" obfervation ; and the wifh to alleviate the diftrefs
" attendant on fuch deprivation muft, it is conceived,
" be univerfal.

" Schemes have been heretofore fuggefted for the
" formation of eftablifhments fimilar to thofe which
" exift in almoft all proteftant ftates on the continent;
" but the difficulties attending the firft foundation of
" fuch inftitutions on an extended fcale have been
" deemed infurmountable.

" It is now propofed that *one* limited eftablifhment
" be formed by the way of trial, and, if fuccefsful,
" of example.

" That a fund be raifed by fubfcriptions of the
" nobility and gentry, applicable, in the firft inftance,
" to promote and fuftain the primary inftitution ;

" and ultimately, to give general extenfion and per-
" manent fecurity to fuch eftablifhments throughout
" the kingdom.

" That fuch fund be invefted on Government
" fecurity in the names of moft highly refpectable
" truftees, and be placed under the control of
" dignified patrons and patroneffes.

" That, with a view to the immediate furtherance
" of this object, an affociation be formed of Ladies,
" among whom twelve will act as patroneffes and
" fuperintendants of the undertaking; and that a
" local committee be appointed to eftablifh a primary
" inftitution in the neighbourhood of Bath.

" That a lady be appointed by this committee
" as fuperintendant of the eftablifhment, and that
" the regulations of the houfhold be placed under
" her direction.

" That no one be admitted into the eftablifhment,
" except on the unanimous agreement of the local
" committee, that the circumftances of the perfon
" propofed for admiffion accord with the object ex-
" preffed in the general propofition.

" That each lady who is regularly admitted as
" inmate of the eftablifhment, fhall be required to
" pay annually fifty pounds for her apartment and
" board.

" That fpare rooms (fhould the houfe be fufficiently
" large) be let at a fixed price to ladies in more
" affluent circumftances, who, preferring fuch refi-
" dence, may thus contribute to its fupport.

" That one of the local committee be annually
" elected prefident; and, as head of the eftablifh-
" ment, vifit the houfe, and direct the due obfervance
" of all the regulations.

" That a report from the local committee be
" annually made to the affociated patrons and
" patroneffes.

" That books be opened, under the direction of
" the truftees, patrons, and patroneffes, at the bank-
" ing-houfes of Meffrs Coutts and Co. London,
" Sir B. Hobhouse and Co. Bath, to receive do-
" nations towards the fund for the promotion and
" permanent maintenance of the undertaking."

This eftablifhment partakes, in a limited degree, of
the nature of a benefit club, under the higheft patronage, and compofed of the firft gentry of the
country, as fome of thofe who contribute may contemplate the poffibility of its benefit being extended
to their own connections ; and it appears to have
been originally intended to imprefs it with this character, that none might be deterred by pride from
accepting its advantages.

No. III.

ACCOUNTS of two charitable focieties, one faid
to have been inftituted in London in the year 1774,
and the other at Nottingham in the year 1776, have
been lately prefented to me, both of which are
founded on principles fo exactly correfponding with
thofe of the Bath Inftitution, as far as inveftigation is
concerned, that they might feem to have fuggefted
the formation of the latter ; although it is probable
that the founders of the Nottingham Society, who
were Quakers, never heard of that in London ; and
I am well affured, that both were unknown at Bath,
when the fociety in that city was eftablifhed.

The London fociety, however, falls fhort of that
in Bath, in not adopting the fyftem of relief by fmall
loans, with fecurities for repayment ; and neither of
the focieties appears to aim at ftimulating the police
officers, by offering bounties on convictions of vaga-

bonds; nor to poſſeſs funds for permanent penſion-
ers ; nor to iſſue tickets for the convenience of a
general reference of all mendicants to their offices.
The Report from Nottingham is dated 1806; that
of the London Society is for 1808. In the London
liſt of ſubſcribers, for 1808, appear the names of the
Duke of Devonſhire, Marquis of Stafford, Lord
Radnor, Lord and Lady Anſon, Mr. Wilberforce,
and Mr. Angerſtein, with ſeveral others of our firſt
nobility and gentry. The books of the London
ſociety are ſaid to be depoſited with Mr. T. S.
Stephenſon, No. 14, Hanway-ſtreet, Oxford-ſtreet,
and ſubſcriptions received by Meſſrs. Drummond and
Co. Charing-Croſs. The inquiry in London was
appointed by five perſons in five different pariſhes.
The number is, perhaps, hardly adequate to the
object ; and this ſyſtem does not produce that com-
munication of the rich with the poor, attempted in
the committees of the Bath and Oxford Societies.

An account of a Society in Weſt-ſtreet, Seven
Dials, for the relief of their poor neighbours in
diſtreſs, inſtituted by the Rev. Mr. Gurney, in 1803,
is publiſhed, and juſtly recommended to the attention
of the public, by the Society for bettering the Condition of the Poor.

In my mention of Bath Charities, I have omitted
to notice one which was founded by Mr. Hervé, in
1810, who collected a general ſubſcription, for the
purpoſe of granting ſmall annuities to perſons labouring under extreme poverty and infirmity, from
old age or ſickneſs, and who have once moved in a
ſomewhat higher ſphere than thoſe who are placed
on the permanent liſt of the Society for Relief of occaſional Diſtreſs, &c. Mr. Hervé, having ſucceeded in
eſtabliſhing ſimilar funds for the ſame purpoſe in
other places, has called each the *National Benevo-*

lent Inftitution, wifhing to promote the general adoption of the plan throughout the kingdom. Thofe who petition for the aid of the fund muft prefent to the truftees, for their inveftigation, certificates figned by nine refpectable houfeholders, vouching for the circumftances detailed in their narratives. Such a fund, under the control, as in Bath, of upright, active, and intelligent truftees, cannot but attain the beft purpofes of charity, according to the extent of the fund. In 1814, the number of penfioners at Bath are ftated to be eleven, and the amount of annual penfions £160.

No. IV.

THE general intent of this Collection being to point out fources of various information, relative to the object of inquiry, I cannot make a more ufeful reference than to the works of Count Rumford, the well-known inftitutor of a public eftablifhment for the poor at Munich in Bavaria ; a man of great intelligence, and moft active in applying various fcience to public utility, and efpecially to the advancement of the caufe of humanity. See his " Effay of the " fundamental principles on which general Efta-" blifhments for the Relief of the Poor may be " formed in all countries."

" It evidently appears, that no body of laws, how-" ever wifely formed, can in any country effectually " provide for the relief of the poor, without the vo-" luntary affiftance of individuals ; for though taxes " may be levied, by the authority of the laws, for the " fupport of the poor, yet thofe kind attentions which " are fo neceffary in the management of the poor,

" as well to reclaim the vicious, as to comfort and
" encourage the defpondent, thofe demonftrations
" of concern, which are always fo great a confola-
" tion to perfons in diftrefs, cannot be commanded
" by force." *Effays, vol. i. p.* 117.

" The greateft difficulty attending the intro-
" duction of any meafure founded upon the vo-
" luntary fupport of the public, for maintaining
" the poor, and putting an end to mendicity, is an
" opinion, generally entertained, that a very heavy
" expenfe would be indifpenfably neceffary to carry
" into execution fuch an undertaking. But this
" difficulty may be fpeedily removed, by fhewing
" (which may eafily be done) that the execution of
" a well-arranged plan for providing for the poor,
" and giving ufeful employment to the idle and
" indolent, fo far from being expenfive, muft, in the
" end, be attended with a very confiderable faving,
" not only to the public collectively, but alfo to
" individuals." P. 120.

" Not only thofe who were formerly ftreet beg-
" gars, but alfo others, without exception, who
" receive alms in the city of Munich, and its fuburbs,
" amounting at this time to more than 1800 perfons,
" are fupported almoft entirely by voluntary fub-
" fcriptions from the inhabitants ; and I have been
" affured, by numbers of the moft opulent and re-
" fpectable citizens, that the fums annually extorted
" from them formerly by beggars alone, exclufive of
" private charities, amounted to more than three
" times the fums now given by them to the fupport
" of the new Inftitution." P. 121.

" Though nothing would be more unjuft
" and tyrannical than to prevent the generous and
" humane from contributing to the relief of the poor,
" yet as giving alms to beggars tends fo directly and

" 'fo powerfully to encourage idlenefs and immorality;
" to difcourage the induftrious poor, and perpetuate
" mendicity, with all its attendant evils, too much
" pains cannot be taken to guard the public againft
" a practice fo fatal in its confequences to fociety.
" All who are defirous of contributing to the
" relief of the poor, fhould be invited to fend their
" charitable donations to be diftributed by thofe, who
" being at the head of a public Inftitution, efta-
" blifhed for taking care of the poor, muft be fup-
" pofed beft acquainted with their wants.   Or if
" individuals fhould prefer diftributing their own
" charities, they ought at leaft to take the trouble
" to enquire after fit objects, and to apply their
" donations in fuch a manner as not to counteract
" the meafures of a public and ufeful eftablifhment."
P. 123.

An account of an eftablifhment at Chaillot, near
Paris, which I have feen in a Bath newfpaper, is
fubjoined, as calculated to excite intereft, and deferving of attention.

" This is an inftitution wholly independent of
" charitable purpofes, in which men and women,
" after they have reached 70 years of age, or fooner
" if infirm, can, *by right*, and without afking the
" favour of any one, *place themfelves*, in order to
" pafs the remainder of their days in comfort and
" repofe.   A fubfcription is the effential and indif-
" penfable condition of acquiring the right of ad-
" miffion, according to which, every fubfcriber muft
" pay, regularly and punctually, 10d. per month,
" from 10 till 30 years of age; 1s. 3d. per month,
" from 30 to 50 ; 1s. 8d. per month from 50 to
" 70 years of age.   Thefe different payments will
" amount to 45l. which muft be completely paid

" before a perſon can acquire the right of admiſſion.
" Hence, if any one more than ten years of age ſhould
" offer as a ſubſcriber, he or ſhe muſt depoſit at the
" time of ſubſcription, and according to his or her
" age, the ſum which would have been paid if the
" ſubſcription had commenced at ten. In order to
" give encouragement to benevolence, all perſons
" who may be diſpoſed to ſubſcribe, may transfer
" their right to as many perſons as they have made
" ſubſcriptions, on condition that the perſon who
" ſhall be benefited by the transfer, ſhall be, as
" nearly as poſſible, of the ſame age as his benefactor,
" and that he ſhall not be admitted before he has
" reached 70 years of age, and paid the 45l. This
" transferred ſubſcription is extinguiſhed by the
" death of the ſubſtitute. The funds are placed on
" ſecurities, and ſubjected to an adminiſtration, which
" is in every reſpect ſafe and undeniable. The
" houſe of M. Duchailla, the governor of this inſti-
" tution, is moſt beautifully ſituated at Chaillot, in
" the Champs Elyſées, about two miles from Paris,
" commanding a moſt extenſive view of the city, the
" Seine, and the Champ de Mars. In front there
" is a very large and elegant parterre, terminating
" in an extenſive kitchen garden; behind, there is
" another large houſe, formerly the monaſtery of St.
" Perine, which alſo belongs to this eſtabliſhment;
" and a field of about four acres, bordered by a
" well-cultivated garden. In this eſtabliſhment are
" nearly 100 aged perſons, male and female, whoſe
" manners and appearance evidently beſpeak that
" they have figured in the genteeler walks of life,
" and whoſe countenances indicate the moſt perfect
" happineſs and contentment."

Since this work has been in the prefs, the Newf-
papers have publiſhed " Reports from the Houſe of
" Commons, upon the ſtate of Mendicity in the
" Metropolis." Theſe will no doubt appear in a
fuller form of publication ſome time hence ; and
cannot fail to excite the ſtrongeſt feeling of intereſt
in the mind of every benevolent inquirer.

FINIS.

Printed by Richard Cruttwell,
Bath Chronicle Office, St. James's-Street.

CPSIA information can be obtained
at www.ICGtesting.com
Printed in the USA
LVHW04s1957040518
576014LV00001B/35/P

9 781108 083935